A BOOTNECK'S FOOTSTEPS

First published in 2007 by
WOODFIELD PUBLISHING LTD
Bognor Regis ~ West Sussex ~ England ~ PO21 5EL
www.woodfieldpublishing.co.uk

© Mike Pinnock, 2007

The right of Mike Pinnock
to be identified as Author of this work
has been asserted in accordance with
the Copyright, Designs and Patents Act 1988

ISBN 1-84683-043-5

A Bootneck's
Footsteps

Retracing my father's Royal Marine exploits 1921-45

MIKE PINNOCK

Woodfield

Woodfield Publishing Ltd

Woodfield House ~ Babsham Lane ~ Bognor Regis ~ West Sussex ~ PO21 5EL
telephone 01243 821234 ~ **e-mail** enquiries@woodfieldpublishing.co.uk

Interesting and informative books on a variety of subjects

For full details of all our published titles, visit our website at
www.woodfieldpublishing.co.uk

~ CONTENTS ~

Acknowledgements

I would like to thank my cousins Eric and Michael who helped me find my roots, and Clive and Steve Nelson for arranging the visit to Southampton docks. I'm also indebted to the Commando Training Centre at Lympstone and to Clydeport in Glasgow for allowing me access to their establishments. My special thanks also go to John Easton for his tremendous help with regards to Weymouth, Portland and Plymouth; similarly to Robert Franks of Dartmouth, Stuart Gough of Arran, Malcolm McDonald of Stornoway, Tom Muir of Orkney, and Margarethe Langfeldt from Odda. Finally I'd like to thank Clive Wignall, Jack Mills and Polly Gardner for their literary advice and for reviewing and proof reading the book.

Mike Pinnock, May 2008

About the Author

Born in 1945, Mike Pinnock spent his childhood within the walls of Portsmouth Royal Dockyard, where his bedroom window overlooked No.12 dock. His youth was also spent there as he then completed an engineering apprenticeship in the dockyard and didn't manage to *escape* until he was 21.

In 1969 he obtained a Higher National Certificate in Engineering and spent the remainder of his working life in industry, for the last 32 years with Calor Gas Ltd, latterly as a Senior Engineer, during which time he travelled extensively both in the UK and in Argentina, China, Pakistan and Taiwan for Calor's Dutch parent company SHV.

He is a widower and has a daughter, son and granddaughter.

Introduction

For as long as I can remember I've been scheming to go somewhere, to pack a few things – sometimes many things – and be off to discover whatever is just around the bend, or over the blue horizon. I believe it's called the travel bug.

Half a century of my life passed before the realisation of how I'd acquired this bug finally dawned upon me – it was the influence, in my early childhood, of my Father. Dad had spent almost twenty-five years travelling the world as a Royal Marine. I also realised that he had been the greatest influence upon my life. In moments of crisis I'm still able to recall some prophetic story or other he related to me as a child, some lesson that he himself had learned about life – and then I know how to deal with the situation. But although I spent the first twenty years of my life under the same roof as he and Mum, I realised that I knew very little, other than a few snippets, about his prime years, the years in which he'd learned the lessons of life he'd handed down to me, the years during which he'd served as a Royal Marine – as a bootneck.

It was the quest to understand something more about my Dad that drove me to research and write this book, but at the same time – that old bug was biting me again.

1.   The Case

It began quite unexpectedly when I was rummaging around in the garage preparing for a car boot sale. I opened the battered old brown suitcase without thinking, and suddenly the life questions screamed out at me from within the case – and I remembered the first time I'd seen Dad open it all those years before…

✦ ✦ ✦

We'd lived inside Portsmouth dockyard, just inside Unicorn Gate. It was a bizarre childhood – living *inside* the dockyard; my Dad was a dockyard copper, a predictable occupation at the time for an ex Royal Marine.

The flats were an old renovated naval prison with barred windows at the top of each dark creepy stone staircase. They were about fifty metres from a boilermakers' yard, so Mum fitted wartime blackouts to the windows at night and covered the three-piece suite with white dustcovers that she only removed on those rare occasions when we had visitors. The blackouts were 'to keep out the smuts,' she'd say and for years I thought that this was what everyone else did in the fifties – it was one of her idiosyncrasies. Another was to preclude certain things from the flat – certain things had to be locked away in a cupboard the size of a small larder in the communal washhouse where her wooden rollered, iron mangle, (or wringer as she called it), and Dad's black pushbike lived. That old brown suitcase of Dad's was one of those things.

I saw the inside of the suitcase for the first time in 1952 when I was seven years old, and remember the thrill I felt was like that of the first Christmas ever remembered…but unlike Christmas, it was a thrill that remained *each time* he opened it. It was fastened by a brown leather belt, and out of it came postcards (almost six-hundred I later discovered), photographs from a Brownie box camera, a knurled old boomerang, a furled crossing-the-line certificate, concertina photo-sets of Pompeii, Naples and Venice within garishly embossed covers, a book about rubber production in Ceylon, a mottled buff booklet entitled Shanghai 1937, Chinese characters scribbled in pencil on a crumpled envelope, a silver cigarette case stuffed with greasy foreign bank notes, a rolled-up photograph of HMS *Nelson* in the Panama Canal – and a brass Nazi cap badge.

The case was, to me, a box of dreams, and each morning I imagined walking on past the school – on and on...to wondrous lands glimpsed from surreal paintings of flying horses and turbaned Turks in magical Arabian Night tales.

But these boyhood dreams didn't die they grew over the next forty years into a gut-wrenching urge to travel – to tread a different part of the earth every day.

◆ ◆ ◆

Now, that day in the garage when I opened the case again and those life questions, (the *why, what, where, when* and *who*) screamed out at me, the answers emerged like hatching chicks. *Why* was I the way I was? – It was because of *what* had happened *there*, in that washhouse *when* I was a boy. Everything had started when Dad had opened that case for the first time; it was then that my life had changed forever. Dad was the person *who* had made it happen. So now, suddenly freed of forty years of confusion, just one question remained in my mind: *Who* was the man who'd been my Dad?

2.   Beef, Pudding and Wine

The wind blew in chilly from Spithead on a bleak November morning in the year 2000, sweeping friskily across the almost empty shingle car park as I made my way to the Royal Marines Museum. On the way I passed photographs of the Cockleshell Heroes encapsulated behind Perspex. I was trying to recall the film, when it began to rain large but infrequent blobs.

The first frisson of expectation hit me as I left the First World War display and scuttled up the stairs, but here it soon left me – for here were... the Second World War cabinets. Where were the inter-war years? Almost everything in that battered old brown suitcase I'd opened in the garage were souvenirs from the inter-war years. Several times I went up and down those stairs searching for the missing years, thinking that there was a room hidden away somewhere, until finally I found a floor plan that confirmed that no such room existed. Of course, it was appropriate that the museum should commemorate the wars in which the Royal Marines had served and in some cases lost their lives, but still...of the inter-war years there was...nothing.

Trekking through the jungles of Borneo and shooting through the Falklands display like an Exocet, I found my way to the Mountbatten Room, where I skirted its long polished table, cocked a pink eye at the oil panoramas recalling the glories of Britain's once massive but now vanished empire, and walked over to the large window to peer through the slashing rods of rain at the playing fields and football pitches below. Had Dad once trodden the turf there? It was a peculiar feeling, the first of many I would experience over the next five years.

The gift shop contained no inter-war gems either. There was only a photographic collection that included a few shots of the great battleship HMS *Nelson* (Nellie) and a brief mention of *Iron Duke* when she was the flagship of Admiral Jellicoe at the battle of Jutland during the First World War, and long before she'd transferred to the Mediterranean Fleet when Dad had boarded her in 1923. Of the rest – the battleships, battle-cruisers and cruisers – there was no mention.

At the museum exit an old man wearing a uniform, and a young receptionist were chatting intently.

'It'll cost you,' chipped in the old man before the receptionist could answer my cumbersome question. Then he smiled and handed me an A4

sheet headed: RECORDS OF NON-COMMISSIONED RANKS OF
THE ROYAL MARINES.

'They're not very far away,' he said, waving an arm westward in the
general direction, 'they're kept over in Gosport.'

◆ ◆ ◆

Outside it was still raining, even harder now, and with the southerly
wind sweeping in cold on my cheeks, I tugged the hood of my anorak
over my head, bent in towards the driving rain and began to jog back
slowly to the car. With wipers swishing, I drove along the esplanade and
turned right to head for the Eastern Road and the route out of the City
passing, on my left the RMA Tavern and on my right the Royal Marine
Barracks with its old main gate and clock tower. It looked the same as
I'd remembered it a quarter of a century before, when I'd first visited the
museum with Dad, except that something – some niggling thing – was
different. It caused me without thinking to veer recklessly left, soliciting
a horn blast from the driver following me.

The rain petered out as I walked back to the barracks that Dad had
first seen in 1921. Then, it had been the home of the Royal Marine Artillery (RMA) until their amalgamation with the Royal Marine Light
Infantry in 1923, when it then became the home of the Royal Marines –
who finally marched out of the barracks behind the band in October
1991. (Dad would have turned in his grave, if it wasn't for the fact that
he'd been cremated). I stopped outside the RMA Tavern in Cromwell
Road, opposite the main gate, where it suddenly dawned on me what
was different about it – you could see right through to what was once the
parade ground; the central pillar of the gateway had been removed, pre-
sumably for automobile access. The hanging sign outside the tavern
depicted the famous badge of the Royal Marines – the *Globe & Laurel*,
but at the time I didn't know the significance of any of the six elements
that made up the badge, each one of which was earned and awarded to
the Corps over a period between 1704 and 1827. (1)

One of Dad's favourite sayings was: *Life's not all beer and skittles.*
But when he'd joined up in 1921 the RMA tavern had been one of 648
drinking establishments on the island of Portsea, a figure that had, even
then, seen a decline by twenty-eight per cent since 1869. It meant that
there was still one such establishment for every twenty sailors and marines on the island at the time. The RMA tavern had once been a beer
house. It had started life as one in the early nineteenth century, becoming
a public house in 1865, four years before the repeal of the Beer House
Act which had allowed a householder, assessed to the poor rate, to sell
beer and cider from his own house on payment of two guineas. (2)

The tavern was still almost a spit and sawdust kind of establishment, with wooden floorboards covering the entire public bar area. A pool table was its most prominent feature, a jukebox guarded its entrance and mounted on a high shelf was what appeared to be either a TV set or karaoke screen. At one end stood a stone fireplace in-filled with a gas fire above which was a framed scroll giving a potted history of the Royal Marine Artillery. This was, as far as I could see, the only artefact relating to the RMA in the place.

I was hungry but there appeared to be no menu, so I tentatively enquired if food was available. Now one of the tests of a good pub, in my view, is whether they're able to provide the simplest of British cuisine at the drop of a hat when it's not on the menu, or when as in this case, a menu doesn't even exist. By this I mean the humble cheese and pickle sandwich. The RMA tavern, on this occasion, passed the test.

It was as I was sitting at the bar, quietly chomping the sandwich and sipping a pint that a leaflet, which had been stuck with blue-tack onto a support column, wafted to the floor. I slid off the stool and picked it up. It was an advertisement for a forthcoming event at the tavern, but it had been stuck over a far more interesting framed document, an enlistment poster for the Royal Marines. It read:

All dashing high spirited YOUNG HEROES
Who wish to obtain **GLORY** in the **SERVICE** of their country
have now the finest opportunity
by entering the enterprizing respectable Corps.
THE ROYAL MARINES.
Everyone must be aware that this Honourable Corps
possesses Advantages superior to any under the Crown.
Good quarters whilst on shore;
on Board, plenty of Beef, Pudding and Wine after Dinner.
Even these Advantages are trifling when compared to the inestimable one
PRIZE MONEY.
Remember the Galloons; when the Private Marine
made sufficient Prize Money
to render himself and Family comfortable for Life.
Remember these Times may return, it is impossible to say how soon.
Loose no time! therefore in repairing to the head Quarters
of the first Lieu. H. B. MENDS
of the Plymouth Division of Royal Marines,
commanded by Lieu. Gen. BRIGHT.
or to Sergeant GREBBLE,
at the BLUE BOWL, PITHAY, BRISTOL,
where every attention will be paid to them
Eleven Guineas Bounty

SEVEN YEARS SERVICE
Sixteen Guineas
UNLIMITED SERVICE
Boys 5 Feet, Eight Guineas, limited Service, Twelve Pounds, unlimited
NOW OR NEVER, ENGLAND FOREVER
The Bringers of Recruits will be handsomely rewarded
GOD SAVE THE KING

Bonner (3)

So here was the first of many mysteries I'd encounter: What, where and when were the Galloons? Had those young recruits known about them? And even if they hadn't, would it have deterred them from joining the Corps then? Beef, pudding and wine alone would surely have done the trick.

I didn't know what had done the trick for Dad in 1921, but if I'd been a young working lad in 1826, I'd have sworn the Oath of Fidelity just as soon as Sergeant Grebble had bought me a pint.

3.   Footsteps

The Public Records Office (PRO) at Kew is an illustrious modern concrete building edged with smartly painted green metal trim and an obviously manufactured lake facade complete with fountains; it was not quite the place in which I'd expected to find myself. It glinted discreetly in the frail February sunshine as I skirted the lake, wondering whether the mallards, Canada geese and swans had been imported or had somehow discovered their new environment by innate instinct − as the pigeons obviously had. Anyway, it was a pleasant enough setting, which was just as well, as I was to visit it many times.

I was there because the records of Royal Marines who'd enlisted prior to 1925 were not at Gosport as I'd been told, but had been relocated to Kew. There were eight and a half million documents in the place, and I was looking for just one − my father's service record. It seemed like the proverbial haystack needle − and it took me a complete day to find that precious single document.

I found it finally on the second floor, in the map and large document room. Delivered from the bowels of the building by three-quarters of a kilometre of conveyor track, it was a document box the size of a small desk that, (if the Manual Handling Regulations pertain to museums), should have required a forklift truck to move it to the reading desk.

Dad's page was in fact located easily by his service number that I'd found on the tissue paper duplicate of a *War Gratuity and Post War Credit of Wages* slip dated 1945. The slip had been lurking unglamorously in a corner of the case, the service number barely discernable along a tear. The page fittingly reflected his twenty-four years of service; it was crammed with the dates of every ship and shore location on which he'd served, arranged chronologically. In addition, his was one of the few pages to which had been pinned a thin piece of brown-stained paper, which was the record of the time he'd spent in the Royal Marine Artillery (RMA) as a blue marine, prior to becoming a Royal Marine (without realising it) whilst serving in Turkey in August 1923. All this was more than I'd dared hope for. Now, for the first time, I could begin to understand the jumbled contents of the old brown case.

The page held a few surprises though: The colour of his eyes upon enlistment was recorded as hazel, but I remember them to have been grey! Do adult's eyes change colour like some babies?

I was also surprised to learn that he'd enlisted as a gunner, as he'd never told me this. Gunners were a legacy from the days of the Spanish Armada in 1588, when they were important men and in short supply – (the IT expert of their time, except that I doubt that the gunners made as many cock-ups – only joking before all you IT buffs log off). Charles the Second had formed the first Marine Regiment in 1664; they were known as the Duke of York and Albany's Maritime Regiment of Foot, but it wasn't until 1804 that the Marine Artillery Divisions were formed, in part due to representations from Lord Nelson. The artillery moved to the Portsmouth area in 1817, (4) so by the time Dad joined them in 1921 there was already a tradition of some 104 years to follow.

My last discovery would lead me to the place from where I'd have to start – to Dad's birthplace. His trade before enlistment had been entered as agricultural labourer – (the same as James Cook's – so I didn't feel so bad.) Below this, was entered his home address: 2 Seal Cottages, Waterlooville. One of my earliest recollections was of visiting this place when I was aged about two; the single occasion upon which I'd met my grandmother. Was the cottage still there?

I sat a long time savouring the page in that massive book and thought about what the world had been like when he'd enlisted in 1921.

✦ ✦ ✦

At the end of December 1921, Dad had been seventeen. He'd been lucky to get to that age perhaps because a worldwide influenza outbreak during late 1918 had killed 220,000 people in Britain alone and over 20 million people worldwide in just 120 days. To put this in some sort of perspective – Aids killed 3 million people in the whole of 2001.

Unemployment in Britain was about to top an unprecedented one million when Dad joined up – one month and seven days after his seventeenth birthday. Fear of unemployment was unlikely to have been the reason for him enlisting though; the only alternative would have been to stay a farm labourer like his father George, who'd died at the age of sixty-three, (Dad said, from hard work). Dad's grandfather Frank was also a farm labourer, so by enlisting Dad was breaking the chain of farm labourers going back generations, probably to the creation of the family surname with its rural connotation, meaning, according to Burke: *Dweller at or near the sign of the hedge sparrow.* (5) The true reason he joined up, I shall never know. Did he too have that gut-wrenching urge to travel? Perhaps he'd seen a recruitment poster? Or maybe he just fancied the uniform – he *had* after all been a boy scout!

✦ ✦ ✦

Passing through the swipe-card security gate of the PRO, I handed in my slim folder for the security check and ambled on through the automatic revolving door, (that's all you can do is amble – you feel you want to push the thing to make it go faster). Then, after a complete day locked away, I emerged back out into the pale yolk February day that was now fast fading.

I knew that there would be many more visits to this place, trawling through the ships' logs of the great battleships and battle cruisers upon which Dad had served. It would be frustrating and tedious but it was something I *had* to do.

✦ ✦ ✦

Dad, aged 36, as a corporal, at his wedding on 2nd November 1940.

Dad's service record showed that upon enlisting, he'd begun his training as a private gunner at Eastney, in February 1921. But a letter from the archivist of the Royal Marines Museum assured me that, as a Royal Marine Artillery Supernumerary, Dad would first have been despatched to Deal. (6) I didn't believe this! Perhaps the old man was letting me know in some spiritually telepathic way or something because I just *felt* that Deal was a place he hadn't seen. James Ladd's book: *By Sea By Land* recorded, somewhat ambiguously perhaps, that after the amalgamation of the Royal Marines Light Infantry (the Red Marines) and the Royal Marine Artillery (the Blue Marines) in October 1923 – Initial training for recruits was concentrated at the Depot (Deal), (7) By this time however Dad had already arrived back from a year's service in Turkey. Deal Library just made the mud thicker by writing that: *he may or may not have been at Deal.* (8) I decided in the end to trust Dad's spiritual telepathy and closed off his training period.

His service in Turkey when he'd been a blue marine was well documented on the thin piece of browning paper pinned to his service record. He'd been in Constantinople from September until November 1922, before being posted to the Gallipoli peninsular where he'd stayed until August 1923 – but it wasn't easy trying to relate the indecipherable place names of the peninsular, written in English eighty years ago, to their modern Turkish equivalents. What the record did clearly tell me though was that he'd embarked for Turkey at Southampton on SS *Kinfauns Castle.*

But most of Dad's service time was spent on board ship and this is where the ships' logs came in, although they too sometimes proved problematic. For instance, the dates when he'd been discharged from, or had joined a ship didn't always coincide with the ship being in his homeport of Portsmouth. I queried this with both the Ministry of Defence and a retired naval captain and they both concurred that on these occasions he'd probably have travelled by train to pick up his ship.

Curiously, the most difficult period to track was at the end of his service, during the war – the time from December 1940, until his discharge in 1945. This proved to be like the pieces of a jigsaw that you pick up and put down tens of times before finding where they fit. There were three pieces of the puzzle that stubbornly refused to be slotted into place – they were labelled MNBDO, Odyssey and HBL.RMTG.

MNBDO was the acronym for Mobile Naval Base Defence Organisation, which some had unfairly and incorrectly dubbed as *Men Not to Be Drafted Overseas.* Dad had spent from December 1940 until his discharge in 1945 attached to it. To complicate things this organisation had during the war been split into two, labelled – MNBDO 1 and (guess what?) – MNBDO 2. My problem was to try to find out to which of these organisations he'd been attached. Once I knew this, I'd be able to find out where he'd been posted and from which UK port he'd sailed.

For a six-week period covering the Normandy landings, Dad had been attached to something that had been scribbled on his service record simply as *Odyssey.* Now, because I'd overheard him telling my Uncle that he'd seen German bodies, and because I'd found that souvenir brass swastika cap badge in the brown case, I made a tenuous connection between the two and assumed that *Odyssey* was a small D-day craft of some sort. Despite an extensive search though, there was no trace of such a craft.

The final difficult piece of the puzzle was another government acronym – HBL.RMTG, and all I could say about this (at that time), was that I had absolutely no idea of who to ask, or where to go to ask it!

❖ ❖ ❖

I decided that none of these problems was going to delay my journey – I was getting old. So I made some plans and set some rules.

Not to fly was the first of a couple of ground rules I made. Dad had never flown in his life and somehow flying seemed out of place with a journey into the past. I knew that this could cause me problems; for a start it would mean that I'd have to confront seasickness.

Dad was never ever seasick, (so he said); he reckoned that it was purely psychological and that if the mind was concentrated sufficiently, it could be overcome. In this, I knew that he'd been wrong; the problem is definitely in the stomach and later in the throat. I'd first been seasick as a boy on a millpond-calm sea in a rowing boat during a fishing trip off the end of South Parade pier. Dad's panacea for seasickness was – a hammock. Hammocks were introduced into the Royal Navy in about 1600, and I seriously considered including one in my travel luggage even though it didn't seem to help Darwin much – he couldn't seem to evolve much of a theory for that one, and was apparently always seasick in his hammock on the Beagle. I consoled myself anyway with the thought that Lord Nelson too had frequently been seasick.

The second rule was to try to re-visit the exact spots Dad had been to, to tread the ground, so that perhaps by some kind of magic I might be transported back seventy or eighty years. To do this I'd need to find anchorage details, so I could decide where Dad had actually stepped ashore. The ship's logs helped here again, usually they gave three-point compass anchorages from prominent features such as lighthouses or church spires; other times they gave details of berth numbers or buoys. But these things change with time and I knew that there was always the possibility I'd be looking for something that was no longer there.

The passage of time had erased so much and there were so many pieces of the jigsaw puzzle that could probably never now be found. But I had to give it my best shot; I had to make that journey in the hope that the pieces would slot into place along the way. I had in effect to…follow in my father's footsteps.

4.   Family Feud

I stood beneath a large sign that read TAMPONS – BABY FOODS – NAPPIES, and gazed down the aisle towards the number nineteen-checkout desk looking for my wife Ruth whom, as usual, I'd lost. At this time I hadn't yet discovered the significance of where I was, but had I done so, I'd have missed some experiences along the way. The reason I didn't make that discovery was that I'd been so excited when I'd finally seen my Dad's service record in the PRO that I hadn't accurately copied down all the information.

If I hadn't made that error, I wouldn't have started my quest at Portsmouth City Museum and Records Office, which was once part of a large barracks complex, built on the site of the former seventeenth century town defences, and known as Clarence Barracks. The Marine Division had occupied the *original* Clarence Barracks, (long since demolished), until they'd re-located in 1848 to Forton Barracks on the Gosport side of the harbour (which later became HMS St Vincent). (9) The Wrens had then inhabited the second Clarence Barracks during and after the Second World War where, after they'd vacated the place, workmen had uncovered their likely antics by the discovery of a multitude of phallic carved candles, fashioned it seems to satisfy every female maritime taste and appetite. I couldn't imagine why they didn't remember to take them with them! (10)

Not surprisingly perhaps, the museum didn't hold a map of Waterlooville dating back to the 1920s on which might have been shown 2 Seal Cottages, where Dad was born and had spent his childhood, but the museum re-directed me helpfully to the City Library where I was to re-discover the Guildhall Square. This was the square, where, as a boy, I'd begged from rich American sailors who gave my ragged friend a silver half-a-crown, (a small fortune), and me a yellow three-penny bit – which was still enough to buy an ice cream cone from Verrecchia's (so cold that it made your head implode).

I'd parked some distance away, approaching the square from an unfamiliar westerly direction, so perhaps it was this that threw me, because at first I didn't recognise the smooth concrete edifice of the Guildhall rolling upwards to where a rope clanged against a flagpole. The silence here was broken only by the rope's constant wind quivering and by two skate-boarders teasing reckless leaps from kerbstones. A polystyrene cup, blown along, turned cartwheels up King Henry the First Street where a solitary pedal-cycle was chained to the railings that ran along the side of the Guildhall. I reached the Fleet & Furkin and looking left was relieved to see the two familiar lions at the top of the Guildhall steps. Local tradition said that these would roar if ever a chaste young woman passed by. All was quiet though, but their presence did confirm that I was on land I must have trodden many times before. I passed some pseudo gas lamps and glancing right, thought I could just pick out the old Theatre Royal in the distance, camouflaged now within a pedestrian precinct.

Seal cottages 1975. The site of an Asda supermarket when visited in 2002.
[Photo: Eric Pinnock].

Verrecchia's was no longer there, hunched under the railway bridge as it had once been. It had been opened in 1933 by Augustus Vericchia and his father as a coffeehouse before these became fashionable in the late fifties and early sixties. I wondered how the late-Mussolini-years must have affected the trade of Augustus and his family, but in the 1950s it was flourishing and I had fond memories of the place and of the ice cream, which was the best ever tasted. Like all things, progress (in this case the re-development of the Guildhall Square) had overtaken Verrecchia's and it was demolished in 1970 (11). I wondered if you could still buy those polar shocks somewhere else, or if the Verricchia family had buried the recipe?

Climbing the steps to the new, (to me anyway), Central Library, flanked by colonnaded white flagpoles and defended by Queen Victoria herself, (or at least her statue), I was impressed by its cleanliness. When I left Portsmouth in the 1960s, the centre was shabby. There were still plenty of bombsites about – huge lunar craters, remnants of the war, which had gradually changed into rubbish tips. These were our play-grounds – and the showers of war-bricks we hurled at each other recklessly, were our toys. Unlike Plymouth – that was totally flattened by bombs and quickly re-built after the war – it took decades to re-develop Portsmouth – but now it was magnificent.

The librarian at the desk almost managed to divert me onto a fruitless microfiche search of the 1891 census, which I soon realised wouldn't help me, but out of deference and politeness I still felt obliged to waste some time in mock search before sneaking up on another librarian. He eventually turned up a 1930s map of Waterlooville on which of course Seal Cottages could once again not be found. At this point he suggested what was retrospectively bloody obvious – I should perhaps search in Waterlooville library itself; he even gave me a contact name.

✦ ✦ ✦

Waterlooville is just north of Portsmouth; it began on the London Road after some of the 11,000 unscathed and wounded troops from Welling-ton's victorious army limping back from the battle of Waterloo in 1815 and set up camp there. In all probability some nineteenth century entre-preneur figured that the soldiers wouldn't fancy spending almost a week's wages and twenty-four hours of valuable drinking time on a stage wagon to London. He backed his hunch by arranging a suitable loadstone in the form of abundant supplies of alcohol from one of five buildings by the side of the London Road, which thereafter became known as the Heroes of Waterloo. (12)

Dad was born just 88 years later, when the population of the village had grown to around 650. When I arrived back there less than 100 years after that, the population had increased some fifteen-fold and had be-come a bustling town; between 1958 and 1973 in fact it had grown faster than any other place in Britain.

As one of six children from a poor rural manual labouring family, sur-vival past childhood was in itself an achievement. If you managed that feat, you had to contend with the many common ailments caused by poor diet and poverty such as rotten teeth, tuberculosis, ringworm, rick-ets and inflamed tonsils.

In those days you could expect peddlars to knock on your door selling plates. Milk was delivered to your door too, but not in bottles; there were large pails suspended from a yoke, and transactions were ladled out in half pint, pint and quart measures to a jug you brought to the doorstep. Family run stores served the remaining needs of the village and horses were the main mode of transport. (13) They would clomp up the chalk and flint main road, which had been hacked from the South Downs at Butser, and had been laid down on top of the London clay that characterised the area. The London Road that passed through the village was lined either side by beech and chestnut trees. Only just over 100 years before Waterloo, the highway between Portsmouth and Petersfield, sixteen miles northeast, had been a quagmire and impassable for nine months of the year. It wasn't possible then to get through the Forest of Bere until the Portsmouth Sheet Bridge Turnpike Trust had been set up in 1710. (12)

When Dad was growing up, in the first decade of the twentieth century, the village had character and characters, like Edwards the builder, Restall the grocer and Pook the postmaster, printer and stationer. (13)

✦ ✦ ✦

I enquired about the location of the library at The Heroes pub, a modern charmless transfiguration of the Heroes of Waterlooville hotel, which had descended from the Heroes of Waterloo, which my Dad would have known. The young barman had no problem in directing me, because the library was just around the corner, but he made me feel as if I had landed by helicopter or via a spaceship from Mars or Southampton or some equally inhospitable place – (oops, a politically unacceptable statement... against the Martians)... You know of course that all Pomponians (natives of Portsmouth) really love the good people of Southampton – especially their football team.

The librarian was helpful; she handed me an envelope containing thirty negatives – each with about 200 christening, marriage and death certificates – before leading me to a microfiche machine locked away in a booth in the corner where I was given instruction on the machine's inherent peculiarities, and left alone. The cardinal clue I'd been looking for I finally found after a one and a half hour search. It was on Aunt Lilly's marriage certificate, and it was that 2 Seal Cottages now had an address in Portland Road; in fact the address was given as: *Seal Cottages, Portland Road*. The affable librarian enthusiastically produced a 1932 map of Waterlooville, no doubt out of sympathy for my labours.

'Here,' she said, pointing out Portland Road to me and photocopying the map.

I found the road easily using the 1932 map as it was opposite St Georges Church. Churches are usually one of the few landmarks that withstand the traumas of town planning and development. Nobody messes about with churches lightly and St George's hadn't broken this rule. But the smart block paved road I was now walking down terminated in the green triangular facade of an Asda store.

Somewhere here had been 2 Seal Cottages, demolished, I later discovered in 1980, having survived for one hundred and fifty years and two world wars before tumbling to the modern shopping system.

Only two detached houses remained on the approach to the store; the first possessed a fine porch supported by four cylindrical white pillars. By the porch, black lettering on a silver plaque on the wall told me that the house was now the office of an architect and interior designer. After some deliberation I plucked up courage and rang the bell, expecting no reply, as it was a Saturday. However a short, grey haired man in his sixties opened the door and once I'd explained my interest in the road, he ushered me inside enthusiastically.

'Come in, come in.' Here I'd struck lucky because it turned out that this gent knew the builder who, he explained 'knows everything there is to know about this road.' Then, despite my embarrassed apprehensions, he even tried to telephone him, although unsuccessfully.

I left, thanking the gent profusely, with much more than I'd ever expected: I had a name, a telephone number and something approaching the level of satisfaction reached in a police investigation when a DNA sample is found to match that of a suspect.

✦ ✦ ✦

I didn't know at the time, as I skimmed through the narrow single-track lanes, but by pure chance the man who I'd arranged to meet at his house was the great great grandson of the founder of Waterlooville's oldest existing business, who had in fact developed much of the village. I turned off the main road at Denmead, known to the sailors from Portsmouth in the eighteenth century for its cockfighting, and was now in the middle of nowhere searching for the builder's house. A signpost told me that I was two miles from the famous Bat and Ball public house, known throughout the world, (so it claimed), as the cradle of cricket. If they signpost a pub, I thought, I must be in the middle of nowhere.

The house was raised above the dip of the lanes at a grassy crossroad, secluded, yet not without views. Tony had selected the spot himself and, being a builder, had also designed and constructed the house. His other business was as a funeral director – so it would have been quite possible to be housed by him in both this life and the next. I was shown in through the kitchen at the rear of the house, with a view across a large neat lawn to a swimming pool at its end, and a backdrop of tall conifers. He led the way into a spacious split-level lounge. The lower level, down two steps, having large bay windows on its north and south facing sides reminded me somewhat of a ship's bridge. (I think that, if I get desperate, I might apply for a job as an estate agent).

Tony was in his mid to late seventies, now retired from both businesses but still very proud of both. Over tea and biscuits brought in on a tray by I supposed his wife, who appeared magically from nowhere and then promptly disappeared, he pinpointed exactly, 2 Seal Cottages on my 1932 map. I'd brought with me the only photograph I had of my parents, when they were married in November 1940, and surprisingly he told me that he remembered my Father when he'd been a Royal Marine.

'Sailors were a common sight in the village, but to see a marine was something special,' he recalled. Then he struggled to remember Dad's nickname. 'Everyone had nicknames in those days... I think your Dad used to be... *Wobble.*' As soon as he said this, I knew that he did in fact remember Dad, because this nickname was descriptive of the family-walking trait of moving from side to side in John Wayne fashion. It crossed my mind though that perhaps he was being polite and that the name had really been *Waddle*!

Now, it was Dad's profound belief that his limbs had somehow stretched, because he'd spent a long time horizontal whilst ill in bed as a teenager, but it was one theory that I've just never found time to verify. Certainly if it were true, the much slighter man in the photograph, standing on my Dad's right, whose head barely reached Dad's shoulder, hadn't received this lifelong benefit. This was my Dad's brother whom I'd discovered, when I was a child, he'd stopped speaking to – because apparently it was he who'd arranged for my Grandmother to be put into a mental institution.

Tony knew Dad's brother George too – said that he'd lived to a ripe old age, into his nineties; but here was the thing – he relayed a story of how he'd recently met George's son Eric. Now I never knew of Eric, my cousin, and for fifty-seven years of my life, the family feud that my Grandmother's despatch to the *loony bin* had started, had deprived me – an only child – of knowing the one cousin who bore my surname.

I respected Dad's decision, but family feuds are terrible things that rip your heart out. They're usually about money, jealousy and power. Family feuds seep into the fabric of life and invade every area of passion within it – from birth to marriage to divorce and finally to death with quarrels over inheritance. They embrace for sure, five of the seven deadly sins with only gluttony and sloth possibly escaping. Avarice and envy feature prominently, and money is always the focal point. In my

Dad's case there was anger followed, as usual, by pride – with stubbornness thrown in to boot.

I thought about all this, considered the adage that life is too short to be taken seriously, decided that it was true and quickly resolved that fifty odd years was long enough for a family feud. I did worry whether Dad would have approved or not, but I wanted to meet my cousin, primarily to find out about the cottage which I'd visited only once as a two-year-old, but which I was sure had been Eric's childhood home. So I wrote to him, sending him a copy of the wedding photograph. Once he'd decided that I wasn't a crank, he left a message on my mobile.

✦ ✦ ✦

Ruth and I stood at the door with some apprehension, and I'm sure these same feelings emanated from the other side of the door as I rang the bell.

'Mike... come in – you've got hair!' this short, bald cousin of mine exclaimed. Well, that was it – a classic icebreaker.

From then on we gradually discovered that our 'invisible' childhood lives had attained some inexplicable entwines that could only have had something to do with the power of genetics. One phenomenon in particular was that as lads we had both owned Norton Jubilee 250cc motorbikes.

This bike was the only 4-stroke twin ever produced and sold at a premier price. It was named to celebrate the Diamond Jubilee of the setting up of the company by Pa Norton. Its selling slogan at the time was: *Go gay with the Norton Jubilee*, but it wasn't targeting a niche market in those days. (14) Now statistically, the chances of us both independently selecting to own this model of bike must lodge, on a probability scale, somewhere between rolling a dice and coming up with six sixes in succession and swimming the Atlantic Ocean. Between 1959 and 1966 there were probably only around 20,000 of these bikes produced. The thing that attracted me to the Jubilee was its appearance, its shiny chromium twin exhausts, its aluminium alloy tappet covers secured by Allen screws and above all its fairing – mine was blue and white; Eric's was apparently red and white. This attraction must have been designed by Norton to detract from the bike's inherent mechanical problems; I spent twice as much time working on it as riding it – those aluminium tappet covers had been off and on more times than a stripper's G-string and the points were just impossible to set and stay set; they had a knack of somehow self-mal-adjusting. The worst mechanical feature by far however were the brakes; the bike could do 80 mph, but you'd need about half a mile to stop at that speed. I once had to slither at the last second between the kerb and a line of traffic for 50 yards before the bike would come to a halt; then there was the time that I crashed into the back bumper of Dad's pale green Ford Poplar at a set of traffic lights. I can't remember what happened about the insurance – we were with the same company, so I bet it brightened up the day of some insurance clerk.

The thing that overshadowed these entwines however was the fact that Eric looked so much like my Father it was positively eerie. As brothers, Dad and George looked nothing like each other, yet a generation apart the image of Dad had somehow transplanted itself within Eric.

I liked Eric straight away; he and his wife Gill were good hosts and produced a generous buffet spread, which was unexpected but very welcome. Albums of photographs were produced some of which depicted Eric's father, George, in old age with long straggly grey hair trailing over his shoulders; as my Mum would have said: 'Like rat's tails.'

'He let himself go at the end,' Eric mused, and I wondered if George had ever, at the end of his life thought about the brother he'd outlived by a good ten years, and had perhaps regretted the family feud? (15)

There were also photographs of the cottage, taken in the 1970s, and later Eric sent these to me. The clay roof tiles were coated with a patchy green moss, whilst the house-bricks were a tired burnt umber colour with mottled areas of white cement due to some shoddy repairs and re-pointing at some time. Remembering that the cottage was around one hundred and fifty years old, the only toilet was in a lean-to at the back. The road at the front was still unmade and potholed, not much changed since 1820, whilst a gate from the garden at the back led out onto allotments. When Eric had grown up there, the cottage had, by then, had one of its bedrooms converted into a bathroom. Before this, bath-time would have been in a tin bath in front of the coal fire, and before the lean-too, other business would have been conducted at the bottom of the garden – if you could somehow bear the stench long enough to visit the place. In 1921,when Dad left home to join up, the three bedroom cottage had housed eight; I imagine that the four sisters, aged from 12 to 21, must somehow have shared one bedroom whilst Dad and his brother perhaps had the relative luxury of sharing another. The family had done their bit to help swell the population of Waterlooville to 1,033; a 60 per cent growth since Dad had been born there 17 years before.

✦ ✦ ✦

It was dark as we left Eric's and felt our way onto the old A3 heading back up north, but the Asda store was still open and we needed some provisions. The other and more important reason for stopping there was that now, having found the exact spot where the cottage had stood and having seen pictures of it, I wanted to stand on that spot and savour it for a small moment. The spot was somewhere close to the sign that read

TAMPONS – BABY FOODS – NAPPIES, which I had unwittingly visited some six months before.

✦ ✦ ✦

One month later, on my next visit to the PRO at Kew I obtained a photocopy of Dad's service record. When I got home and studied it closely I noticed for the first time, on an accompanying *Service and Casualty Form (Part 1)*, that the address given for his next of kin, (his mother), was 2 Seal Cottages, Portland Road, Waterlooville. Had I known initially that the cottage had been in Portland Road, I would have arrived there earlier, the architect and interior designer's office may have been closed – then I'd not have taken the road to Tony's house, but instead would have gone straight to Asda, (would not have passed Go, collecting £200), and wouldn't have met my Cousin!

5.   Roads

The first road Dad took in his life was at the age of seventeen when he caught a Green Car from the village of Waterlooville down the A3 to Cosham on the outskirts of Portsmouth; it was Monday the 7th February 1921 and he was on his way to sign up.

Green Cars was a colloquial term used to describe the emerald green and cream trams that had been operated on that route since 1902 by the Portsdown and Horndean Light Railway. The trams, with their overhead electric lines, ran for the most part on tracks through the grass at the west side of the A3 until they reached Purbrook where they formed a coalition with the main road. Then, just south of the George, a public house at the top of Portsdown Hill, the tracks split off again onto their own embankment and the trams shuddered down the hill to terminate just south of Cosham Station. (16) In 1921 Dad would have changed here, because these trams were then still prevented by Portsmouth Corporation from running on into town; he'd had to have caught a motorbus, operated by Portsmouth and District Motor Services Ltd., from Cosham to Eastney.

✦ ✦ ✦

To 'tread the ground', I decided to re-enact this journey and sauntered down the pedestrian precinct to what was once the original village cross-roads to the bus stop at Waterlooville. It was a Saturday and there was the usual assortment of passengers, mostly either young or old. The young bussed because they hadn't accumulated enough money to buy a car, or hadn't passed their test and the old bussed because they hadn't enough money to run a car or couldn't see any more to read a number plate from whatever distance it is these days. The young this day comprised two ear-ringed, open-shirted, lads with hairy chests, who swaggered to the back of the bus to join two of their mates, both wearing baseball caps and sprawling sideways in their seats. The old stayed at the front of the bus either for ease of escape or because they were too infirm or scared to make it to the back. I selected my place appropriately, (I thought), between the two age groups. There were about a dozen of us in all.

I found myself thinking back, wondering if Dad had simply stared out of the window at the dissolving views, savouring images of the countryside he might not see for a long time – perhaps would never even see again? Then I imagined *that* old suitcase sitting on the seat beside him, a polished mirror brown then, measuring 50cm by 30cm by 16cm deep and carrying everything he would need and most of what he possessed.

Was he sure that he'd be accepted in the Corps in 1921, or had he bought a return ticket just in case? He was probably confident of passing the medical, because he was certainly over five feet seven and a half inches tall. The other requirements being that he should be strong, vigorous, healthy, free from bodily infirmity and be able to read and write with a fair knowledge of the four rules of arithmetic. His chest must have measured at least thirty-five inches. Today, the adverts try to attract recruits by proclaiming that if selected, you really *are* someone special – one in ten thousand; '99.99 per cent need not apply', the website baits; and the TV advert shows a commando almost drowning as he negotiates the rigours of an underwater burrow.

Had Dad fallen into conversation with a fellow passenger? Knowing him, he might have. Or would he have been reading a newspaper purchased at Pook's for 3d? The newspaper columns, on the 7th February 1921, were still preoccupied with the Great War. Britain was trying to come to terms with the loss of 680,000 of its young men. Reparations were required and there was a feeling in Britain at the time that the Germans should be squeezed until the pips squeaked, whilst the French wanted to pulverise the apple completely. Even the King, fifty-five year old George V, had diplomatically changed his surname four years earlier from the German Saxe-Cobourg-Gotha to Windsor – after the castle.

Other news that day was of Mustafa Kemal Pasha who, from his Angoran headquarters, was pressurising the cabinet of Ahmed Tewfik Pasha in Constantinople, declaring that Constantinople had become a mere province in enemy occupation – like Smyrna. Dad, if he'd read about Kemal, couldn't have guessed, as he rode the Light Railway, that he'd soon be spending a year of his life in Turkey; as far down the road as he could see, he was going to Portsmouth. (17)

As the doors hissed open and I hit the pavement I checked my watch – the whole journey of about eight miles from Waterlooville had taken about one and a half hours. I pondered a while on how long that same journey would have taken Dad eighty years before?

✦ ✦ ✦

Britain was in the process of change the day Dad had stepped off the motorbus at Eastney to enlist in the Royal Marine Artillery. She still controlled over a quarter of the human race then but her mastery was beginning to be questioned by the Sinn Feiners in Ireland and by Mr Gandhi in India.

The armed services were being reduced too. It was perhaps surprising that Dad, a farm labourer, managed to get into the Corps at all, as its strength had fallen from a war-time high of 55,000 to around 20,000. He must have managed it just in time, because *the Geddes Axe* was just about to fall. Sir Eric Geddes, First Lord of the Admiralty, appointed by Lloyd George, chairing the 1921 Committee on National Expenditure had attacked the service estimates and was proposing to get rid of redundant personnel. A year later the numbers of the Corps fell again to less than 10,000.

◆ ◆ ◆

I had an appointment with the archivist at The Royal Marines Museum and with time to spare thought I'd see if I could get to the museum via the old main gate entrance to the barracks. The barracks had been built between 1862 and 1867 and was, in its time, state of the art. Within its bounds were the existing musketry and gunnery training fields, whilst a large parade ground had later been added. The gate entrance, (no gates now of course), was opposite the RMA Tavern. I crossed the road, which was originally built in 1865 by fatigue parties of the Royal Marine Artillery, and read a large sign that glared the message:
PRIVATE ESTATE – NO THOROUGHFARE.
Inside the walls I was on Gunners Row, and recalled that the last time I'd been there was with Dad when he was 72, in 1975, when we'd visited the museum together. For him, returning there must have been like a nostalgic glimpse back to a previous life – but he'd said nothing!
The museum had then been located in one of a complex of buildings near the gate and close to the spot where the guard mounting ceremony regularly took place in the 1920s. Now though, there was no sign of the past. Even the 19th century mortars and mortar ball pyramids that had for so long stood guard along the parade were no longer there. Perhaps the freezing balls had rolled away one cold day when the brass monkey had contracted! (18)
I sauntered with a disguised air of nonchalance up Gunners Row, feeling like a burglar or a spy, fervently clutching a Dictaphone hidden in my pocket. On the seaboard side the original barrack block had been retained; this once housed the Sergeant's mess, canteen and laundry. The single block, now high-priced prime accommodation, stretched the length of the road, its facade punctuated by half a dozen elegant arched canopies each supported by two white columns and stepped entrances, above which hung two black coach lamps. Every entrance had been christened with a nautical name such as Hardy House. There was nobody around and only the sprinkling of BMWs and Jaguars indicated that the place might be inhabited. Suddenly, as I tried to make out the

name over the next entrance, a large dog, luckily chained, began to bark aggressively; he knew that I was up to no good! I veered as casually as I could to the left of the road, almost tripping over a speed ramp and expected at any moment to be interrogated by a retired resident admiral. Mature shrubberies, sprouting cabbage palms, pampas grass and ferns were broken only by the entrances to neat sparkling white garage blocks, which bordered the footpath. Green wheelie bins were discreetly dotted around in pairs, partly hidden by the foliage. Palm rosettes encroached over the pavement and brushed my legs as I walked on – eventually coming to a large square with a green. This was Mountbatten Square.

✦ ✦ ✦

I tried to imagine the scene eighty years before when Dad had enlisted. In those days the Eastney Barracks site had stretched from the clock tower, one and a half miles to the east, as far as Fort Cumberland. There were accommodation blocks, a church, a theatre, parade grounds, sports fields, a gunnery school and a rifle range. Dad joined a company of Royal Marine Artillery created at the suggestion of Lord Nelson to man the Royal Bomb-Vessels, after the Admiralty had endorsed his idea by the Order in Council of the 18th of August 1804. The formation of the RMA had followed years of discussion and conflict between the Admiralty and Horse Guards after the attempted naval court martial of a land force officer, Lieutenant Fitzgerald, to which the Duke of York had subsequently objected. (19)

Eastney barracks main gate circa 1920s.

The marines had at different times been given very contradictory references. General Wolfe had described them as dirty, drunken, insolent rascals, (20) whilst Kaiser Wilhelm, when visiting Eastney Barracks in 1890 had called them the best all round fighting men in the world, (21) (I suppose they could have been both). Each marine had, upon enlisting, to swear an oath of fidelity – something that a sailor was never required to do. It would have been something like:

I do make Oath, that I will be faithful and bear true Allegiance to His Majesty, His Heirs, and Successors, and that I will, as in duty bound, honestly and faithfully defend His Majesty, His Heirs, and Successors, in Person, Crown and Dignity, against all Enemies, and will observe and obey all Orders of His Majesty, His Heirs, and Successors, and of the Generals and Officers set over me. So help me God. (22)

In a previous age the oath had committed a man to unlimited service, which I suppose could mean for as long as the Corps required him. When Dad joined, it was initially for a term of twelve years, which was still a grave undertaking, bearing in mind that if he'd found things unbearable it would have been impossible for him, coming from the working class, to be able to afford to buy himself out. At that time too, he must have known that he might be committing himself to a life at sea – *the* most dangerous life that anyone could choose; several hundred men were lost in British ships each year during the first decades of the twentieth century. (23) This oath was similar to, and reminded me of the deed of apprenticeship I'd signed at the age of fifteen, witnessed and signed too by Dad. I can still hear the old man's proud reply when he was asked if he'd served in the Royal Navy.

'Royal Marines Sir,' he almost bellowed without hesitation, and I half expected him to stand to attention and salute. There were times though during the next five years when I hated him for signing that piece of paper.

In 1921, Dad's initial training would have included doubling around the parade ground, (somewhere very close to where I now stood), with rifle at the slope, at least seven times. Harder still would have been running up and down the pebble beach, again with a rifle, or the ultimate weekly route march with full pack. (24) This he'd have had to encounter in one of the hottest of English summers. It wasn't unusual for Q Company to march to Purbrook, a distance of around seven miles. I remember him recounting such route marches to me with a strange kind of pride, as if only *very special* people could ever have endured those tortures. Intermixed with all this physical stuff would have been the usual housewifery chores such as making beds, cleaning, preparing food, polishing, and sweeping. A bit of education was thrown in as well and

Dad's service record noted that after five months in the Corps he'd achieved a third class school certificate, something he obviously hadn't managed to gain whilst at school! Later would come naval gunnery and musketry instruction.

✦ ✦ ✦

Several roads branched out from Mountbatten square, but I suspected that each would be a cul-de-sac and that it wouldn't be possible to continue east to emerge at the museum. Reluctantly, (and with some relief that I hadn't been arrested for loitering with intent), I retraced my steps out of the estate towards Cromwell Road. Again I saw nobody except a paperboy, who looked as fearful as I no doubt did. As I rounded the corner at the end of Gunners Row I heard the dog barking again and imagined the poor paperboy tripping over the speed ramps.

✦ ✦ ✦

I'd got off to a bad start with the archivist of the museum two years before, so I wasn't unduly surprised when it appeared that he'd forgotten our appointment and I was asked to wait in the Mountbatten Room. After about a fifteen-minute wait, a small slightly stout, balding, tanned man approached and shook my hand, his short-sleeved shirt revealing ginger freckled arms. He was not at all as I'd imagined, as is very often the case with people you speak to on the telephone. He led the way by unhooking a scarlet twisted rope cordon and we descended the uncertain staircase to the basement, passing framed glass-covered photographs of Royal Marine events and past times, hanging dangerously off the walls.

I'd prepared a list of questions. The Galloons? An optimistic question to start with I knew, and it drew the expected blank. My next question concerned Dad's 11th battalion's service in Turkey in 1922 -23, (which James D Ladd's book had referenced back to the archive files of the museum). I was to be disappointed here too though as it appeared that the archives were being re-organised and so the files were unavailable.

Perhaps by way of compensation the archivist asked if I had with me Dad's service record. I fished it out and he spotted the reference to HBL. R.M.T.G. This was one of the three difficult jigsaw pieces that covered the period from August 1944 to Dad's discharge in 1945. The archivist told me that it stood for Home Based Ledger – Royal Marines Training Group and produced a book titled: *Royal Marines in Wales*, indicating that there had been a number of training camps in that country.

But the suggestion that he'd been somewhere in Wales didn't gel with me because of a grubby little yellow booklet titled: *Depot Royal Marines – Lympstone* that I'd found in the case. This booklet had first led me, in my ignorance, to think that Dad had undergone his basic training there, as the introduction read: *You are joining the Royal Marines at a critical time in its long and honourable history.* But on page thirty-five I'd read: *Post War Credit of 6d. a day will be credited to you as from 1st January 1942.* One conundrum had been solved but another was posed.

No light could be shed upon *Odyssey*, which left me still sailing that long unknown course and brought me to my last question – MNBDO?

I was convinced, after reading Ladd's book, that Dad had, in January1941, joined MNBDO 2, which would have meant his involvement in the invasion of Sicily. On this hunch I spent a further two hours engrossed in excerpts from *Royal Marine Business No 1*, which the archivist handed me. It described in detail the Sicilian campaign, the landing for which had taken place at Marzamemi in July1943. I imagined Dad marching the forty miles north to Buccheri and finally into Catania as the Germans were driven back onto the foothills of mount Etna. It was only at the end of this long foray that the archivist casually asked about Dad's medals and like a magician, produced the book *Ribbons and Medals*. Now in hindsight, I should have known about Dad's medals, they were on display in my study at home; I saw them almost every day. I was pretty sure that he had been awarded the Africa Star – but when the archivist showed me a photograph of the Italy Star I was certain that this was a medal he didn't have. The thing was if he *had* been with MNBDO 2 in Sicily he would undoubtedly have been awarded this medal and, as MNBDO 1 were in North Africa, it now seemed almost certain that this was where he'd served. I'd used most of my time in the archives to make this obvious deduction when in fact, if I'd thought about it, I could have saved myself the visit – except of course that I'd learned the meaning of HBL. R.M.T.G.

I'd been standing, like Robert Frost, at diverging roads in the yellow wood, looking down a road that I couldn't now take to a bend in the undergrowth. For three hours I'd become excited by the exploits of 7 R.M. under the command of MNBDO2; I'd learnt for instance that in Catania they'd had to contend with booby traps disguised as a bed of luscious ripe tomatoes, each one of which when touched would detonate a mine. (25) For three hours, in my mind I'd been lost in the yellow wood beyond the bend in the undergrowth – but now, it was a different road I had to take.

6.   A Foreign Country

My idea had been to stuff everything we'd need for a long weekend into a rucksack and throw out less essential things in accordance with the law of Bryson's *A Walk in the Woods*. But Ruth had won the argument and as I staggered and stumbled my way the 500 metres back from the Wight Link car park to the ferry terminal with bags laden with what appeared to be several kitchen sinks, I regretted my easy surrender. Then the teasing drizzle turned into a steady rain, so that I was unpleasantly wet as we finally made it to the haven of the cantilevered blue-framed shelter that draped itself along the edge of the pier. Ruth was dry; she was carrying the umbrella.

Dad had sailed out of Portsmouth Harbour into Spithead twenty-five times on seven different ships over a period of sixteen years. I'd sailed out three times previously, and on each occasion it was to visit the Isle of Wight. Dad always used to joke that you needed a passport to go there and certainly it always seemed like visiting a foreign country even though there's only a two-mile stretch of water between Portsmouth and Ryde.

As a Royal he'd made three visits to the island's waters. The first was in 1927 aboard the battle cruiser HMS *Tiger*. The second visit was in 1935 aboard HMS *Effingham*, a Hawkins class heavy cruiser, during which a landing was made at either Sandown or Shanklin (I couldn't be sure which), whilst the third was as part of the Normandy landings in 1944. My plan was to re-visit all three events.

We were about to board the great yellow monster, flying saucer-like Fastcat. I'd considered whether a catamaran breached my first rule of not flying; a hovercraft would have as it's completely supported on a cushion of air, but I felt fairly comfortable with the pure catamaran. It just uses accelerated water flow via its water jet unit to propel it faster. In my book that still made it a boat. Nobody was allowed on deck (if their was indeed one) and the saloon looked more like the cabin of a jumbo jet than of a ship – wide and spacious with a refreshment servery. Two television screens spat out the usual airline safety spiel. All that was missing was the instruction on how to buckle and unbuckle your safety belt; this will follow once the Brussels bureaucrats pick up on it. I peered out through the splashed plastic porthole at the dark, secret, ancient almost, barnacle-caked piles of The Hard's landing stage. It was the only thing that reminded me of my last trip across the Solent thirty years before.

Aweigh! Up anchor! Weigh anchor! (There is no anchor on these things anyway is there?) – Slip! Unmoor! Cast off! Unhook the damned hawser – whatever! That *real* sea experience – I never saw any of it. Somehow though we were moving…we quickly passed the opulent new Gun Wharf Quays Shopping Centre (once HMS Vernon) and the Still and West public house which Britain's last battleship HMS *Vanguard* almost entered for a quick drink on her way to the scrap-yard. Within a couple of minutes we'd already passed through the narrow channel between Fort Blockhouse on the Gosport side and Point Battery at Sally Port on the Portsmouth side, where Dad and I used to fish from when I was a boy.

The battlecruiser HMS Tiger

In the seventies I thought I'd remembered that the old British Railway ferries used to continue parallel to the shore past Southsea Castle before curling around in a large clockwise loop to approach Ryde pier from the east. I'd been expecting this so that I could take a peek at the Castle from the sea but now, before reaching it, we swung decisively to the south – perhaps the *Fastcat*, with a shallower draught, could take a different channel?

Southsea Castle was built in 1544 from money raised by dissolution of the monasteries, under direction of Henry VIII and as part of his war effort against France. He hadn't yet thought of a State lottery – England had to wait another twenty-five years before his daughter Elizabeth

dreamed that one up, (a 'major' achievement no less). From the castle
Henry had watched his fleet engage the French invasion fleet and had
heard the cries from some of the 600 to 700 men of his flagship, *Mary
Rose* as she sank a mile away. (26)

My clearest recollection of the castle was, as a boy of seven, being
taken there by my parents one night to see the fleet illuminated in Spithead and the firework display. It was the Coronation Review of the Fleet
by the new Queen in June1953 and it transfused into my mind and remained there as a single image of a glistering array of tiny lights –
glinting flecks hung upon the black backdrop of the Isle of Wight. The
number of ships then assuring us that Britain still ruled the waves.

Royal Reviews at Spithead were a British tradition going back to
George III in 1773 – the one I was seeing was in fact the thirty-fifth.
Queen Victoria held the record for attending the most; she witnessed
seventeen over a span of fifty-seven years; perhaps the most impressive
being her Diamond Jubilee Review of 1897, when the British empire
was at its height. It was described as the greatest assembly of warships
ever gathered at anchorage; 165 ships of the Royal Navy were there, in
lines that aggregated to nearly 30 miles. (27).

What I also didn't know when I was seven, or until I was fifty-seven,
was that Dad had himself taken part in a Review seventeen years before
– it was the Silver Jubilee Review by King George V, in July 1935, and
he'd joined the flagship of the Reserve Fleet, HMS *Effingham* for a
three-week period – just for the review.

It had been foggy when the Reserve Fleet had gathered in Spithead
and the fog buoy had to be streamed. Thick fog came in again that night
and didn't disperse until late morning of the following day. The plan had
been for the ships to visit Weymouth and return in time for the Review
on the 16th but at some point the decision was made, due to the uncertainty of the weather, to sail instead around the corner to Sandown Bay.

Now it's an ill wind that blows no good, and the fog had the same effect – the loss to the trades-people of Weymouth was to be the gain to
those of Sandown and Shanklin because, after entering yet another fog
belt, *Effingham* and the other forty ships of the Reserve Fleet crept quietly into Sandown Bay and anchored at 1657 on Thursday 11th July
1935. (28) It was one of the three reasons I had for being aboard Fastcat
now.

◆ ◆ ◆

Part way across Spithead we passed one of the forts, and between it and
us were half a dozen yachts with wet-suited crews struggling to control
things in the lively water. I'd expected to see a few seagulls following
us, but at a speed of 40 knots a super breed of jet-propelled gull capable

of crashing through the plastic porthole and grabbing the sandwiches had yet to evolve. Dad had told me all about seagulls – how they were supposed to be reincarnated dockies and matelots. I kind of believed him.

As we pulled into Ryde and the slick hydraulic drawbridge, (replacing the previous rickety gang-plank), was lowered swiftly and precisely into place, I remembered that the pier was the oldest and fourth longest in the British Isles. Older than Brighton's chain pier, it was opened in 1814 and is 703 metres long. (29) Fortunately we, (or rather I), didn't have to walk the entire length of it lugging our lead cases because as we emerged from the covered canopy tube, which attached itself almost magnetically to the drawbridge, two options presented themselves – train or bus? The question, which I'd pondered for some time when I'd envisaged the trip, resolved itself in a split second – outside was the bus stop, inside was the train terminal – outside it was raining, inside it was dry.

At Sandown station the results of my *incoordination strategy theory* were forthcoming. This dictated that nothing be pre-booked so that the spontaneity and unpredictability of events could unfold naturally. So it was that slowly and laboriously we trudged along Station Avenue with its truncated shorn off trees, I periodically changing the left hand concrete bag for the right hand kitchen sink one, whilst Ruth similarly juggled her umbrella. Then we began to see the NO VACANCIES signs, and as the rain and mucus dripped from the end of my nose, we reached Albert Road and took shelter in a shop doorway.

'So this is your idea of an adventure is it?' She moaned.

'Well it's different.' I said.

'Different! It's different alright – that's for sure – what are we going to do if we can't get in anywhere?'

'Sleep under the pier I suppose.' I said, attempting some light relief... It didn't go down well.

Whilst Ruth remained in the doorway, I spent half an hour scouting around Sandown in a attempt to find somewhere to stay until finally I came upon the patron saint of bedraggled, wet, lost and miserable travellers – the tourist information centre. I returned to Ruth, we returned to the centre, and within five minutes we'd made a booking in a hotel just around the corner.

We'd secured a bed for the night, but couldn't get into the hotel because the proprietor wouldn't be back for two hours. If it'd been sunny and warm, we could have spent the time pleasantly sitting on a bench on the promenade with our bags, but it was still raining – that dank fine drizzly rain that you don't realise is happening, which seems to occur about eighty percent of the time in Britain. We sat despondently in the café opposite the hotel and tried to beat the slow coffee drinking record. Failing even at this, we left our bags at the café and wondered off down the hill to the pier.

Sandown pier was completed in 1879 and extended in 1895 to a length of 875 feet; it has a large pavilion at the land end, built in 1933 and opened on the 23rd of October 1934 by the Admiral of the Fleet – Lord Jellicoe; famous or infamous, (history still hasn't quite decided), for his role at the battle of Jutland during the First World War. (30) Ruth had some sort of phobia about walking over planks with the sea foaming below and elected to stay in the pavilion, so I ventured alone along the narrow corridor bordered each side by those impossible to win fairground attractions and emerged into the rain.

At the very end of the pier, some steps led down to a concrete C shaped atoll where a solitary man was fishing. He didn't look up as I passed, probably – and with some justification – thinking that I was as crazy as he was. I walked to the end of each of the extremes of the C, to the chained-off concrete steps leading down into the grey sea. In 1965 the Queen had boarded the Royal Barge from one of these sets of steps when she'd toured the Isle of Wight and Lord Louis Mountbatten had been installed Lord Lieutenant of the island. (30) Dad, I thought, thirty years before her, might well have ascended these same steps in July 1935 having alighted from a drifter and, much later and less steadily perhaps, may have descended them again.

◆ ◆ ◆

Now here was the proof that my *incoordination strategy theory* really worked – the hotel, The Montpelier, turned out to be on Pier Street, overlooking the pier. From the window of our room was a perfect view of the coast sweeping around to Nansen Hill in the south that dropped abruptly down the cliffs to Dunnose and then ran on to Monks Bay. The whole of Sandown Bay and Shanklin was spread out below us like candied peel on a Sandown donut.

The Reserve Fleet had anchored somewhere out there in 1935, but it had been difficult to gauge its exact location from the shore. Viewed from Sandown some ships appeared to be almost off the end of the pier, whilst when viewed from Shanklin they appeared to be well away from Sandown. It was, as the local newspaper said at the time, a maritime optical illusion (31). The fleet was actually anchored in a fairly central position between the two towns about three miles out. From our hotel window and using a scaled map, three miles along the coast brought me to the end of the viewable land, terminating at Dunnose, so by visualising a convex line swinging out anti-clockwise from this point across the sea I was able to pinpoint the approximate position of the Fleet and conjure up its ghostly image. (32)

Three thousand sailors and marines of the Reserve Fleet had piled into the two towns over that weekend in 1935. The trades-people had to take emergency action to obtain fresh cases of supplies – but there was no trouble. The newspaper reported: *The sailors made their presence felt with their joviality and heartiness unstintingly bestowed on all and sundry.* This, I thought, was a wonderfully graphic piece of journalism, with a modality that captured the era perfectly. Accommodation ashore was scarce for the navy, so although some slept rough, most returned aboard for the night. (33) The ships were open to visitors and people from the two towns eagerly grabbed the opportunity by crowding into all manner of small craft. The boat proprietors made a quick killing, although their profits were nicely wiped out by the courts three weeks later when they were prosecuted for carrying more than the certified twelve passengers. (34)

By the morning of Monday 15th *Effingham* had been dressed with masthead flags and was back at anchor again in Spithead, completing the clan gathering of the Mediterranean, Home and Reserve fleets for the review the following day.

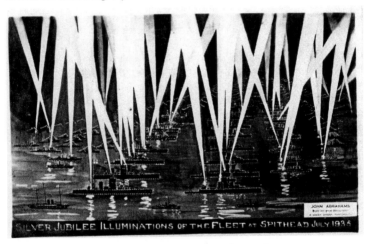

King George V silver jubilee fleet review – July 1935.

✦ ✦ ✦

Next morning as I peered warily out of the window of the Montpeliar It was as if we'd been transported overnight to the Mediterranean – well almost! Anyway it was pleasantly sunny, although there were still a few white clouds and it was a little fresh. I left Ruth and caught a bus less than two miles north to the crossroads at Morton. Then, checking the map, I puffed my way up the hill to Brading Down, breaking into a sweat by the time I reached the car park viewing point, at a height of around 120 metres. I was there because it was to this point, on the night of Tuesday the 16th of July 1935, that hundreds of Caulkheads (a Pompey nickname for residents of the island – as they were once renowned for caulking the decks of ships with tar and hemp to make them watertight) and visitors had climbed by car, cycle, on foot and by charabanc to view the Fleet spectacularly illuminated in Spithead. At Morton, it was said that: *for fifteen minutes there was no appreciable break in the line of vehicles and crossing the road called for extreme nimbleness* (31), and this was remember – in 1935. The distance from the anchorage somehow added an ingredient of completeness and quiescence that those at Ryde or Portsmouth probably missed.

From Brading Down I looked out past the kissing gate across the mustard coloured rape and arable green fields to the roof tops of Sandown, picturing the scene sixty-eight years before, with less roof tops and forty ships arrayed across the silver and cobalt blue sea. Then after ten minutes I slowly moved off across the downs road and through the gorse, heading vaguely towards Brading Harbour and then on to Bembridge – and in those three miles I moved on in time nine years, to June 1944.

✦ ✦ ✦

Between May and August 1944 Dad was attached to HMS *Odyssey*, which I'd initially thought to be a craft used during the Normandy landings. I knew he had been somehow involved in the landings because this was the only time he could have earned The France and Germany Star – one of six medals on his medal bar (35) But *Odyssey* turned out to have been a shore establishment – based at the Collingwood Hotel in Ilfracombe. It had been an accounting unit, set up to cover men who were assigned to various detachments. The difficulty was in finding exactly *where* Dad's detachment had been sent. My inquiries had led up several blind alleys (36) and all I knew for sure was that the British had sailed from the Southampton area, landing on Gold beach, and from the Shoreham area, landing on Sword beach. I knew Dad's background had been in gunnery and, from a book I'd read, (37) had deduced that either he'd been a gunner providing support in one of the fifty-four landing craft involved or, as one of the older members of the service, might have been part of the crew of an assault craft, or have been involved in the build-up phase after the actual assault. Then, at the PRO I discovered some landing craft report papers written by flotilla officers, most of whom had sailed from the Beaulieu River and had rendezvoused off St Catherine's

Point at the southern tip of the island, about twelve miles from Bembridge. (38 / 39)

These were the most tenuous of facts but they were all I had as I tried to convince myself that, at the very least, I could capture the mood of those times when Dad had been anchored off Bembridge, with a nighttime view of the island, on a foaming force-four sea with young *hostility-only* marines puking up all around him.

Many of the landing craft report papers had mentioned rendezvousing off the Nab Tower, so my wistful idea had been to see if there was a boat trip out to it. I'd reached the southeast corner of Bembridge harbour when I noticed the kiosk advertising fishing trips. The lady was polite enough and didn't laugh at my inquiry, (at least not then). Yes, there was a boat going out tomorrow – a 12-hour fishing trip – and it *did* go out around the Nab. Many things I could think of doing for 12 hours, but fishing wasn't one of them. I declined with equal politeness and asked if there was anywhere else I could catch such a tourist boat. She shook her head. I was glad my initial aspirations hadn't been too high.

The Nab tower was originally intended to reside in the Straights of Dover as one of a group of six such towers to be linked together with steel nets designed to repel German U-boats during the First World War. The armistice defeated this plan, but the Admiralty had expended a lot of money already on the first of these towers, so no doubt the Board sat around dripping their scrambled-egg gold braid onto one of their magnificent polished oak tables and brainstormed what to do with it. Somebody decided that at 92 feet tall, the tower would make quite a nice lighthouse, and because at that time the Nab Rock was only guarded by a lightship, the tower had finished up off Bembridge in this role. (40)

Opposite the kiosk I noticed a café and decided to grab a sandwich and a can of Coke. I sat outside at a wooden picnic table, soaking up the first of the summer sun. It was a lovely day; the cumulus clouds had moved away towards Portsmouth, leaving a blue zenith that whitened as it reached the line of the horizon. I sipped my Coke from the can, telephoned Ruth on the mobile and waited for my sandwich to be brought out to me.

Well, I thought, if I can't actually sail out to the Nab, the best I can do is to see it from the shore; I knew it was located a couple of miles to the south-east of Bembridge, so set off across the sands and shingle around the shore. I picked my way gingerly through the strange remnants of old staging post stumps, their short slimy, bright green bases thick with long brownish seaweed-hung 'hair' drooping almost down to the shiny sand and rocks – looking back on them from a distance, they seemed almost animalistic. Then I wondered whether the staging had been in tact almost sixty years before, remembering then the landing craft reports I'd read – 606 flotilla had reported that some craft never made it to Normandy, in fact they never made it further than somewhere close to here. They'd made the mistake of anchoring too near to the coast on a falling tide and had been left beached. (38) Not too clever a story to relate to grandchildren!

It was just after I'd passed the lifeboat station, perched on the end of a 250 metre long pier that I caught sight of the Nab. There was no mistaking it, it was in the right place and its distinct rectangular shape etched itself into the horizon. Up close though, I knew, that the tower actually leaned at three degrees; not as much as Pisa, which inclines at just over five degrees, but still noticeable. At last I felt a modicum of satisfaction, slung off my rucksack, slumped down on a rock, hauled out my spanking-new camcorder and scanned the horizon until I pinpointed it. Then I zoomed in – it was the closest I could get to Dad's Normandy departure point.

◆ ◆ ◆

From Bembridge, I picked up the coastal path and passed the elevated white coastguard station before reaching, around the corner, the Crab and Lobster pub, its picnic tables now brimming with people lunching and drinking in the sunshine whilst children played and screamed, and dogs sheltered under the tables. I supposed that the pub pre-dated the coastguard station, as the former was a well-known smuggler's haunt. The views from the coastal path between the pub and Culver Cliff were stunning, and at Nab Bars I caught a last glimpse of the Nab. On my map the walk was described as strenuous, and a steep climb out of Whitecliffe Bay Caravan Park soon justified the description.

On the high and breezy Culver Down just to the seaward of the Yarborough monument I flopped down in the grass. From here I had a good view of the bay from which Dad had first glimpsed the Island aboard HMS *Tiger*. The ship had in fact used the monument as a fix point in 1935. Looking out over the steely pale-blue rippled sea, I pictured the great grey hulk of the warship quietly sitting there like a guard-dog. Now, in its place were the bright multi-coloured triangles of yachts busily scudding about the sea like frightened ants.

Tiger was at that time described as a seagoing gunnery training ship. She'd been built just before the start of the First World War and had immediately joined the First Battle-Cruiser Squadron of the Grand Fleet at Scapa Flow in November 1914, seeing action at Dogger Bank and Jutland. She wasn't designed to fight battleships – some gun power and hull protection had been sacrificed in order to give her extra speed; the space which otherwise would have been devoted to guns and armour was taken up by an additional engine and boiler room. She was the brainchild of Lord Jackie Fisher who, in his enthusiasm for speed and firepower, had forgotten the third basic element of warship design – protection. Because of this, she'd sustained some major damage at Jutland; ten heavy projectiles had struck her in various places and she'd lost two officers and twenty-two men. (41) Despite this, she was then the fastest and largest capital ship of her time, easily making a good 30 knots. She was manned by up to 1,447 officers and men, more than attend many football league matches.

Tiger was also the last naval ship to burn coal; she required 1,245 tons of coal a day at speed, but after the First World War some of the coalbunkers were converted to oil tanks and she ran on oil, burning 1,200 tons each day. (42) An ex-stoker of 101 wrote to me saying that one of the old coalbunkers had been transferred to the stoker's mess – but he didn't say why, and it's perhaps too late to ask him now. Maybe it was to remind the stokers of how much hard graft it had taken to shovel all that coal. He'd joined her he said, just after her conversion – and even then, in 1919, there had been three messes each of 16 stokers to serve her 39 boilers. (43) I couldn't imagine a ship with that many boilers, but I checked it out – he was right.

The great battle-cruiser carried eight, 13.5-inch guns in four gun turrets, which Dad would have been more than familiar with. She also had twelve 6-inch guns and a couple of 3-inch anti-aircraft guns. Her gunhouses were small and were fitted with radial overhead cranes. The main cordite and shell hoists were combined and there was stowage for eight rounds per gun within the gun-house itself, which was protected by armour on its front, sides and rear. There were also anti-flash doors that sealed the gun-loading cages and magazines from the gun-houses. (44) The problem was, that at Jutland, most of the battle-cruisers, including *Tiger*, over-rode the designed safety of the anti-flash doors by clipping them back or taking them off completely so that they could increase the flow of shell and charge to the turret, a practice condoned and even encouraged it seems by senior officers. This ultimately caused the loss of two battle cruisers (45) and is a classic case of productivity overriding safety.

Anyway, the American naval lawyers finished the poor old girl off prematurely with some obscure clause in the Washington Treaty and, a few years after Dad left her, HMS *Tiger* was sold and scrapped. When Dad sailed with her, she was part of the Home Fleet; the furthest south and west she would sail would be to The Scilly Isles, the furthest north to Lamlash on the Isle of Arran and the furthest east would be to Shoeburyness. My idea was to follow her ports of call clockwise from Portsmouth around the UK.

From Culver Down the walk was pleasantly downhill to reach Culver Parade at Sandown then of course flat along the promenade until the Montpeliar. I felt pleased with my day's trek, which I estimated to be about eight miles. To celebrate, I treated myself to a kid's iced lolly and sucked it slowly, making it last all the way to the High Street where I turned left and dropped down along the Espanade towards the pier and the Montpeliar.

Ruth was sunning herself on the veranda of the hotel. She didn't ask if I'd had a good day – and I didn't say.

✦ ✦ ✦

The next morning we caught a tourist bus to the old village of Shanklin. Ruth was in her element; she'd spent much of the previous day here poking around in its quaint little craft and antique shops and sitting in thatched, black and white fronted tea shops with their leaded windows. My only ambition for the day was to see the remains of Shanklin pier. My gut feeling was that Dad had stepped ashore at Sandown and not here, but I wasn't *sure* and could never be sure, so I was here – covering all the angles.

I left Ruth in the Village Inn and walked, following the beach signs, past the Chine up the lane towards the sea where I reached and descended the 155 Rylstone Steps that deposited me at sea level. Then I walked along, past the bottom of the gorge and Fisherman's Cottage (now a pub) up onto the Esplanade with its modern waterfront pubs, restaurants and hotels to reach the stubby buttress remnants of Shanklin pier with its flowerbeds, flagpole, seats and commemorative plaque.

The pier had begun to die by the 1970s from frequent change of ownership, but the final blow came on a night that will be engraved in most Britain's minds – the night of the hurricane of 16th October 1987 – Mr Fish remembers it well! I stood facing the commemorative plaque, whipped out my Dictaphone and was just about to speak into it when I became aware of a young lady staring pensively out to sea.

'Um, don't think I'm mad,' I warned, 'but I'm just going to use my Dictaphone for a while.' She smiled demurely with an air of embarrassed disinterest and then continued to stare out to sea. I began to read quietly, almost mumbling to myself –

'Work commenced in August 1888. The pier was constructed of an iron girder framework and cast iron columns to a length of 1,200 ft. and a width of 30 ft. It was timber decked and the cost of construction was around eighteen thousand quid...' The plaque didn't say quid though – it said pounds, and maybe it was this transgression that prompted the young lady to slowly and casually stand up, sling her handbag over her shoulder and saunter off. Perhaps it was the 'quid' that had convincing her that I really was a nutter, but still I carried on to the end of the inscription, with one ear cocked for the sound of a siren:

'The pier's hardwood decking was re-cycled for sea defence work, the steel re-cycled on the mainland and the cement re-processed for road improvement alterations...' I suppose this is what happens to all things eventually – piers, battleships, people...everything gets re-cycled.

✦ ✦ ✦

Ruth seemed unusually cheery when I met her. The assortment of bags soon told me why; she'd re-cycled a large chunk of money from our bank account into the accounts of the craft and antique shops of the old village of Shanklin. I decided to ditch my *incoordination strategy theory* forthwith – it was too damned successful!

7.   The House that Jack Built

The Hampshire countryside flooded past me; it was like watching an old movie – scenes from a past life, decades before – familiar yet strangely unfamiliar – real yet surreal. Then although not exactly lost, I somehow took a wrong turning or two and was up the proverbial creek at Fareham without a paddle. I think it must have been somewhere near Knowle village where the pauper lunatic asylum had been until 1996, and where, when I was a recalcitrant boy, Mum had always threatened to send me.

I arrived at a set of traffic lights that seemed to be forever stuck on red and my wild imagination began to wander to the events that had brought me here... The sequence of those events reminded me of the nursery rhyme – *This is the house that Jack built*. Remember – *This is the farmer sowing his corn, who kept the cock that crowed in the morn, that waked the priest*... People and things were linked in the rhyme to form a chain.

✦ ✦ ✦

My chain began perhaps benignly enough when George Milne, a British Major General, acquired a pet Alsatian dog called Fritz that had been captured from the enemy. Milne was promoted to General and posted, together with Fritz, to Salonica, which had previously belonged to Turkey but was returned to Greece in 1912. Greece, under the rule of King Alexander and the premiership of a man called Venizelos, finally joined the Great War in 1917 on the side of the British, and Milne thus gifted Fritz to Alexander – the consequences of which did not become apparent until after the war. (46)

In 1918 Greece, (who were on the winning side) pushed, at the Paris Peace Conference, their claims against Turkey, (who were on the loosing side), for the territory of Smyrna and Thrace. Lloyd George, the British Prime Minister, supported them to the hilt; maybe he'd developed a secret liking for mousakka or something, although he actually claimed to believe that the Greeks were a strong and prolific race, and predicted years of peace for the Balkans under Greek rule. Lloyd George eventually won over the Supreme Council and encouraged Greece in pursuit of her Hellenic dream, which she began to fulfil soon enough by occupying Smyrna (now Izmir, on the Mediterranean coast).

Turkey was at that time in an arrant mess; a puppet government operated from Constantinople whilst the Italians, French and British each occupied different parts of the country. (47) Meanwhile, in March 1920, some Turkish Nationalists under the leadership of Mustafa Kemal managed to bring down the Sultan's government and force the resignation of the Sultan, which prompted the British to occupy Constantinople. To rub salt into a festering wound, in May, the Allies produced the final draft of the Turkish peace terms – a document that effectively spelled the end of the Ottoman Empire – whilst Lloyd George compounded the Turk's plight by conspiring with Venizelos for the Greeks to advance further into Turkish territory.

It was then that the consequences of Milne's gift of Fritz to Alexander became apparent. Fritz got himself involved in a fight with two pet monkeys and King Alexander, in trying to separate them, was bitten on the leg by one of them. The wound turned septic and four weeks later the King died. His death in consequence influenced Venizelos who, foolishly both overestimating his own prestige and underestimating the fickle nature of the Greek electorate, declared a general election. This he promptly lost, and in consequence in less than a month a plebiscite had been called for the restoration of the pro-German King Constantine (who had been forced in 1917 to abdicate under threat of invasion by the Allies). (46)

The French had been fishing, looking for an excuse to abandon the Greeks, and this was the bite they'd been waiting for. It didn't take much for the Italians to follow suit, they were never that happy at the prospect of fighting anyone – and this left Lloyd *Zorba* George alone in support of the Greek's dream of ruling Byzantium. (48)

In June 1921 the Greeks prepared a further offensive against the Turks, and pushed east towards Kemal's headquarters at Angora (now Ankara), where thirty miles from that target and three months later they were defeated by one of Kemal's crafty strategies. In the same month, the French were engaged in secret negotiations with the Turks, and signed an agreement with the Nationalists in the October that resulted in the French gifting Mustafa large stocks of arms that would now, in consequence tip the military balance in favour of the Turks.

Kemal and the Turkish Nationalists unpredictably attacked the Greeks in the south at Dumlupinar, defeating them decisively and driving them all the way to Smyrna and the Mediterranean, where most boarded warships before the Turks could reach the city.

In consequence of his victory, Kemal's objectives were now Constantinople and Adrianople and he moved his troops towards Chanak on the Asiatic shores of the Dardanelles, where the frontier was the Neutral Zone that the Allies had imposed around Constantinople. It was to Chanak that my Dad had been sent in September 1922 – the British proposed to defend it alone. (49) The House that Jack built chain had led from Milne to Chanak.

✦ ✦ ✦

...Beep – beep – beep...Suddenly, I realised that the lights had changed and in the rear view mirror I could lip-read the profanities of the driver behind. My wild imagination had run away with me it seemed.

✦ ✦ ✦

It was precisely 10 a.m. when I arrived at the freight handling company to meet Steve. I sat in a small reception area waiting for around ten minutes for him to appear. Normally I'd have been spitting blood with impatience, but as it was I felt relaxed and sat browsing through a copy of *A Pictorial History of Southampton Docks* that had been left on a small table.

The foundation stone for the docks had been laid in October 1838, the same year as Queen Victoria's Coronation, whilst the port's association with troop transportation had begun with the Crimea War, which broke out in 1854, when 90,000 men and up to 20,000 horses were shipped from the port in requisitioned steamers. The port's busiest period was during the First World War when seven million officers and men were embarked and disembarked. It had remained the principal port for peacetime troopship movements until 1962. (50)

For the first time ever I experienced an odd diffusion of emotions when Steve finally appeared – relief, and annoyance – I'd only made it as far as page ten.

Steve drove along Albert Road towards the Eastern Docks, past Southampton's new St Mary's football ground, and then turned onto Canute Road, named after the Viking king who in 1014 defeated Ethelred the Redeless (commonly known to every schoolboy as the unready). He pointed out the Queens Hotel as we passed, which he said had been used as the backdrop for the opening sequence of the film *Titanic*. Then, as we approached dock gate 4, I relayed to Steve the trouble I'd had in trying to gain official entry through these gates.

The docks were now privately owned and I'd written with some optimism requesting an escorted tour. It was an approach that had received positive responses from other establishments, including the Commando Training Establishment at Lympstone – but not Southampton docks, run now by Associated British Ports. 'For safety and security reasons', they'd written, my visit would not be possible. Undeterred, I wrote again offering to sign a safety disclaimer, but again they replied that their priority in such a busy port must be 'safety and security'. Short of trespass, which I *did* fleetingly consider, I appeared to have hit the proverbial brick wall. I worried about this, but not unduly because I knew that the problem would either somehow solve itself, or would lose its importance.

It was during the crispy aromatic duck course in a Chinese restaurant that the brick wall crumbled.

'My brother has access to the docks – I'm sure he could get you in,' Clive had said when I mentioned my problem – So here I was...

The security guard either knew Steve or there was a pass on his windscreen that I hadn't noticed, because suddenly we were inside the docks.

'Things have tightened up quite a bit since September the eleventh,' he said.

We drove along Central Road towards the end of Test Road and berths 38 and 39 that were used by Union-Castle Line ships until 1956 when they moved to 102 berth in the Western Docks. We parked by the grain terminal between 37 and 38 berths, and Steve pointed across to the Western Docks.

'When I started in the 1970s, Union-Castle ships were lined up over there waiting to be sold off,' he said. This was the graveyard initiated by the world oil crisis of 1974, which increased bunker prices resulted in a 10 percent surcharge on mail-ship fares. A year later the run-down of the weekly mail service had begun and by 1977 it was all over; if a ship was lucky, she was sold for some bizarre foreign use, or if she was unlucky she went straight to the breakers yard.

✦ ✦ ✦

The Union-Castle Mail Steamship Company was formed in 1900 with the merger of two previously deadly competitors – The Castle Mail Packet Company and The Union Line, whose first mail-ship sailed from Southampton to Cape Town in 1857. In the year of that merger many of the Company's ships were requisitioned by the government to carry troops to the Boer War. (51) The sister ship to 'my' ship – *Kinfauns Castle* – was *Kildonan Castle*; she carried 3,000 troops off to that war, with the soldiers photographed leaving Southampton festooning the ship's decks and rigging. (52) The Company played its part in both World Wars, loosing eight ships in the First World War and 13 in the Second.

In September1922 there was much public concern that Chanak would be the tinderbox that would start a Second World War, and on 19th September *Kinfauns Castle* was hastily prepared for her departure, which would take place from Southampton four days later.

✦ ✦ ✦

I left Steve in the car and ambled along the dockside. It and the QEII cruise terminal were both deserted; I saw not a soul. So much for the 'such a busy port' statement of Associated British Ports, although apparently almost 400,000 cruise passengers pass through the port each year. On this day anyway, berths 38 and 39 were empty – the six lonely cranes sat impotently on their yellow and black diagonally striped feet, glued into their rail-tracks with their pointed skeletal jibs seeming to probe hopelessly up into the cloudy sky. The only other dockside features were a stack of rickety wooden pallets and a stalwart row of about a dozen black mooring bollards standing like soldiers two metres from the edge of the dockside.

✦ ✦ ✦

Just over eighty years before, real soldiers – 1,000 sea soldiers of the 11th Battalion of the Royal Marine Artillery, including my Dad, had assembled where I now walked. The terminal had then been a great warehouse into which, during the morning of Saturday the 23rd of September 1922, company after company of fully equipped men dressed in khaki had trickled. *The Southern Daily Echo* reported that the scene: *Recalled the familiar sights of the Great War. Though at first there appeared to be confusion, there was a certain orderliness, which soon created an impression in the files of men who passed to and from the boat.* Dad would have winced at the reporter's description of *Kinfauns Castle* as a boat. The report continued: *Men wearing sun helmets and carrying heavy kit bags went on board, to re-appear later with ordinary field service caps, and in fatigue dress, to convey the hundreds of well-filled valises to the crane, which hoisted them on board.* The headline of the article was: *Kinfauns Castle – Vessel Sails for Unknown Destination.* (53)

You wouldn't have to be Sherlock Holmes though to have worked out where that somewhere destination was likely to have been. For days the newspapers had been full of little snippets. On the 20th of September the *Southern Daily Echo* reported the withdrawal of the French and Italian troops from Chanak. In a column below that, the newspaper reported that the leader of the Kemalist delegation in Paris had declared that they wouldn't recognise the neutral zones created by the Treaty of Sevres and that their intentions were to occupy all positions previously occupied by the Greeks. The Kemalists were carrying on towards Chanak even though the British were there and the shit was about to hit the fan!

Now, apart from the reaction of the French and Italians, there were a few other reactions to be noted that same day: The White House stated that the US would take no part in the allied action against the Turks at Constantinople or in the Dardanelles – well there was a surprise! The National Council of the Independent Labour Party adopted a manifesto that cited British capitalistic greed for oil and minerals and ended: *No more war; down with the Government.* The Russians stated that Britain's idea of freedom of the Straights, (the Dardanelles), was that she could send warships there whenever she liked. Sir Claude Hill, (later to become Lieutenant Governor of the Isle of Man), thought Britain had made: *A hideous mistake that would alienate the sympathies of Moslems.* The Assembly of the League of Nations in Geneva took a pro-active approach by referring proposals for the League's intervention to council. The Press Association issued a statement that they'd learned from an authoritative source in London that there was no truth in the rumour that Britain had declared war on Turkey. This just left the Church. They requested that all congregations of the Free Churches engage that coming Sunday… *In special prayer to God that the threatening horrors of war may be averted.* (54)

The 11th Battalion Royal Marine Artillery returning from service in Turkey, September 1923.

Curiously it seems that the Churches' request must have been heeded and God must have, on this occasion, listened and been on everybody's side, because on the following Monday, two days after *Kinfauns Castle* and Dad had sailed from Southampton, *The Southern Daily Echo* reported… *Kemalists disposed to accept terms,* referring to a proposal by the allies for the establishment of a Nationalist Ministry at Constantinople. There was an even more optimistic piece below this. It seems that 1,100 Turks, thinking the British had withdrawn, had entered the prohibited neutral zone, but when it was hinted that perhaps this wasn't the case they'd quietly retired. (55)

However, on the 29th of September the British Cabinet panicked because Mustaffa hadn't replied to their invitation to a conference. They drew up an ultimatum and tasked General Harrington (commanding the British troops) to deliver it to the Turkish commander, threatening war unless the Kemalists withdrew. Harrington, being a soldier and not a politician, never delivered the ultimatum, if he had I might not have been here on that dockside; in fact I might not have ever existed. (56) But Dad wouldn't have known any of this. A senior officer interviewed by *The Southern Daily Echo* reporter denied that he knew where they were going, let alone what for.

✦ ✦ ✦

As I took photographs of 38 and 39 berths, I pictured Dad as one of 500 young men. Some of the others were: *Old soldiers with the red and two, three or four blue stripes upon their forearm, and not a few wearing decorations testifying to their gallantry and devotion to duty. (53) They were men from Eastney, Chatham and Plymouth, and some had only received orders to prepare to leave the day before.*

I tried to imagine the scene of the towering two-funnelled Royal Mail ship alongside, coaled up, smoking, ready to go – and of the 1,000 bodies moving around on the dockside below her. It would be fifty weeks before Dad and many of the others would return to England. I wondered exactly how far I was from where his boots had walked twenty-six years before I was born. Then I turned and walked back to Steve and the car.

'I'll drive around to the other end of the terminal,' Steve said, and began to back-up.

'Over there is Dibden Bay.' He pointed out across the River Test.

'It's reclaimed land, formed from dredging Southampton water; the Port Authority got hold of it in the 1960s. There's a plan to develop a new deep sea terminal there, but its being resisted by a lobby group.'

'Is it an environmental thing?' I asked.

'Yes, its a bird sanctuary, but the terminal would be right next door to the Hythe Marina Village over there,' he pointed again. 'Its a case of anywhere, but not in my backyard – there was a public enquiry; I think they're waiting the outcome, but I don't think the lobby stand much of a chance – they claim that these berths could be used instead.'

'If your Dad arrived here by train he would have come along here,' said Steve, pointing out the railway tracks that ran parallel to, and terminated at, the unloading platform of the closed, steel shuttered terminal building, as we drove along its front. 'The terminal was opened by the Queen in July 1966 – they had to get Royal consent in order to call it the QE II terminal,' Steve said.

I got out of the car again, armed with the camera. At this end of the dock area there were a pair of red gates topped with barbed wire, one of which had been lazily left open – but again there was nobody in sight. Fixed to the gate was a large red lettered sign on a white background that read: *AVIATION & MARITIME SECURITY ACT, 1990. This is a restricted place... Unauthorised persons proceeding beyond this point are liable to PROSECUTION.*

'A bit late now,' I thought, 'I've just been in there at the other end.'

I walked back to the railway lines that ran to the front of the terminal building and crouched between the tracks to take a photograph. I was sure in my mind that Dad had arrived here by *train* during the morning of Saturday the 23rd of September 1922, and that at a certain moment in time he would have passed within a foot or so of where I now was.

Steve asked doubtfully if I'd seen everything I'd wanted to see. I told him I was more than happy, which was true. But as we drove out through dock gate 4 a thought crossed my twisted, suspicious mind – had I been refused entry into this place because Associated British Ports thought I might be a spy for the *Residents Against Dibden Bay Port Action Group* – or was it just my wild imagination again! (57)

8. Tug-O-War

With which European city are Romulus and Remus associated? If I'd answered this question correctly the local team, to which I'd attached myself like a lonely limpet, would have won the pub quiz star prize – a year's supply of cheese and onion crisps I think it was, (or it might have been salt and vinegar). The team surprisingly and unequivocally accepted my answer with a kind of respectful reticence reserved for strangers.

It soon became obvious that the duo were expert quizzers. The one with the thin features, shoulder length curled-up hair, striped pirate's tee shirt and black leather skin-tight trousers certainly knew his stuff. I put him down as an unemployed social worker. He'd have been a dead ringer for *Who Wants To Be A Millionaire* if only he'd been able to release the index and middle fingers of his left hand from his cigarette, and his right hand from around his beer glass, for long enough to win fastest finger. Unfortunately the answer I gave only served to expose my lack of a rounded education, and this galling experience ensured that the correct answer would be forever scored into a distant long-term memory cell somewhere. The suggestion I proffered was – Athens – the correct answer was, of course, Rome.

This would I swore, be the one and only time I'd ever take part in a pub quiz.

✦ ✦ ✦

I'd left Ruth in her native Wales and had pitched my one-man-tent late on a May night at a campsite near Rufus Stone, situated on the eastern edge of the New Forest. The place had obtained its name because somebody killed poor Rufus there, (William the Conqueror's son), by accident or otherwise, whilst the poor man was innocently trying to kill a few deer and wild boar.

The venison I'd ordered took so long to come that I began to think they'd been out hunting for it in the forest with blunt arrows, so that by the time it finally arrived, I'd already downed a couple of pints and by then, things were starting to happen. The quizmaster had begun to unfold a table and set up a laptop, after which he proceeded to unveil and arrange all manner of flourishing electrical and electronic paraphernalia and gizmos into their allotted positions. So hypnotically seduced was I, that I barely took note of the person seated next to me. She was it seemed the landlady's infirm and lonely mother who'd apparently decided to target me for the evening. Anyway it was she who knew longhair the pirate and his mate – and then, before I'd realised it, I'd been irrevocably sucked into the quiz – tossing my entrance fee recklessly onto the table.

✦ ✦ ✦

Romulus and Remus lost the quiz for our team and the evening ended *crispless*! I shook hands with longhair, taking care to avoid his eyes, and niftily made my escape from the landlady's mother to begin the hazardous drive back to the campsite in a legally unfit condition, with those Roman twins stuck fearfully and now permanently in my mind. The car slithered secretly and lost through the forsaken, wild, bootblack forest lanes like a firefly, guided only by God and the dubious directions of the landlady's mother. At any moment I expected wild ponies to wander across the road and prance onto my bonnet.

I stumbled upon the entrance to the campsite by a blessed amalgam of intuition and luck and tentatively eased my way into the claustrophobic blackness of my tent. Luck it seems can come either in one large dollop or in a series of smidgens. If it's a dollop, you either win the lottery, or you're in the wrong spot in the fast lane when a drowsy trucker careers through the central barrier and hits you head-on. So smidgens are generally to be preferred.

Anyway, it was then that I made this obscure pub-quiz-question connection with the reason for my being at Rufus Stone. The connection was a question that I wanted all quizmasters throughout the UK to tap into their laptops. It was: In which sport did the British police win gold, silver and bronze medals in the Olympic games? The answer is – tug-of-war and, driving between Rufus Stone and Dorchester, I pondered why it was that police teams from London and Liverpool had swept up all the medals at the 1908 Olympics and what had happened to the sport and the police since then. Tug-of-war had apparently been dropped from the Olympics after 1920 to reduce the number of participants and was never re-instated, which seems a shame as its a sport that dates back to the ancient ceremonies and cults of prehistoric times and was more latterly practiced by Greek athletes as early as 500BC. In the 1920s the police still competed keenly in every tug-of-war event being staged and Dad as a member of *Tiger's* 1928 United Services winning team at Portland Sports pulled against them in events held later that year at Bournemouth, Poole and Dorchester.

✦ ✦ ✦

I'd developed a certain obsession with time; there's never enough of it, and as you get older it seems to diminish exponentially. I was late again then, as I arrived at Dorchester's County Council Offices, scuttled towards the library and zipped up the stairs two at a time.

'I've booked a microfiche reader for 9 o'clock,' I said, trying to regulate my breathing, 'sorry I'm a bit late.'

My first smidgen of good luck was that the bespectacled middle aged lady librarian was prepared to assist me in my search rather than leave me to spend the next fifteen minutes trying to thread the film through the appropriate slot.

'What document are you looking for exactly?'

'Well – a local Dorchester newspaper for 1928,' I said hopefully.

'Right, I think we should try *The Dorset Chronicle* first,' she suggested, pulling open a filing cabinet.

So now it was time for the first smidgen of bad luck – the 1926 to 1927 reels were there in place, as were the 1929 to 1930 ones, but the 1928 reel had grown legs and walked off somewhere. Before I could begin to fret about this though, the next smidgen of good luck emerged – she found the reel, all by itself, alone in an otherwise empty cabinet.

'Tt, tt – How did that find its way in there?'

She clicked-on the machine, and now came the next smidgen of bad luck – the film was in negative, white on black instead of the usual black on white; not only that, but the edges of some of the pages were faded and appeared to be illegible.

'I wonder if that's why it was in the other cabinet?' She speculated, almost to herself.

I knew from previous research that the date of the Dorchester event was probably somewhere between March and June 1928. There were two choices – I could either start searching from March and go forward in time, or begin at June and go back in time. I chose the latter and was immediately blessed with my next smidgen of good luck as I read: *(58)*

TUG-OF-WAR
*(Eight Men, Captain and reserve Man). Open
to any Amateur Team in the United Kingdom,
the average weight not to exceed 12 ½ stone per
man. Twelve foot pull under A.A.A. Laws.
Prizes Value £20 and £10
ENTRIES POSITIVELY CLOSE JUNE 14TH*

The event was scheduled to take place on Wednesday 27th of June 1928 in Dorchester, as part of Dorset Constabulary Athletic Club's Twenty Eighth Annual Sports.

The bad luck followed immediately, in line with classical probability theory; when I wound the reel forward to the newspaper report of the 28th of June I couldn't read much of the article. I tried fitting all three magnification glasses, fiddled with the focus, pulling a lever to make the print larger but still large areas of it were faded, blurred and would require interpretation by a blind professor of hieroglyphics high on LSD! Snippets of it only were decipherable:

Great Tug-of-War Contest... at the Dorchester Recreation Ground... interesting programme of events...one of the most ambitious in the club's history... well trimmed grass track of about four laps to the mile... the centre served admirably for the shorter distance races and tug of war contests... small marquee, and here the Chief Constable entertained a number of guests... programme contained in all 14 events... weight 12 ½ stone there were no fewer than 14 entries... Dorset Constabulary appreciated the spirit of comradeship which existed between the military units and the police (Applause)... the county was to be congratulated on having such a splendid fellow at the head of the force (Applause)... He thought it was a wonderful thing that today there were no fewer than 22 teams entered in the tug of war competitions, and although two had scratched he thought that 20 was a record for any sports meeting in England (Applause). (59)

A report in *The Globe and Laurel*, (the magazine of the Royal Marines), said that the HMS *Tiger*, 8 men, 100 stone team won first prize from the Bristol Police, which prompted the Chief Constable from Bristol to concede grudgingly in his presentation speech that it was the first time in 24 years that anyone other than a police team had won there. What the *Globe and Laurel* failed to point out was that *Tiger* had received a bye in the first round and had a walkover in the second owing to Hoyal Works not arriving. They were therefore automatically through to the semi-finals without having made a pull – so by the time they met Bristol Police in the final they had only made two pulls compared to as many as nine endured by the bushed bobbies. Now that's what I call a small dollop of good luck! I wondered how many drinks they'd managed to buy with the £20 prize money.

I discovered from *The Bournemouth Daily Echo* that the Bournemouth event was a gala held at Meyrick Park, whilst I gleaned from *The Poole and Dorset Herald* that the final event was held at Poole on the 6th of August 1928:

Labour's Day Out – Fun and Frolic on the Football Ground – Visit from North Country M.P. – Who Declares Socialism as Only Hope of Salvation. (60)

Now I was set to visit all three venues.

HMS Tiger tug of war team after their victory at Poole Sports on 6th August 1928.
Dad pictured seated, far right. Medals at top are from US Athletic meetings held at
Portland 1927 and 1929.

The Dorchester Corporation Recreation Ground of 1928 was now called Weymouth Avenue Recreation Ground and sat between a cemetery that was there then, and a Tesco store that definitely wasn't. The two were separated by a two-metre high brick wall that had been ingeniously painted white over its middle section to act as a cricket screen. To the east was the railway line, running south from a point where the old Western and Southern Region tracks of British Rail still merged, (as they had in 1928). To the east of the railway line had sprouted a housing estate.

I trod the ground – wondering where the Chief Constable's marquee had been located in June 1928 – whilst casting a wary eye out for people whose curiosity might be stirred in these sad days by a lone man walking around a recreation ground without a dog, where children were playing football.

✦ ✦ ✦

Ten minutes later I threw my Dorchester detective kit into the passenger-side foot-well of the car, pulled out a street map of Bournemouth &

Poole and headed off back east towards my second venue at Meyrick Park in Bournemouth.

Meyrick Park was named after Lord Meyrick, a local landowner, whose grandfather had bought land in the area in 1805. Lord Meyrick had previously been known simply as Sir George Augustus Eliott Tapps-Gervis Meyrick 3rd Bart, when he opened Bournemouth's new pier in 1861. (61) This poor devil was saddled with Tapps Gervis from his father and Meyrick from his mother. It must have been quite a relief to him when he became plain Lord Meyrick.

After the treading bit, I climbed an incline to a track, looked down on the recreation ground, and pulling out the photocopied extract I'd taken that morning from *The Bournemouth Daily Echo*, I tried to imagine the 5,000 people assembled on the 8th of August 1928 for the gala, described by the newspaper as: *A Splendid & Well Organised Show*.

Tug-O-War, as it was described, was not the star feature of this fete however; that honour was bestowed upon the gymkhana organised by the Bournemouth Motor Cycle and Light Car Club. The simple pleasures of the 1920s seem to have been more than adequately satisfied by the delights of riders trying to avoid deluges of water from booby-trapped buckets whist endeavouring to plant balls in pots; Tug-O-War was in fact forced into third place in the pecking order by the Comic Dog Show. This competition awarded prizes for the largest, smallest, handsomest, ugliest and fattest dogs, as well as for the dog with the longest tail, and the one with the most sympathetic eyes. Randy, winner of the ugliest dog prize, won the day overall for me though, and I fantasized about how he might have celebrated his victory – the old rascal.

A tug-of-war pull is won when a team pulls a marker on their opponent's rope beyond a centre line marking on the ground, but there are, as in most sports, a string of rules (almost a pun –that!) about equipment, infringements and ways of holding the rope. *The Daily Echo* reporting the Tug-O-War at the gala commented that:

The 'Tigers' were a fine team and had a knack of making nearly a foot on the word 'heave'. They rarely gave back any rope they had gained, and skilfully coached, they took the final two pulls amidst the rousing approval of the spectators – (who obviously favoured the seafarers over the Bristol Bobbies). The report concluded: *It was 'noticeable' that the service teams did not lie on the rope like some of the others.* (62)

✦ ✦ ✦

The six miles of urban driving to the last *footsteps*, tug-of-war stop at Fernside Road, Poole could have been lifted straight from the *Midtown Madness* game on my laptop, except that I just managed not to hit any lampposts or pillar boxes that sprayed letters everywhere. If you've ever tried to navigate and drive simultaneously through a strange town whilst keeping a wary eye out for speed cameras, you'll know where I'm coming from here. But at Fernside Road there was no sign of a football ground, so a little further on I pulled up outside a small library and the librarian re-directed me to the Local History Centre at the Waterfront, Poole.

Two and a half hours later I was back at Fernside Road again, this time armed with a photocopied A4 sheet of the area taken from a 1933 Ordnance Survey Map that showed the football ground. The ground had disappeared it seemed, replaced by Linthorpe Road and forty-one detached houses. I parked outside a house with a prodigious black and white sign declaring it as – The Grange – (perhaps it *had* once been a country house with farm buildings attached, but it hadn't existed on my 1933 map so I thought it a little ostentatious). Anyway, it kind-of set the tone for the road. Linthorpe Road was a quite cul-de-sac of neat, mature, similar but individually modified, detached houses with a mixture of painted and natural brick frontages, a sprinkling of bay windows and the odd BMW.

The entrance to the road had once been the entrance to the ground, situated between two older houses on Fernside Road, and I wondered if the owners of these two houses had each made a killing by selling the strip of land between to the developers. I walked up the road to the turning eye at its end, effectively walking the length of the 1928 pitch between the goalposts. Then, as I walked back down the road to my car, I approached a man unloading groceries from the boot of his car parked up his drive. He was in his forties, with blond wispy, slightly thinning hair and thin gold-rimmed glasses. He'd heard me approaching and turned his head surreptitiously to the side to see who it was.

'Hello,' I said as casually as I could.

'Hello,' he mumbled back, burying his head busily back into his car boot and no-doubt thinking, 'Oh God, I hope he's not going to talk to me – what's he selling? – I hope he's not one of those perishing Jehovah Witnesses or worst still, canvassing for the Labour Party.' There was, I thought a real irony here; this was quintessential middle class, middle England with, in all probability, not a single Labour voter living on the road, yet this was where, seventy-five years before, in 1928, the East Dorset Labour Party had held their annual field day.

✦ ✦ ✦

In 1928 the Labour Party was just over 28 years old and already had an eventful history. It had been formed as a limited political experiment on the site of an old prison in London – (some might say that they're still experimenting and that it should have stayed in the prison)! It was then an uncomfortable fusion of the Marxist-orientated Social Democratic Federation, the less radical Fabian Society and an assortment of trade unionists. (63)

The field day at Fernside Road comprised an eleven-hour programme that included the unlikely combination of sports, a baby show and a political meeting. About 5,000 people were reported to have turned up, (60) with music provided by the Nine Mile Point Colliery Band. This colliery, in Cwmfelinfach, (I'm not sure where that is, but it probably rains a lot!), was later to become famous for its 164 man stay-down strike of October 1935 in protest at the importation of scab labour. The National Coal Board finally closed it down in July 1964. (64) At the political meeting the large gathering were reminded that:

With a General Election in the offing, every party was making preparations. The Conservative and Liberal parties were raking up the old dummies they had used for the past twenty years, namely Free Trade and Tariff Reform, but the latter had been given a new name – safeguarding. They were safeguarding their own pockets to the detriment of the working class, and it was the duty of the working- man and woman to return a Labour government, which would look after their interests. The terrible question of unemployment was still unsolved and they had a government in office which had made a definite promise to do their utmost, but which had actually done nothing. (60) There was something vaguely familiar about that last statement!

✦ ✦ ✦

As I passed by gold-rimmed glasses, I turned back as casually as I could to look at him.

'Excuse me, but how much would these houses sell for?' I inquired, as indifferently as possible. He caught site of the A4 papers in my hand and drew the conclusion that they must be estate agents brochures.

'Are you looking to buy a house here then?' he asked, looking me suspiciously up and down and no doubt noting the wrinkled clothes that I'd thrown on in the tent early that morning.

'I'm thinking about it – yes,' I lied, as it was a lot simpler than trying to explain my real amorphous motive. He nodded towards his neighbour's house...

'Well that one there was up for a quarter of a million – I don't know if they got that for it though.' he added.

'Thanks very much,' I said, forcing a smile and then escaping quickly down the road. The houses here weren't *that* special either, but it was a fact – you could buy twelve-and-a-half two bed-roomed terraced houses in Oldham for the price of one here.

There were, I thought, as I turned the car back onto the road to Dorchester, a few historical points worthy of note that had emerged from this *event in a field day* – If you, Anthony Boniwell are still alive, congratulations! Did anyone ever tell you that you were well named and that you won first prize in the bonny baby show at Labour's day of fun and frolic on the 6th of August 1928?

The Royal Marines of HMS *Tiger*, the *Tigers* as they were known, won first prize in the tug-of-war by beating the glamorously named team of Gas Works – each marine being presented with a set of fish knives and forks. (65) Now, when I'd read this in the *Globe & Laurel*, I'd remembered selling, or more accurately having 'stolen' from me, a set of fishy cutlery, at a car boot sale, by one of those dastardly early morning people – (upset all you car-booters too now I suppose)!

The coming 1929 general election was to be a stalemate, but Tory Prime Minister Baldwin knew it would be untenable for him to remain in power with reliance upon the Liberals (decimated after the 1922 General Election) for support. He duly resigned, and on June the 7th 1929, a year and a day after the field day at Fernside, Ramsey MacDonald formed his second Labour cabinet. By then Dad was back at Portsmouth Division, Eastney and I wondered how he'd voted? When I was a boy I knew what his politics had been, but I'd only recently discovered why; the event, which was to influence the way he voted for the rest of his life, was still to occur over three years later in Invergordon.

The previous night at Rufus Stone had been one of questions. This day had seen some answers, although there hadn't really been enough time to savour the visits properly. But the smidgens of good luck had outweighed the bad and in the end had turned into a medium-sized dollop.

At Lytchet Minster I turned wearily onto the A351 and headed for Weymouth; it'd been a long day.

9.   Near Misses and Minor Hits

Weymouth came to prominence as an upper class holiday resort after mad King George III had first stayed there to convalesce in 1789. This was six years after he'd been forced to endure the final recognition that he'd lost a 'small' chunk of land across the Atlantic. Well, he got the blame for it anyway! But whatever his popularity had been at the time, (he was known as the people's king), Charlotte his wife thought him wonderful because she managed to gift him fifteen children.

The Weymouth people also thought the world of him and erected – a good word in this case – his statue near the beach. They were more than grateful to him for tempering their previous black reputation as being the place where the first bubonic flees had hopped out of the fur of rats that had scurried from ships that had moored up in Weymouth in 1348. Actually they'd moored up in the then separate village of Melcombe Regis, but the two places were later merged and are now known as the Borough of Weymouth and Melcombe Regis – the Regis bit was awarded because of George. At any rate, the plague spread to the rest of Britain and Weymouth had become known as the Black Death epicentre of Britain. (66)

◆ ◆ ◆

Dad had spent 570 days as a Royal Marine looking out across Weymouth Bay in all seasons and in all weathers – mostly on HMS *Tiger* between 1926 and 1929, and mostly tied up to Admiralty buoy D4 in the centre lane of Portland Harbour inside the breakwater, although sometimes anchored at J berth outside the harbour in Weymouth Bay itself. (67)

The great capital ships of the fleet had all been here then, spread out like stars in the Milky Way; accompanying *Tiger* had been *Nelson, Rodney, Iron Duke, Benbow, Emperor of India, Marlborough, Hood, Repulse* and *Renown*; (68) names that screamed out the rule of Britannia, (the name co-incidentally given to the training ship that in 1862 was the first naval establishment at Portland). (69) There had been a definitive mooring protocol, with each ship being designated its unique buoy and setting up its ship to shore telephone cables that required continual adjustment with the tide in order that they didn't tangle around the mooring chains. (70)

Life on board was tough; there would have been little space between the casings of ventilator shafts, ship's machinery and the low deck-head for Dad to sling his hammock. If it had been the twenty-first century, the conditions would be reported in the Sunday newspapers as being intolerable. Marines who couldn't cut it would be selling their stories to *The News of the World* or would be engaging an American lawyer to sue the Admiralty for causing them to walk with a stoop or suffer claustrophobia. But this was not *that* long ago – in the 1920s – and marines would both live and eat in their mess deck known as 'the barracks'. Today's Health and Safety Executive would probably insist that entry into confined space permits be issued, together with movement detectors. Dad would also have had to take his turn as cook of the mess, which included keeping the mess clean and collecting meals from the galley. This might explain why, in later life, he left the cooking to Mum. (71) Nobody asked if you minded if they smoked – tobacco was first issued in the navy around 1800, and in the 1920s it wouldn't have been much good complaining if you were a non-smoker about the effects of passive smoking because almost everyone smoked. In fact the UK was the greatest cigarette smoking nation in the world at that time and in 1927 consumed 3.4 lbs of the stuff per head that year. (72) The routine and drudgery of life on board, especially when in base port, was broken only by the occasional – 'make and mend clothes'. I'd seen this frequently entered in the ships' logs at the PRO – at first finding it surprising that the sailors had all been trained as part time tailors – then I discovered it was a naval term for a half-holiday, although originally it had meant exactly what it said. (73)

Apart from shore leave, (and the solace found in extraordinary drinking feats), relief from the monotony for seamen and marines came mainly in the form of sport – Dixie Dean was the hero of the day, he scored sixty goals for Everton during the 1927-28 season. One of Dad's greatest loves was sport; any sport – football was his real passion, but he also had a penchant for rugby, cricket, snooker, boxing, athletics and swimming. The only sports that he never watched on TV were tennis and golf; these were 'officer sports' and ones that Dad couldn't seem to get into. He was an armchair macho-man of the Hemingway mould; he'd once said that he thought a man couldn't be a man unless he had a love of sport. And swimming was something special to him – I remember him once saying, (whilst floating on his back), that swimming was one of the most beautiful sensations in the world.

To be a non-swimmer in the Royal Navy or Royal Marines, (it seemed to me from reading the ships' logs), was a liability thought to be of deserving a suitable persecution. Non-swimmers were thought weird, (grouped together perhaps with the 'fancy religions' like Calithumpains and Anabaptists); they of course had to attend swimming instruction, and perhaps this was the reason why *I* was 'encouraged' at a premature age to enrol at a swimming club. Perhaps this was why I'd suffered the torture of standing on tiptoe, neck-deep in the shallow end, clinging to a rail, splashing around and ingesting huge quantities of chlorinated water with the voracity of a hydrophobic canine. Perhaps this was why when this failed, Dad tried desperately to teach me to swim in the sea by supporting me from beneath whilst I splashed around, clinging to him like an octopus that'd had all but one tentacle amputated and, for something of a change, ingested huge quantities of seawater. Eventually, despite all his attempts, I'd taught myself to swim. But I could never be as naturally aquatic as Dad. His party trick at the seaside was to stand on his head in the sea with just his legs sticking out of the water; I tried to do this for my children but failing miserably. Dad *was* a hero – my hero anyway – a natural amphibian!

♦ ♦ ♦

I reached the tourist information centre with quite a sweat on, as the day had now become warm and sunny with just a few fluffy cotton-wool clouds scudding about in an otherwise clear blue sky. I'd prepared a mini-list of questions, the inaugural one of which immediately floored the young girl, so that she had to call to a male assistant who obviously dealt with difficult customers like me. He was very friendly and helpful, without appearing condescending, and managed to answer every question I posed – except for the one about the whereabouts of Wey Harbour steps, where Dad may well have disembarked, but even here he hazarded a guess:

'They could be somewhere along Trinity Road – across the Town Bridge,' he said, unfolding a pictorial map of Weymouth and jabbing at the spot. Wey Harbour steps, as with a lot of my leads, was a name obtained from a Weymouth based retired ex sailor, prolific letter writer and I suspected, amateur local historian called John. My opening question had been about the Gloucester Hotel and it soon became clear why the young girl had struggled, because it was now known as the Cork and Bottle pub and restaurant and was in fact just across the road. I bought the map, thanked the assistant and wandered over.

The Gloucester Hotel was on my list of places to visit because on the 3rd of March 1927 a fire had broken out there and a fire party from *Tiger* had been landed to assist; a pretty tenuous connection I know. But it was around lunchtime anyway, so I thought I'd stop in for a pint and a sandwich, (cheese and pickle, if they had it).

The place had an interesting enough history – The Duke of Gloucester, mad King George's younger brother, had built and named it Gloucester Lodge in 1780. The King liked it so much he bought it from his brother as a holiday retreat. From here he'd cross the Esplanade to take a dip from his bathing machine accompanied by a small orchestra who broke out spontaneously into *God Save The King* as his royal willy hit the chilly waters of the bay. The cold didn't seem to have harmed its reproductive capability though, but might have had something to do with his stammer. (75)

In 1927 the front grounds of the hotel had been bounded by a three-foot high wall, whilst its main entrance had comprised a sun terrace and a grand looking ornate porch. All this had changed; the wall had gone, replaced by a pavement and a row of pseudo-gas lamps, a modern fenestrated façade replaced the old sun terrace, whilst the porch too had been replaced by a slimmer sleeker version. Recently, the upper floor of the old hotel had been converted into private flats named – surprise! – Gloucester Lodge.

The bar of the pub was in the basement of the old hotel and what a shock this would have been to anyone who'd remembered what the place had once been like – still more so for poor old George! Now, the ceiling and flooring were of a polished wood decking, the floor draped with a garish red patterned carpet whilst pale amber emulsion walls dropped to a pale green border which met more polished wood sprouting up from the floor. The other accoutrements mixed in with the mahogany furniture included a flashing electronic armless though not harmless one-armed bandit, a polished beer barrel positioned on end and adorned with wicker baskets and a huge floor-supported sprawling potted plant. The worst feature I thought was a huge TV screen flashing music videos, accompanied by music so loud that even Beethoven would have heard it if he'd been buried alive in a lead coffin fifty metres under the sea at the nadir of the Philippine Trench in the Pacific Ocean!

The place was empty, apart from a scruffy middle-aged couple and two staff. In this ear-shattering environment I ate my toasted cheese and pickle sandwich whilst simultaneously peering through reading glasses, plugging my ears with my fingers and poring over the information I'd been given at the Tourist Information Centre.

A sweet peace descended as I ascended the steps from the basement of the pub and walked west along the Esplanade to pass a Punch & Judy show set up on the sand. An arc of chanting and screaming spellbound children surrounding it. It took me back to my childhood; I'd always been a bit of a fan of the crocodile when I was a boy, which probably explains a few things to any psychotherapists who might be reading this. I was hung up on the sausages as well – so make something of that boys and girls! But there was no time to linger for more than seconds because there was serious ground to tread.

I headed for the Weymouth Pavilion because I figured that it was a good bet that the Pavilion steps, where again Dad might have disembarked, would be nearby. The Pavilion still sported a BALLROOM sign, but concert hoardings advertised Rick Wakeman, The Drifters and The Blues Brothers.

Past the Pavilion I looked for the steps on the harbour side but it seemed that it wasn't possible to get any further along because the ferry operator Condor owned the land. Instead I walked inland along Custom House Quay where a blackboard advertising a boat trip caught my eye.

'Do you fancy a trip around Portland Harbour Sir?' asked a dark haired, dark skinned, middle-aged man in a blue and yellow chequered shirt, with that distinctive curled-tongue, West Country accent.

'Yes, I might be interested,' I said hesitantly, trying not to sound too committed.

'Well we should be sailing at two – if enough people want to go.'

I'd read something in the tourist information centre about a ferry that went across to Castletown and thought this might be cheaper –

'There's a ferry isn't there?' I enquired as casually as I could.

'Yes, but he's not running today – Dorset is closed today Sir,' he added with a chuckle.

'OK – Thanks – I'll probably see you at two then,' I said, checking my wristwatch. There was about twenty minutes to spare. Across Town Bridge on Trinity Road, the ferry, which turned out to be the poetical White's Boats, was closed, but *was* apparently running, (chequered shirt was a little liar it seemed) – DON'T GO AWAY, WE'RE SAILING TODAY, a chalked blackboard proclaimed, KIOSK OPENS IN TIME FOR THE NEXT SAILING AT 3 P. M. – But the price wasn't much cheaper than old chequered-shirt's.

I'd never visited Portland before and my Weymouth based contact – John, had written to me with a concern that I'd be starting my quest backwards if I arrived in Portland by road. *Your Dad's ship would have sailed-in around Portland Bill and would have saluted Osprey by custom,* he'd written – (Osprey would then have been the Anti-submarine warfare establishment). *He'd have stood high on a deck looking out on a very bleak countryside before the present housing estates had been built. There would have been just a few houses over on the Wyke side, but the Dockyard would have been a busy, smoke filled area, with huge mountains of coal piled on the piers.* (75)

I took his point and, if I could have both afforded and arranged it, would have chartered a boat. The next best thing, and the compromise I'd settled on in my mind, was a boat trip from Weymouth – so this trip was important.

As I looked from the narrow Cove Row, along both sides of the river, there were several possible contenders for the Wey Harbour steps title. The great warships like *Tiger* and *Nelson* moored in deep water bays usually a few miles out from the towns they visited. They were frequently open to visitors who, to get to the ships, boarded small tenders known, as drifters. One of the other functions of the drifter was as a liberty boat, to take the crew on shore leave – the marines always congregating, by tradition, at the fore.

A lady of over 90 wrote to me in very shaky handwriting, that it was pure luck which warship was visited – *it depended on which drifter you happened to board*. She must have either been very lucky or have had tremendous stamina, because she wrote that she'd visited *Revenge, Repulse, Hood, Tiger* and *King George V: This would have been when I was about 10 in 1920*, she wrote, adding a post-script: *I forgot to mention Nelson, which I also visited*. (76) Another lady of 85 described how at the age of 13 she'd boarded *Nelson: There was quite a swell on so, as we neared the platform and steps up onto the boat, we were grabbed by a sailor and handed to another one. We youngsters thought this was very exciting*. She added – *There were no stabilisers in those days and some of the people were feeling seasick*. (77) A gent wrote to me that he: *Was greatly impressed by the vast size of the warships and their huge guns. I was given a large lump of ship's cocoa by one of the ratings. This could be eaten like chocolate*. (78) This chocolate or cocoa seems to have been a memorable feature of navy rations at the time, as a lady who'd gone on board HMS *Nelson* whilst the ship was in Guernsey also remembered it, and wrote: *We were given mugs of cocoa (and very dark chocolate).'* (79)

Outside a RNLI boathouse a grey bearded character stood by a boat, talking. He was wearing a sea captain's hat with a brocaded mock gold insignia, but surprisingly there was no clay pipe hanging from the corner of his mouth. I waited for a suitable moment to interrupt, then sprung the question. The sea captain was puzzled; then, when I'd explained further about the 1920s and 1930s, an even deeper furrow began to etch itself into his brow, but I sensed he'd become interested.

'Mmm…could have been those over there, where the harbour boat trips go from,' he said, stroking his curly grey mat and pointing over to the other side of the river where, not long before, I'd been standing – 'or they could be the Admiralty steps – at the end there, by *Condor*.' He waived his arm haphazardly in the general direction.

✦ ✦ ✦

Descending the Pier Steps, which *could* have been those used by the liberty boats and by Dad, I boarded the MV *Lorna J*. This craft was licensed to carry 12 persons within 3 miles of Weymouth, so a blue sign fixed to the varnished burnt-umber wood of the skipper's cabin declared. There were actually eleven of us: The skipper, three couples, all in their thirties, two children and a baby. We were soon underway and putting out of the harbour. Two of the couples appeared to be together because the two women chatted away incessantly. The men were quieter and tended to look more at the seascapes, which I thought was supposed to be the whole purpose of the trip. One of the children, a boy of about three I'd noticed was wearing National Health spectacles and an orange cap with what I at first excitedly thought was the word 'Tiger' marked on it. On closer inspection though this turned out to be 'Tigger', an altogether less interesting word in the circumstances.

We edged out past Nothe Fort to the breakwater and although the water was quite calm it became a shade colder as the wind hit us. All three of the women had long blonde hair that they continually struggled to keep it out of their eyes. The skipper gave a commentary on a tannoy system as we passed interesting features, whilst the breakwater was our constant companion.

The breakwater encircles four square miles of sea within the Bay and is the largest man-made harbour in Europe, if not the world. It had been promoted by a Captain Manning, was started in 1849 and was finally completed in 1872. (80) Over the years many soldiers and sailors were stationed on the breakwater and in the breakwater fort, manning the defences. Marines also frequently landed on the breakwater during exercises and knew well its intimate sheltered recesses. French prisoners constructed these and carved their names into the stone, but the marines used them as hidey-holes in which to sneak a quiet smoke. (75)

Shortly, we passed a rectangular tube-shaped structure poking out into the sea from the breakwater. This was once, (our skipper announced), a torpedo testing station but was now used for testing sonar. Ferrybridge near Wyke Regis, between Weymouth and Portland, had a torpedo history whose roots lay with Robert Whitehead, the son of a cotton-bleacher from Bolton who'd produced the first self-propelled torpedo (81) Whitehead's Torpedo Works was apparently once a complex of huge buildings that started at the imposing dockyard-type gates, branched off from the main road, and finished at the end of the breakwater in a flurry of little piers and rafts. (75) All that's left now are some torpedo remnants, collected and held in Northe Fort.

My interest in torpedoes, nicknamed 'Tinfish' by the Navy, had been generated by entries in the ship's logs at Kew that had recorded many torpedo practices. Not only did the records give details of their firings but also of their recovery, and in some cases of their loss. The recovery aspect intrigued me, but as the cost of a torpedo was in those days about the same as the cost of a medium-sized house it was fairly crucial that it was recovered after use. I'd received two differing reports about how this was achieved The first claimed that the torpedo was rigged to float on the surface at the end of its run, (82) whilst the second stated that it would be filled with compressed air instead of explosives so that it floated at the end of its run. (83) I'd read yet a third account that the warheads were replaced by collision heads filled with sand – carrying flares that burnt at the end of a run. (84) I suppose all the reports may have been true. Live torpedoes were of course programmed to sink or explode at the end of their run if they'd missed their target.

The man with the close-shaven temples he'd had cut that way to match his bald crown or emulate a billiard ball was giving me a steely evil eye. He wore a lilac tee shirt and a camera dangled down over it from straps. I'd first noticed his look as we'd swung in through the breakwater and were snooping around the South Ship Channel.

We passed close to the dockyard and Castletown and I was excited that here I was, actually seeing this place from the sea for the first time – although obviously now much changed – exactly as Dad had once done. There were no stacks of coal now but, even in Dad's day, the oilers were gradually replacing the smokers. (75)

Then I half caught billiard ball's eye on me again. I'd been pulling my camcorder in and out of its carrying case and recklessly aiming it with wild abandon since we'd left Weymouth and now he was suspecting that either I was trying to secretly film his partner's tits or that I didn't know what the hell I was doing with the thing. The latter was actually true – it was a fairly new acquisition, purchased just before my trip to the Isle of Wight, and my video record of the boat trip, I later discovered, included more footage of people's feet than of the scenery.

It was whilst I'd been video-panning crazily around that I'd noticed the orange and red lifebuoys contained in what appeared to be rope bags stacked in two piles on the roof of the skipper's cabin. I'd also noticed a red sign next to the blue one, which said – IN CASE OF EMERGENCY CARRY OUT ALL INSTRUCTIONS FROM THE SKIPPER. Now, what do you think this could possibly mean? There were eleven of us, including the skipper, and only an absolute maximum of seven lifebuoys that I could see; so what instruction would the skipper give? – 'Two to a lifebuoy please! Women, children and baby first!' 'Those who can't swim, grab a lifebuoy!' 'Have you got a lifebuoy boy, if not grab one!' 'I think I'm having a heart attack, anyone who thinks they can sail this tub – take over now!' I hope that the Health & Safety Executive don't read this and descend on the poor dark haired, dark skinned man with the curled West Country tongue – because he seemed like a nice man trying to earn a honest living. Still, I remembered something I'd read about a pleasure boat called *Skylark 6* carrying tourists around Poole Bay that had sunk back in 1946 and in which a knocking noise had developed that was later thought to have been a fracture in the propeller shaft. I strained my ears for any unusual sounds and checked the floorboards for seeping water, but we seemed to be all right.

These thoughts of nautical disaster brought me back to my reason for this boat-trip because it was about then that we'd passed the centre lane of the harbour and I thought again about *Tiger*, imagining her moored there.

✦ ✦ ✦

An earlier HMS *Tiger* had been sunk in 1908, close to the Isle of Wight, after crossing the bow of the cruiser HMS *Berwick* and being almost sliced in half by her. The *Tiger* that Dad had sailed on also had a disastrous reputation founded upon her exploits in Weymouth Bay in November 1920. John had written in a letter that the Signals Section at Portland had a standing joke about her – *Watch out mate, the Tiger's taking up station – Clear the area!* (75) On the 23rd of November 1920 she'd collided with submarine R4. Her ship's log read:

0847 Sighted submarine Red 15° – 300 yds.
0848 Hard a port. Full astern starboard.
0849 Full astern port
Sub. R4 collided with Tiger on port bow
Away lifeboats

Unfortunately, this wasn't to be last of her ordeals; a day later she was at it again:

1136 ½ stop port
Hard astern port
Full astern port
Full astern both
1139 Collided with Royal Sovereign in D4 birth
Helm and engines as required to clear (85)

Between 1136 and 1139, the words – 'Oh shit' – were reportedly overheard several times, but not actually recorded in the log! I'd remembered noting that *Tiger's* logbook had then continued on regardless until the 4th of December, when a Rogue's Salute would have been fired at colours, a single gun to indicate that a court martial was to be heard onboard. On the 5th of December, however a new logbook had been begun – perhaps coinciding with a new Captain.

The submarine *R4* was a bit of a nightmare herself though and seemed to have some sort of a weird affinity with *Tiger*. In March 1928, when

Dad was on her in Portland, *R4* had popped-up again close by, surfacing from a dive of 40 ft., but this time she'd missed *Tiger*, rising instead beneath the destroyer *Thruster*, smashing and bending her own periscopes. It was more dangerous being a sub mariner in those days than driving blindfold the wrong way up the M6. In these waters we now chugged through, there had been, between the wars, no less than six incidents involving submarines – including three total losses. (86)

♦ ♦ ♦

The MV *Lorna J* at any-rate made a safe return to Pier Steps without a submarine incident, which was just as bloody well, bearing in mind the orange and red lifebuoy situation. I was last up the steps and looked back down to the boat, in part at least because I didn't want to be accused of filming billiard ball's partner's bum and being head butted or throttled by his camera straps. On *Lorna J* I saw the dark haired, dark skinned, curled West Country tongue man hauling a green tarpaulin over the seats. It'd been his last, and maybe only, trip of the day. I mentally calculated his takings – deducted his diesel cost and all the other hidden burdens of mooring fees and boat maintenance. He'd not made a fortune.

Back on dry land, I walked west again, over the Town Bridge, (which was once the boundary between Melcombe and Weymouth), hunting for, and eventually finding, the famous Boot Inn situated in steep-sloping High Street. This pub was on my visit-list because I'd received a reply from an advert I'd placed in *The Dorset Echo* regarding HMS *Tiger*. The writer had sent me a copy of his parent's marriage certificate dated 1927 that showed that his father was at that time a Leading Stoker aboard *Tiger* and his mother was the daughter of the proprietor of this pub – although it was then a hotel. He also claimed, and I later verified at the PRO, that his sister, who was born at The Boot, was baptised in the chapel on board *Tiger* when she was anchored in Portland Harbour. He'd e-mailed me that he thought that, before *Tiger* was scrapped, the chapel had been taken from her and re-installed in Portsmouth dockyard. (87) But although I'd written both to the Royal Naval Museum and to the chaplain at the naval base his claim couldn't be verified.

An Inn or Alehouse had been sited here since 1346 and sign writing on the wall outside claimed it to be a: REAL PUB WHERE CONVERSATION RULES. Well, perhaps sometimes this might have been the case, but when I visited it, the pub must have recently been blessed by a visit from the entire ancient order of silent Northamptonshire shoe-making nuns! It was the quietest pub I'd ever been in. Nobody spoke to me! Their claim was a *load of old cobblers*. Not even the reported lady ghost of easy virtue, who supposedly sits in the corner waiting for her lost lover, put in an appearance – let alone (to my great disappointment) chatted me up. I felt as disillusioned as the customs officer who came to the Inn searching for smuggled goods but who was beaten up and booted out by the landlord instead – thus its said, giving the pub its name. (74)

I left with some reluctance, hanging-on in case some event should occur which would change my view of the place – but it didn't and I wearily wound my way down the slope, back across Town Bridge once again and along St Thomas Street. The day had actually turned out OK; I'd seen the remains of the Gloucester Hotel, had covered the various landing steps used by the packed liberty boats and had seen the breakwater, the dockyard and Castletown, all for the first time, from the sea – just as Dad would have done seventy-five years before. I'd even got some good shots of billiard ball's partner's tits as well, and had rounded off the afternoon with a couple of cosy pints. Magic!

10. The Old Wooden Hut

If you are adventurous enough to head out from the industrial city of Almaty in Kyrgyzstan in winter, south towards the Tien Shan Mountains, you'll come across lake Issyk Kul – and here on its western shore, if you're lucky and haven't frozen stiff by then, you might see a duck-like bird waddling across the icy marsh – it goes by the name of a bald coot. On Friday the 25th of August 1944, French women, who'd thought that the Third Reich was going to last, (as Hitler had predicted), for a thousand years and had slept with German officers, found themselves being shorn to vaguely resemble that bird. On that Friday, news came crackling through on the radio that French tanks were clattering through the streets of Paris and that collaborators were being dragged out of their houses, and beaten.

Dad had arrived at Lympstone on the preceding Tuesday, the day that Florence had fallen to the allies and all over Europe the Germans were in retreat. Dad, like thousands of others, had returned from Normandy and was immediately despatched to Exeter where he'd changed trains and journeyed on, rattling through the pleasant red-clay Devon countryside down the branch line to Exton station, (once known as Woodbury Road), and to the camp.

Although the end of the war in Europe seemed to be in sight, the Japanese were fighting on and Lympstone camp, known initially as Exton, (the village to the camp's north), together with Dalditch, three or so miles to the south-east, (and nicknamed by some marines as the hell hole), were both part of the production line set up to turn Hostilities Only (HO) recruits into fighting Royals.

I'd found the small orange booklet decorated with the Globe & Laurel badge in that old brown case, titled: *Depot Royal Marines – Lympstone*. Then, at the Royal Marine's Museum, (several years ago now), had discovered what HBL. R.M.T.G. scrawled on Dad's service record had meant. Taking into account Dad's age, experience, the fact that he was by this time a sergeant and that he'd spent a full year at the depot, I concluded that he'd been assigned to the Royal Marine Infantry Training Centre at Lympstone as an instructor.

The orange booklet was crammed with classic statements like: *The proper answer in acknowledgement of an order from a superior is: Very*

Good Sir, Colour Sergeant and so on. Not only are such answers as Right, Righto or, worst of all O.K. forbidden, but you will soon discover that they sound unsoldierly. (Especially after you've been made to double a few times around the parade ground in full kit as punishment).

I liked the saluting rules too: *If you happen to have a cigarette in your mouth, take it out before saluting.* This instruction should, I felt, have specified that the cigarette be taken from the mouth with the left hand to avoid the possibility of setting fire to your cap whilst saluting with your right. Then there was: *Always try to make the correct salute with the right hand. If you are carrying anything in your right hand, transfer it to your left before saluting.* OK, so it's raining, you're carrying blankets under your right arm *and* smoking a cigarette, now what? Do you transfer the blankets and spit out the cigarette – or take out the cigarette with your left hand and drop the blankets into the puddles – or take out the cigarette, transfer the blankets and set fire to them whilst saluting with your right hand? The worst dilemma was what to do if officers approached on both sides simultaneously, which one did you salute first?

In the centre of the booklet fastened by four corroded staples, that had stained the paper around them brown, was a map of the camp. I sent a copy to a recently retired marine who'd been at Lympstone, who suggested a contact name at the camp, (which was now known as The Commando Training Centre). I wrote requesting a visit, but didn't hold my breath for a reply.

✦ ✦ ✦

It was a short walk from the car park, where the captain had suggested I should park, across the A376 from the Centre. I carefully and slowly pulled the letter I'd received from my rucksack, taking care not to alarm either of the armed commandos standing in the cabin at the entrance to the Centre. There was a conversation on a short wave radio; apparently the guard was being changed in a minute and I was to be escorted into the guardroom by the commando going off guard duty. A contractor I'd worked with, who said that he had 'been through' Lympstone, later told me that hidden above the guardroom were two more commandos with their guns trained on me. As I didn't know this at the time, it didn't bother me.

In the guardroom my arrival was expected and I only had to wait a couple of minutes before a young marine arrived. I was told in the letter that the Duty Officer was to take me around the Centre, but it appeared he was unavailable to escort such an inconsequential visitor – so this young marine had been detailed. The problem was, he'd been detailed but he hadn't been briefed on his 'mission'.

'I've just been told to take him down to POC,' the young commando named Bob said to the guard, as I followed him outside.

On CTCRM's website I'd read that one of the old wooden huts had been retained as a mark of respect to the pioneers of World War Two and I was particularly anxious to see it.

'What's POC?' I asked Bob.

'Potential Officer's Course.' We passed the parade ground and the Royal Marine band were formed up and receiving instruction.

'I don't suppose I can take photographs, can I?' I asked meekly.

'No,' he hesitated, 'not without permission – and you'd have to fill in some paperwork...'

'Oh – it's OK, it doesn't matter.' Then I thought – This might be the right time to manoeuvre a slight edge – he didn't seem a hard enough nut to refuse two consecutive requests...

'I've got a Dictaphone though – you wouldn't mind if I use it to record some stuff would you – it's bloody difficult to remember things when you get home?'

'No – umm, that's OK I suppose.'

We stopped outside of a red brick-built single storey block just past the parade ground and I began to wonder how I'd ever managed to get that little recording gizmo to this point and why I hadn't been asked to leave my rucksack in the guardroom. After all, only about a month had passed since Bush had stood on the carrier USS *Abraham Lincoln* and had announced – 'Mission Accomplished,' that was supposed to signify the end of the war in Iraq, and let's face it, they even make you leave your rucksack at the desk in the public library these days in case you're about to nick a book or two. I slipped the rucksack off my shoulders, unclipped the straps and fumbled around, taking care not to activate the timing mechanism of the suicide bomb just yet though. I calmly and casually pocketed the Dictaphone, so as not to alarm Bob too much or make him change his mind, then I took out the small orange booklet decorated with the Globe & Laurel badge and opened it to the rust stained centre pages.

'This is what my Dad was issued with when he was here in 1944,' I said, leaning across so Bob could see the map,

'Where exactly are we? – Oh, I can see, we're here, look!' I'd answered my own question. We were outside of what was, in 1944, H block. I was confused – surely this wasn't the hut I'd come to see; even I was sure that this building was of brick and not wood.

'Is the original wooden hut around here somewhere?' I asked, as we were about to enter the POC building, 'I was hoping to see it – it was built in the 1940s.'

'I don't know – I was just told to take you down to the POC, that's all – this block was an original building though I think,' Bob said apologetically.

Inside, we stalked up and down the stark, whitewashed brick-walled, narrow claustrophobic corridors that reminded me both of a Victorian hospital and of similar buildings I'd encountered in Portsmouth dockyard in the 1960s; the architect must have produced a standard blueprint that was used throughout government establishments. A door off the corridor had blinked open enough for me to see a small rectangular room, a bit like a prison cell, with the bed spanning the complete width of the room and taking up half its length. Well, I suppose the occupants, (of whom there was no sign), were only 'potential' officers, so were expected to rough it a bit!

As we were about to leave, an elderly civilian appeared and Bob briefly explained my historical interest in the building.

'Yes, this block was built in the early 1940s – in about 1941, I think.' In that year I knew in fact that the building had witnessed queues of raw HO recruits at the start of their initial six-week course, awaiting their inoculations where the most stalwart sporty types regularly fainted. (88)

'Some of the lads reckon they've seen ghosts through the windows – It was probably me – I'm here at 5 a.m.,' he joked.

❖ ❖ ❖

In 1939, as war and conscription seemed increasingly inevitable, there had been a lot of debate over the selection of the site for what was to become the Training Centre. Tankerton on the North Kent coast was at first considered, as was Littleham, between Exmouth and Budleigh Salterton, but the Admiralty had set their sights on Exton. The Parliamentary Private Secretary to the Minister of Agriculture was however particularly worried about the adverse effects on the local winkle industry if Exton were chosen, but The Civil Lord of the Admiralty wasn't too impressed by this argument and dismissed it as a load of mollusc, accrediting no import to the half pint winkle man's handcart. The Civil Lord of course had no idea of the things that could be done with a bent pin. (89)

The Admiralty made an inspection of the proposed site without the owner being present. The site was part of the Nutwell Court Estate and was owned by a Captain Meyrick, who was a descendant by marriage of Sir Francis Drake. At any rate the Civil Lord got his way and in February 1940 the first trainees arrived, moving from their billets in the local villages into the wooden huts as they were completed. The huts were furnished, and contained coke-fired stoves that sat in the middle, surrounded by white painted bricks, white enamel kit lockers and beds –

complete with white naval counterpanes. Covered walkways connected the huts to the ablution rooms. The rough serge, buttoned up to the neck, ginger suited *hostility only* recruits wearily tramped the muddy tracks that passed for roads. (90)

After the war, the Training Centre underwent a major re-development programme in five stages, beginning with…wait for it…stage one – the Officers Mess. The building of five new barrack blocks, each to house 100 men to replace the wooden huts, followed this, whilst the last stage, completed in around 1966, included the guardroom I'd passed through, a swimming pool and a new church. (91) Dad would have known the old church, St Albans, (demolished in 1968), but I wondered if he'd realised that the two frosted 'Corps Crest' windows had originally come from the sergeant's mess at the old red marine's barracks at Forton, Gosport after it'd closed, at the time of the merger with his blue marines in 1923. (92)

✦ ✦ ✦

From the POC building we moved around to the Tarzan assault course bordering the perimeter fence which was topped with bloated loops of razor wire; I wasn't sure whether this was to keep intruders out or the trainees in. Bob was very proud of having made it through this course, with its thirty-foot high wall to scale as a finale.

'I had to have several goes at this,' he said, '…just managed to beat the 15 minute time limit – the course record's up there on the board look!' I looked; it was marked as 7 minutes 37 seconds. 'God knows how anyone could do it as quick as that. Some guys do it in good style right down as far as the wall, but just can't get over it.'

'What happens to them then?'

'They fail – some guys get up there too,' he pointed. 'But they can't make it across the rope ladder – fear of heights see – they fail too.'

We walked on, anti-clockwise around the camp, at one point crossing in front of marines lying prone with rifles pointed at us.

'We're not going to get shot at out here are we?' I jested nervously, noticing that I seemed to be kind-of ducking and bobbing as I walked.

'No, the rifles aren't loaded,' said Bob reassuringly, with a smile.

We walked out towards the western boundary that sloped down to give an appealing view over the River Exe. I sensed that Dad hadn't had such a bad time here in 1944 and 1945. It seemed to me, at that moment anyway, like a pretty good place to see out the last year of the war and the last year of his twenty-four years as a Royal.

There would still have been the rude awakening of reveille at 0600 hours of course, with the morning ritual of shit, shave, shower and a shoeshine, but there were compensations and little treats. The RMITC were Football League Champions then, and on August bank holiday Dad would have gone with the rest to the big public sports day at Exmouth's cricket ground. It must also have seemed a bit strange to him to be back in the soldierly role of the marine, which he hadn't experienced since his return from Turkey in September 1923.Generally though things were OK. He'd been married to Mum for four years by then, but hadn't seen much of her – but now, around the end of September 1944, she'd caught the train down to Exeter where he'd taken some leave and had met her. They'd spent some time west of Lymstone, on the other side of the Exe – at Dawlish, four miles away as the sober crow flies – and this was where I'd been conceived.

The war in Europe trickled on; in October 1944 the British had landed in Greece, in November the RAF sunk Germany's last major warship – the Tirpitz and by the beginning of May the following year the war with Germany was over. On July the first 1945 Dad got slightly pissed in the sergeant's mess at Lympstone to wet the baby's head, and six weeks later he was back in Portsmouth Division, Eastney. Then, on the 17th of October 1945 he was released Class A into Civvy Street – well almost, he joined the Admiralty Constabulary.

◆ ◆ ◆

I looked at my map in the centre of the old orange booklet; it showed this area as 'S', the lower fields. Now, it was 'S' assault course, and a marine came steaming up the slope towards us, panting heavily.

'He's just practicing – timing himself – when he does it for real he'll be loaded up with full kit,' said Bob.

Bob was from Barnsley and he told me he'd signed up for four years and had done one-and-a-half so far.

'I joined because I wanted to travel but all I've seen so far is this place,' He beefed.

'Are you going to be here much longer then?' I asked.

'No I've passed out like – but I'm waiting to go on a course at the moment – that's why I'm still here.' We passed back along the other side of the parade ground where the band had struck up.

'They're practicing for the King's Squad pass out,' Bob said, 'that's when you get the Green Beret.'

'How many marines are here then?' Bob paused and thought... perhaps deciding whether this was classified information – more likely trying to work out the number?

'There's about nine hundred training – they start in groups of sixty – usually about twenty finish. Some of em decide it's not for them, and others like – repeat.'

Two marines marched past side-by-side, one black and the other white, swinging their arms together rhythmically and vigorously as if they were on parade. I wondered if they walked everywhere like that? Dad always boasted that the Royal Marines were the smartest and best marching men of all the services. I couldn't argue with that – though some might.

As we passed the Spar shop, which for some reason I was surprised to find on the camp, I thought that Bob might at least be a little curious as to why he'd been detailed to escort this old bloke around the camp, so I told him a bit about my mission and my future travel plans. Now suddenly, he must have thought – what the hell, I may as well tell this guy what it's all about, so he started – whilst I clicked on the Dictaphone:

'First you have to do a six mile route march on Woodbury Common – two miles across – like hills, through fully submerged water tunnels and lengthy underground tunnels, then a four-mile run back. Then there's shooting on the 25mm. range, then a nine-mile speed march around Woodbury Common, then the Tarzan assault course, then 30 miles across Dartmoor to be completed in eight hours.'

Sounds bloody good to me I thought; what's the age limit to join? – Is fifty-seven too old? It is – Oh shit! This is the problem isn't it – you only actually get one stab at life and then before you know where you are, about forty years have slipped by and there are lots of things you can never do. George Eliot wrote: *It is never too late to be what you might have been.* This isn't true if you want to become a Royal Marine.

Now we were back at the guardroom – the tour had only taken about half an hour, but the 'treading' had been done. I thanked Bob and motioned to shake his hand, sensing that this was something he'd not done more than a couple of times in his young life.

Within a few minutes, I was back in the large gravel car park, had slung off my rucksack containing the mythical suicide bomb and was scribbling down some notes before my sad short-term memory had switched to automatic delete mode. In 1940, this car park had been part of the original tented Exton site and in 1978 it was a sports ground, now it had finally bowed to the almighty automobile.

It was then – too late as usual – that I realised I hadn't seen the original 1940 wooden hut. I cursed – just a little…

The sound of crackling gunfire came from the camp. I sighed and thought about those marines lying prone with their rifles pointed at us as we'd crossed in front of them – wondering if Bob had been telling the truth. Then, a beautiful thing happened – faintly, almost imperceptivity I heard it; rising and falling as the breeze drifted softly across the road towards me – the Royal Marine band were playing their signature tune:

A life on the Ocean Wave
A home on the rolling deep,

When the scatter'd waters rave,
And the winds their revels keep.
Like an eagle caged, I pine,
On this dull unchanging shore,
Oh, give me the flashing brine
The spray and the tempest's roar. (93)

I could feel a lump forming in my throat and something welled up inside of me; it was almost as if the old man's ashes were swirling around gently in the air outside – and then, in that moment, the hard old man I'd become turned back into a soft young boy again.

Suddenly, missing the old wooden hut didn't seem to matter much… (94)

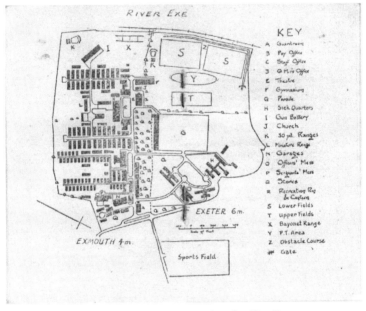

Centre page from 'Depot Royal Marines' booklet,
showing plan of Lympstone camp circa 1944.

11.   Dad, Horatio and the Bogeyman

At dawn on the morning of Monday the 24th of July 1815 the seventy-four-gun frigate HMS *Bellerophon*, known to her sailors as Billy Ruffian, sailed past Dartmouth and anchored in Torbay for a two-day visit. Almost 115 years later, on the afternoon of Friday the 18th of July 1930 the nine, sixteen-inch gun, triple-turreted battleship HMS *Nelson* followed in the long-gone wake of *Bellerophon* and dropped her anchor at 1723 hours in the bay for a four-day visit. Both ships had sailed from France; *Nelson* had arrived with my Dad on board, via Falmouth from Brest where she'd been on a showing the flag visit. *Bellerophon* had arrived with Napoleon Bonaparte on board, from Rochefort, near the present day seaside resort of La Rochelle, where the British Navy had blockaded any thoughts the once-Emperor might have harboured of setting sail to gain asylum in the United States.

I was intrigued that two of Dad's ships had been named after English heroes both made famous as adversaries of his – HMS *Iron Duke* and HMS *Nelson*. This little fat man who'd stood on the deck of *Bellerophon* with hands clasped behind his back like Prince Charles, had looked across to Torquay, then just a small fishing village, and had remarked that it reminded him of Porto Ferraio on Elba. In a few month's time, or perhaps even then, his wish might have been that he'd have stayed on that small island off the southern coast of France of which he'd been granted sovereignty under the Treaty of Fontainbleau.

Newspapers can change lives and sometimes the course of history. A sixty-four-year-old man who was about to retire, one day brought me, completely unsolicited, a cutting from a local newspaper – it was a job advertisement; I applied and got the job that, unknown to me then, would become my life for the next thirty-two years.

A similar thing happened to Napoleon. Lady Holland, who'd been an admirer of Napoleon since she'd met him in Paris in 1802 during the brief *Peace of Amiens* which may well have changed the course of history. She'd wheedled permission from the chief allied representative on Elba, Colonel Neil Campbell, to send Napoleon a parcel of newspapers. In one of these he'd read that his cosy little exile on Elba might be about to be exchanged for a remote island, ten and a half miles long and six and a half miles wide, located in the mid South Atlantic Ocean – 1,200 miles off the coast of Africa. (95) Now, this may well have been the straw that gave the camel the hump – or something like that, because on the premise that it's always better to attack before being attacked, Napoleon escaped from Elba and raised the army that would fight what would be known as the Hundred Days Campaign, with bloody battles at Ligny, Quatre Bras and finally Waterloo, which together claimed almost 84,000 casualties. (96)

What other losses might there have been if Lady Holland hadn't sent Napoleon the newspapers? Well, Wellington probably wouldn't have become so famous, which might have deprived us of the name – wellies, and Billy Connolly of a hit song, Waterloo Station might have been called Vitoria, (after Wellington's 1813 victory against Napoleon's brother Joseph in northern Spain), which would have been confusing to say the least when you came to buy a train ticket... and then there was Waterlooville, where I'd been born, which might not have existed, or at least would certainly have been called something different.

Napoleon, a trained captain, hated but also beheld a secret admiration for the English military – on *Bellerophon* he'd remarked to General Bertrand about the marines – *How much might be done with a hundred thousand such soldiers as these*! He'd also patted Captain Maitland on the shoulder and observed that if it hadn't been for the English Navy he would have been Emperor of the East and that wherever he went he was sure to find English ships in the way. (97) This was so; it was the navy who'd prevented him from transferring troops and settlers to Louisiana, (named after Louis XIV), forcing him to sell it in 1803 for $15,000,000. More specifically it was Horatio Nelson and the navy who'd prevented Napoleon in 1798 at the Battle of the Nile from realising his Pharaonic ambitions of conquering Egypt that would have made life very difficult, if not impossible, for the British in India. It was Nelson again who, by winning at Trafalgar in 1805, had gained control of the high seas by destroying the combined French and Spanish fleets to ensure that Britain wouldn't be invaded. The British had, before this, been frozen into a state of paranoia by Napoleonic invasion, *waves-of-fear* that had rolled ashore like a tsunami in 1798 and again in 1803.

Nelson and Napoleon were inextricably intertwined for most of their lives. Nelson was born in September 1758, the sixth son of a rector, in Burnham Thorpe, a village on the edge of the salt marshes around the Wash, bitten hard by the cold east winds. Bonaparte was born in May 1768, almost ten years later, the second son of a family of thirteen, in Ajaccio, Corsica, (then a province of France – for just a year), licked by the warm Mediterranean and occasionally breezed by the Mistral. At the time when Napoleon was baptised, (curiously not, as was usual – soon after birth, but at two years of age), the sickly Horatio had been rated on the books of *Raisonable*, captained by his uncle and had travelled on the stage coach from King's Lynn to Chatham to board her. (98) Their two paths had first crossed when Major Bonaparte was a 26-year-old revolutionary artillery officer in action at Toulon. Career progression was quick in those days, as all the officers of noble birth had already been hauled off to meet *Madame Guillotine*. Horatio was a 35-year-old captain involved in the defence of that same naval port before the British retreated, (strangely enough), to Corsica. It was during the siege of Calvi in Corsica that Horatio received a wound that resulted in the loss of sight in his right eye, following which everyone had to be especially careful as to the context of use of the term *Aye Aye Sir*!

Quite obviously HMS *Nelson*, affectionately known as Nellie, was named after Horatio, but she and her sister ship HMS *Rodney* were also nicknamed The Cherry Tree Class because they were cut down by the hatchet men of the 1922 Washington Treaty. George Washington was, as a boy, supposed to have taken a hatchet to his father's favourite cherry tree. Anyway, the treaty, signed by Britain, the United States, Japan, France and Italy, officially sought to control worldwide naval expansion by limiting the displacements and the main armaments of capital ships, aircraft carriers and cruisers, as well as the total tonnage and age of the first two. Unofficially, every nation had its own agenda to try to gain some advantage from it. The US in particular was extremely worried about Japanese expansion in the Far East. The moral to be gleaned from treaties generally is that they promote lateral thinking into ways in which the desired ends may be achieved by adapting or manipulating the rules. The rules of the 1922 Washington Naval Treaty were laid down in 24 articles, two of which restricted the construction of new ships to 35,360-tons and to guns of 16-inch calibre maximum. But Britain had by this time already built HMS *Hood* with detailed plans drawn up for Super Hoods – 47,200-ton battle cruisers that included three 16inch triple turreted guns with a 12-mile range. Not wanting to tear up their designs they decided to squash all three triple guns forward onto a reduced tonnage ship by cutting down the length of the quarterdeck and placing the bridge towards the stern. This policy unfolded in the cutting down in length of *Nelson* and *Rodney*, (which were both still twice the length of a football pitch), giving them their truncated appearance and the epithet of Cherry Tree Class. (99) The Americans, French, Japanese and Soviets all later copied the design.

✦ ✦ ✦

The only snippet of information I could find regarding the visit of *Nelson* to Torquay in July 1930 was from *The Torquay Times* on the 25th of that month. It referred to a cricket match held between Torquay and the ship's company at the recreation ground. Figuring that it was a near certainty Dad would have attended this if he'd managed to get shore leave, the problem I then faced was trying to determine where this ground, if it still existed, was actually located. The librarian, an attractive lady wearing a long flower-patterned, hippy dress, was very helpful, and we spent twenty pleasant minutes together searching old reference books. Finally we stumbled across an oblique reference to the repair of the sea wall – near the recreation ground that was close to Torre Abbey. Once a monastery and now the Mayor's official residence, it was easy to locate on Torquay's street map, and bingo! There *was* a recreation ground wedged between the Mayor's residence and Torquay Station.

Armed with a photocopy of the not-too-clear map, I started out by crossing Union Street and climbing up Albert Steps, passing through a narrow alley flanked by high brick walls, sprayed with non-artistic graffiti, that overlooked the (usually unseen) backside of Torquay. I felt more unsafe here than anywhere else I'd ever been in my life; menacing looking youths in reversed baseball caps lounged around smoking, snickering and gripping bottles of beer that might soon become weapons. One lad had somehow managed to climb onto the wall and swaggered around on it, possibly in an inebriated state or otherwise as high as the wall itself – on something or other. I meanwhile tried to look as mean as possible, hoped he wasn't about to leap or, more likely, fall on top of me. I kept my eyes staring into space somewhere ahead and sauntered by as casually as possible.

Emerging, to my surprise safely on Burridge Lane, I crossed Abbey Road and bowled down Hill Road with some relief, towards Torre Abbey and the sea. It was from Torre Abbey Meadows in 1910 that Mr Graham White performed two daredevil flights in his frail biplane over the British fleet anchored in the bay, to demonstrate the potentialities of the airplane in wartime; no ship's guns could be elevated high enough to reach him. Surprisingly it took the Japanese, some thirty-one years later, to prove how correct White had been about the fleet's vulnerability to aerial attack. (100) Now, along the wide promenade path in front of the Meadows, teenage skateboarders performed daredevil tricks for their even younger girl admirers, whilst over on the grass, fairground lorries loitered with intent to set up or set off.

Kings Gardens bordered what was once the recreation ground that I was seeking; it was another world. I was completely alone as I wandered its neat, rock-bordered paths that edged a man-made stream running through a series of ponds fed from a culvert. Across the path, palm trees and other tropical and English foliage lazily lurched in a yesteryear tranquillity that I inadvertently shattered by disturbing the torpor of several mallards that quacked and flapped away noisily into the water. A wagtail sat on the path ahead quietly living up to its name. I crossed a little bridge, turned a corner and almost missed the partially hidden, green corrugated tin door, buried in a wall between trees. It was slightly ajar, so gingerly I prodded it, then pushed it and crept in.

I'd entered a quite, it seemed – almost secret, corner of the cricket ground, overhung by a mixture of conifer and deciduous trees where, on patchy grass, dotted with fallen yellow and bronze leaves, sat half-a-dozen staunch oak benches overlooking a deserted pitch. I flopped down on one and swept a look in a slow anti-clockwise arc around the ground. To the right stood the wooden, white clubhouse, the black-and-white scoreboard and a sightscreen. Ahead was the browner green rectangle of the pitch where the only play was from a lone oscillating sprinkler.

✦ ✦ ✦

Torquay had run out easy winners here in 1930 against the XI from HMS *Nelson*, beating them by 145 runs to 55 in the first innings, Sub Lieutenant White being the only one of the ship's company to score double figures. In the follow-on *Nelson* made a dismal 72 for 9, though I couldn't understand why they didn't let the eleventh man have a go – unless it was because he was the bowler – Marine Jules. (101) Typically, the marines would have comprised about 9 percent of the ships complement of 1,314, so the lone marine in the XI was statistically a fair representation. Not so the officers – they'd have accounted for about 7 percent of the complement, but the XI consisted of 9 officers and potential officers (midshipmen), when statistically you'd have expected there to have been just one of them. This reflected the fact that cricket had first emerged from gentlemen's clubs and was later adopted by public schools who believed it was synonymous with manliness and leadership, although to exert oneself to the point of perspiration was felt to be unbecoming of a gentleman. Perhaps *Nelson* might have done better if they'd carried out trials amongst the lower deck.

✦ ✦ ✦

To be sure that I'd crossed Dad's route into the ground, I completed the triangular walk around it, along King's Drive, Falkland Road and Rathmore Road. An intricate black and gold painted wrought iron gateway at the seaward end verified that Torquay Athletic Rugby Club now occupied this end, whilst the other end was the domain of Torquay Cricket Club. Satisfied, I walked back eastward around the bay to my next target – Haldon Pier.

It was at this pier that the marines and bluejackets would have come ashore on leave, crowded up to the gunwales in picket-boats and pinnaces. (102) At Beacon Hill I hit a snag – major construction works precluded entry onto Haldon Pier; across the road a sign attached to the wire fence told me that inside, 'Living Coasts' was in the final stages of creation. This £21 million harbour redevelopment, described as a marine aviary, formed part of a plan to turn the English Riviera into a world-class waterfront. It was a development that Torquay's Resorts Action Group was glad to see, but which I wasn't – not at that moment at least. Now, the best I could do, and the closest I could get to tread the ground would be a wistful peep from Princess Pier across the water to *my* pier.

So I dawdled off disconsolately around the Old Harbour lined with its union jack flying flagpoles and rows of old people slumped in wheelchairs gazing out to sea – (a refreshing change for them from being slumped in wheelchairs gazing out from a home). At the landing stage of Princess Pier a notice rudely screamed – NO DECKCHAIRS ARE TO BE TAKEN BEYOND THIS POINT, and once I was beyond the point in question I quickly deduced that this was because, if they had been, they'd pretty soon finish up in the sea, judging from the strength of the wind. Torquay is reportedly sheltered from the prevailing southwest winds – but it wasn't that day. I looked across to Haldon Pier with the wind whipping across my face. The New Harbour, as it had been known in 1930, was now just – The Harbour, laid out echeloned style as yacht berths. I looked back across to the messed up, mass construction site of Living Coast; Torquay was still developing, adapting as it always had done, to survive; moving on from being just a nice place to retire to. Looking up to the tors of Torquay from Princess Pier I could see why Napoleon had remarked on its similarity to Porto Ferraio, then I began to think of its history.

✦ ✦ ✦

I thought of the post-war days of mass tourism which had grown out of its Victorian roots as a holiday destination for the wealthy. At one time in the 1920s there'd been a proposal to get the Government to make it a permanent station for the Royal Navy by constructing a breakwater between Berry Head and Hope's Nose. This was vehemently opposed by: *Some of the most important seaside chambers*, and the project had to be dropped, although in 1928 there were still some local hopes that things might go ahead – It didn't. (103) The snooty inhabitants didn't approve of visits of the riffraff navy to the town.

Before this, it had made a name for itself as a seaside health resort. It owed a debt to a treatise written by Dr Richard Russell who'd expounded the virtues of the use of seawater and warm fresh air in the treatment of glandular consumption, notably tuberculosis – a common disease of the day in Britain.

But Torquay's real birth was due to Napoleon. The Royal Navy had been stationed in Torbay for extended periods during the Napoleonic War and the wives of naval officers, who'd come to stay near their husbands to deter them from temptations that might otherwise have led to the threat of indelicate mercurial treatment, found the climate mild, pleasant and most agreeable. They spread the word, which was an improvement on what their husbands might otherwise have spread, and soon the place was dripping with the *filthy*, wealthy rich.

Napoleon's two-day visit on HMS *Bellerophon* on the 24th of July 1815 created a mini boom in Torquay. People were curious to catch a glimpse of Boney, who they'd learned to think of as the devil himself; they travelled from all over the country, from as far away as Glasgow, to catch a glimpse of him. It was reported that: *The ship was soon surrounded with a flotilla of boats and yachts from Dartmouth, Brixham, Teignmouth, Dawlish, Exeter and Sidmouth. Torbay presented just such an animated appearance as is often witnessed on regatta day. (104)*

Napoleon was every bit the actor; he showed himself on deck, took off his hat and bowed. (105)

But during his time in Torquay and later in Plymouth, through until the end of July, Napoleon was cheered by the thought that he might be allowed to stay in England in some style as a country gentleman, much as his brother Lucian had done for four years after being captured in Sardinia. He'd dictated a letter on the 13th of July, when he was still off Rochefort, in which he appealed to the Prince Regent to be able to *share the hospitality of the British people*. The General entrusted to deliver this letter was, however, not allowed to land in Plymouth and returned with it to *Bellerophon* anchored in Torbay. Napoleon had miscalculated; he'd not realised the pervasion of *Bonaphobia* that had gripped the country – that was about to become *Bonamania*. Parents would terrorise their children into silence with threats that otherwise:

Bonaparte will pass this way – who, sups and dines and lives reliant every day on naughty people – And he'll eat you, eat you, eat you, gobble you, gobble you, snap! snap! snap! (106)

The Boney-man will get you – became – The Bogeyman will get you.

He had no chance.

On Wednesday the 26th of July 1815 HMS *Bellerophon* set sail for Plymouth where Napoleon was soon to receive the sympathy of the British people when they'd learnt of his proposed fate. It's said that: *The hats of the men and the handkerchiefs of the ladies were waving in every direction. The people actually cheered him and treated him with respect and consideration.* (107) The navy, on orders of the government, actually broke the law by preventing him from applying for a writ of habeas corpus, thus ensuring that he didn't step foot on British soil and therefore would not be subject to the laws of the land. (108) If he *had* set foot in Torquay he might have become one of the first asylum seekers, but as it was, the British treated him more as a terrorist than as a prisoner of war, to be incarcerated not in Guatánamo Bay, but on an English sanitised version of Devil's Island. And like three-quarters of the prisoners on that island he'd never see the civilised world – (let alone France – oops!) – ever again.

On the 31st of July, Napoleon knew his final destination, the place he'd escaped Elba to avoid. On the 7th of August he'd transferred to HMS *Northumberland*, and she'd sailed off south on the sixty-seven day voyage to the basalt rock of St Helena.

Later, HMS *Bellerophon* was to sail east to her final destination on the River Medway, where five weeks later she was paid off and sadly spent her last ten years as a prison hulk.

✦ ✦ ✦

HMS *Nelson* also steamed east from Torbay – to her home base of Portsmouth and to Navy Week where, ironically, (the old brown case had revealed), the Royal Marines from *Nelson*, including Dad, donned the uniforms of their predecessors from Napoleonic (or Nelsonian) times and marched the cobbled, train-line trammelled dockyard roads to perform the Relieving the Guard Ceremony under the bow of Horatio's flagship.

Having met at the same place, but at different times, the way divided again now for everyone.

I'd stood windswept on Princess Pier for what seemed like a long time whilst Torquay's past swirled around inside my head. I looked out to sea and visualised briefly once more the departure of both old sailing ships and the battleship. Then I bent my body into the wind and left the pier to set off myself – west to Dartmouth.

HMS Nelson in Panama Canal, February 1931.

Royal Marines from HMS Nelson marching through Portsmouth Dockyard during Navy Week (30th July to 6th August 1930).

12. Strawberry Tea

The Royal Castle Hotel was, in 1630, two private houses built by prosperous merchants engaged in the Newfoundland cod trade. Within a century one of the houses had become know as The New Inn and by 1782 the houses had been combined to form The Castle Inn, which became a hotel in 1841. Finally in1902, following visits by the Prince of Wales, it added the prefix 'Royal' to its name (109) (110) It gazes out regally over Dartmouth's small, enclosed quay, known as the boat float, cluttered with fendered and tarpaulined small craft, its River Dart entrance locked in by the embankment and surmounted by a dainty pedestrian bridge.

Wearily checking in, I repaired noisily up the creaky old oak staircase to my 'cabin' on the 'quarterdeck'. The wallpaper outside the room was scribed with latitudinal and longitudinal lines, cascading a seventeenth century nautical collage of compasses, sextants and sailing ships that set the tone for the room itself, which had been cleverly designed to emulate a ship's cabin. The single bed, giving the appearance of a bunk, was wedged snugly in-between walls, enclosed by wood panelling, lit with spotlights at bow and stern and catenary draped with rope along its length. Below the window, which looked out onto a courtyard, was a fake porthole in-filled with a seascape horizon line, below which swam a dodgy and unsurprisingly bemused looking fish. The décor was completed by a solid looking brass lamp standard with a brass porthole screwed onto a twenty-four toothed bevel gearwheel base. Even the deep blue cushions were embellished with a baroque navigational interlace of compasses and Latin like *Septentrio – 80* inscriptions.

That squiffy porthole and an oncoming feeling of seasickness soon sent me scuttling out of the cabin (sorry- room, where incidentally there wasn't room to swing a cat, not even a furry one) to first explore the hotel's cuisine, followed by the pubs of Dartmouth.

In the hotel's restaurant, which overlooked the river, I ordered a spicy beef dish on a bed of saffron rice accompanied by a bottle of Uruguayan Chardonnay wine, which I hadn't planned to finish, but which in an unplanned, reckless fashion I'm afraid to say – I did. Unfortunately, the spicy beef should have been described on the menu as – gristly spicy beef, because it necessitated furtive glances to ascertain that other diners were suitably preoccupied, before I could squirm out the offending gristle pieces and hide them under the parsley.

Suitably victualled, I made my way through the Royal Avenue Gardens, past the bandstand and fountain to the embankment, then east towards the Britannia Royal Naval College, which I wanted to take a look at because I'd received a letter from a ninety-year old retired captain who'd been a cadet there. Dad had only spent two days in Dartmouth at the end of May 1927 on HMS *Tiger*, but the captain had written that he'd remembered visiting the ship: *I think she was an old three-funnelled battle-cruiser and she was accompanied by HMS Iron Duke, the flagship – with an admiral on board,* he'd written: *We were shown around and then all gathered in the Admiral's cabin for a strawberry tea.* (111)

On College Way, just down from the Naval College, was the Ship in Dock, not an actual ship, but a pub in which I'd thought of having a quick drink simply because a local historian had written to me suggesting that this would have been a pub favoured by the sailors and marines. A sign outside described it as – A SMALL INN WITH A BIG WELCOME, and looking in, the half-a-dozen customers made it seem crowded and undoubtedly verified the first part of the statement. I never did test the second part because it appeared to be a 'what r y doin in our pub' type of establishment. Now, I may well have been wrong here but decided to give it a miss anyway, and instead took a long walk west along the almost deserted embankment, strolling through hugger-mugger old town Dartmouth, (as the guide book had described the feel of the place) (112). None of the pubs appealed, and I was in grave danger of running out of town and finishing up in darkness, when I came upon the Dartmouth Arms.

First impressions were that it looked nautical enough to have been selected by Dad, (who at the time was a twenty-four year old marine), on a one-night *dicky* run ashore. Behind the bar around fifty mugs of varying design dripped from the ceiling. Young people and loud music pervaded the place, which coupled with original oil paintings of clipper ships and photographs of four-man clipper rowing crews, made for a strange brew. I sat myself at a table facing two ships' wall plaques labelled *Carron* and *Venub* and pretended to take notes from the book I was pretending to read.

In a corner, four, thirty-something ladies noisily compared weddings and then a bit later compared divorces, but when a man joined them the conversation changed to more mundane subjects such as body piercing and women's hockey. On an adjacent table a businessman and his much younger secretary sat. He was grey-haired with a paunch and podgy ring-less fingers. She was around thirty, slim and sleek, wearing a long black dress with a choker and showing a bit of cleavage – and a wedding ring. She nudged him a couple of times playfully and smiled into his eyes as her foot slid slowly up and down his leg. One thing was for sure – they weren't married. I felt slightly embarrassed and had already decided to leave when the gristly spicy beef began to stir things up in the alimentary canal, forcing an emergency visit to the toilet.

Now, from photographs displayed on the wall as I very swiftly left the establishment, it appears that the Dartmouth Arms are famous for and proud of the fact that they were featured in *The Onedin Line* TV series and the film *The Sailor Who Fell From Grace*. One thing I can guarantee – in those days I bet there was no shortage of toilet paper for the stars! Not so on this night.

Back at the Royal Castle Hotel, and after a desperate enforced return to my *cabin*, I took a double dark rum tot and ginger beer nightcap in the hotel's Galleon Bar before creeping back up the staircase to my *cabin* where the floor now seemed to be sloping and the doorway angled much as they were in the early nineteenth century – but this may well have been due to the excess mixture of wine, beer and rum I'd consumed.

The clock on St Saviour's church tower, which seemed as if it were two feet from my window, struck twelve o' clock as I fell into my bunk. Oh no! Not all-night I thought! But after the one o'clock strike I heard nothing until five bells. Then I fell back to sleep again, dreaming of mutiny at the Nore.

◆ ◆ ◆

A smart, angled, Perspex covered placard proclaimed Warfleet's potted history. Its first industries had served the three basic human needs: A flourmill and a bake house provided food, a brew-house, drink and lime kilns that made cement, shelter. Later, these had all disappeared in favour of the more sophisticated hankerings of paper and pottery. Now, I looked out on that pleasant sunny August day over the millpond creek to the whitewashed walls and apexes of the houses set into the hillside against a pastel blue rinsed sky, through clumps of trees, to Kingswear beyond. The whiteness of the houses were perhaps a remnant, and reminiscent of the limestone cottage walls that the kilns below this point had once also produced.

It was now mid afternoon. I'd spent the entire morning in nearby Newton Abbot trawling through copies of *The Dartmouth Chronicle*, to make the single discovery of exactly where HMS *Tiger* had anchored on the 31st of May 1927. The extract I found was a mere snippet of twenty-one words in length hidden in a column entitled Local Intelligence. It read: *HMS Tiger arrived at Dartmouth on Tuesday afternoon, from Portland, and anchored in the Range. The warship left yesterday for Torbay.* (113) I chuckled to myself – I knew exactly where the Range was; it was shown on a map that the Dart Harbour & Navigation Authority had sent me.

There were fleeting glimpses of Dartmouth seen through the trees from the coastal path, as I made my way from Warfleet. A rise led up from the footpath to the road at a small promontory, skirted at its seaward end by a stone wall, with Dartmouth Castle wedged into its southeast corner, overlooking the estuary. The small car park was packed full, and arriving cars had to turn awkwardly around, driving back down the narrow road and squeezing into the side, tight to a bank for other arrivals to make the same useless journey. Knots of people were sitting everywhere – on seats, grass banks, walls and car bonnets.

The Range was out there, over the stone wall, past long-stalked magenta coloured flowers, (colours, I'd learnt from my schoolboy philately days – but not alas flowers), that shot out wildly under the base of the wall from a steep bank leading down to the surf-less rocks that on that particular day sat frozen in the still, windless sea. The mouth of the River Dart snakes past Dittisham, with the jagged creeks of Noss, Old Mill and Waterhead strewn out over its length as it widens approaching the river's mouth where the castles of Dartmouth and Kingswear stand. They were built on both banks of the river to guard the port from French pirates. The Dart widens again at Compass Cove and Newfoundland Cove, before flowing out into the roadstead – a stretch of water that sits neatly between the castles and coves. The roadstead is called the Range. I stood for a good five minutes just staring at it and thinking about *Tiger* anchored there, picturing the drifters moving off to disgorge their maritime human cargoes three-quarters of a mile up-river at the South Embankment. (114) That day, a single yacht was anchored in the Range, close to a single buoy with a colour that matched the bank-side flowers.

I briefly considered visiting the crenellated castle, but was easily dissuaded by the cost, for which I could purchase the equivalent of three and a half rum and raisin ice creams from the kiosk at the shop. I settled for one – then, sneakily managing to purloin a seat, leaned back, closed my eyes, and enjoyed the sun tanning the outside of my face, whilst a large bitten-off piece of ice cream cooled the inside of my cheek as it slowly dissolved. There was plenty of time... and I had nothing much else to do now until my evening appointment.

✦ ✦ ✦

Subject-changes can occur in subtle ways on the Internet. One thing can lead to another and then on to another, so that the subject you finish up with bears no relationship to your start point. This is what happened to me one night when somehow I managed the mutation from the subject of Dartmouth Royal Naval College to that of corporal punishment.

The flogging of boys was once an integral part of naval culture, and the training hulk *Britannia*, the predecessor of Dartmouth Royal Naval College, which was moored in the town from 1863, was no exception. In 1864 there had been a total of 279 boys flogged in the Royal Navy with each boy receiving an average of 31 lashes. *Britannia*, reflected perhaps either a better class of boy or a higher degree of leniency, as it only accounted for two floggings that year, with an average of 18 lashes per boy. (115) From 1901 until 1992, 241 birchings and 8,000 canings were recorded in naval training establishments (116) If I'd been a boy in the navy in those days there's no doubt I'd have been amongst those statistics; I'd infamously received the cane from the head whilst still in primary school – and held the class record in senior school. Punishment by the cat was stopped for naval cadets in special regulations of 1858 in which the more genteel punishment of the birch rod, as favoured by public schools, was substituted. (117)

In 1941 George Orwell recorded in his wartime essay *The Lion and the Unicorn* that Britain had 10,000 such public schools. In 2004 that number, (largely because of *that* war), had reduced to around 2,400, although they're now re-named as Independents. Dartmouth Royal Naval College was in effect a specialised public school until 1941 when a scholarship scheme was introduced.

Robert, the ninety-two-year old man I had an appointment with that evening had first sampled the privileges that Dartmouth College beheld in 1925, as a thirteen-year-old boy; that meant that he'd been just fifteen when he'd gone aboard *Iron Duke* for his strawberry tea in the Admiral's cabin.

✦ ✦ ✦

As the late August darkness crept in, I had some difficulty in finding the house, unassisted by the narrow, steep, rural and bendy road, so I parked up and decided in desperation to knock on some doors. A stranger knocking on the door of a country house in the dark seemed like a risky undertaking for both parties, but I tapped loudly on the first door I came to and immediately a small, frail old man appeared at a window and motioned me towards a side door.

'I'm sorry to trouble you,' I started, as the door edged ajar, 'but…'

'You must be Mr…' he interrupted. We looked at each other – and then I realised that not only had I by chance picked on the very house I'd been searching for, but that also the old man had momentarily forgotten my name.

'…Mr Pinnock,' he finished – suddenly remembering.

'Robert?' I enquired with mixed incredulity and relief.

I'd expected a rotund, ruddy-complexioned sea-captain type – which had in fact been the rank he'd reached upon retirement.

'Mike,' I said offering my hand.

'Come in' he said, as we shook hands. As I entered the kitchen a spaniel jumped up and licked my hand and Robert busied with some saucepans on a cooker.

He was remarkable; we'd first made contact through a local lady historian, and in his letter he'd given me his e-mail address, (I found it amazing that he'd learnt to use a computer at the age of ninety), and we'd exchanged e-mails over the past two years. In the latest of these, he'd invited me to a scratch supper. I wasn't too sure what that was.

In the event he first offered me a sherry and then led the way to a polished wooden table, which he'd laid with a tablecloth, place-mats, plates, wine glasses and a cheese-platter in the large dining room which spread the length of the house and which would in daylight have afforded a splendid view out over the Range. Here he served us both up a thick, slightly cold, mushroom soup accompanied by an assortment of different bread rolls, butter, cheeses and a bottle of red wine, which he seemed anxious for me to share with him. Throughout the meal, the spaniel, whose name was apparently Blackie, licked my hand whenever he could get it – he was either very friendly, very lonely, had a fetish about hands or had some strange oral affliction.

The house was I suspected, decorated much as it would have been when his wife had been alive – there were old, original oil paintings, alabaster statues and a large heavy looking bottle-green curtain that divided this room from the lounge with its open fireplace and cat sprawled on the coffee table. In truth I wasn't hungry, but ate up gracefully. It was good.

He asked about *footsteps* and if I'd brought the book with me, which of course I hadn't. I was more interested in *his* life; he was nine years younger than Dad would have been if he'd still been alive, and like Dad, would have experienced the last days of the British Empire. This recently much maligned institution still embraced – in 1939 – an unbelievable *quarter* of the world – both its population and land surface. (118) France ran second with her territories in Africa and South-east Asia, but the population of the French territories was less than half that of the British Empire. (119) I'd been born at a time when the Empire had started to fade from the six million it had once administered to the less than 125,000 it is today.

Our discussions were limited during supper, mainly because, after a good deal of repeated conversation, I finally realised that Robert was actually very deaf. Then I suddenly noticed that he wore hearing aids in both ears and, as everyone does – I began to shout. In fact we had little time to finish our supper before a Second World War documentary about Dunkirk, (which Robert suggested we might watch together), came on the TV.

We retired to the lounge, and I sunk deep into an armchair, which allowed Blackie to get into a much better hand-licking position; I tried to wriggle free several times, but after I'd almost knocked over the coffee table and catapulting the poor cat into the fireplace, I gave up and just let him lick away. The television volume was set to an equivalent level you'd get from placing your ear hard up against the main speaker at a hip hop concert, and just in case the odd elusive word was still unheard, the screen ran a text for the hard of hearing. Robert was engrossed in the documentary so I sipped my second glass of wine and looked around the room. On the wall below a window were photographs, perhaps about twenty, all nicely framed and mainly in black and white. Some were of a younger Robert at various periods in his life, ranging from when he was a young lieutenant, to a photograph of him with his wife, which I suspected had been taken much later, perhaps even when he'd retired from the navy. I noticed a cross of four photographs taken of a naval officer at various stages of being introduced to, and shaking hands with, the Queen. Below the photographs were several rows of old, dusty, hard-backed books.

After the programme, came the peace – as the TV was switched off, and here – across from the fireplace and the cat – we began to talk.

Robert explained that the ships' guns had been the cause of his deafness.

'In those days if you put cotton wool in your ears you were considered to be a sissy,' he said.

'Didn't they provide you with ear defenders then?' I asked.

'No, nobody gave it a thought,' he said. There was enough here to keep a court full of American lawyers busy for years, I thought to myself, but asked him if he was the naval officer in the four photographs taken with the Queen.

'No, that's one of my sons,' he said, 'he's in the navy too'

'Were you at Dunkirk?' I asked, thinking of the documentary. He was sitting opposite me now and I was pretty sure he must be lip-reading, because he seemed to have no trouble at all understanding me – and now I wasn't shouting.

'Yes, I was a young lieutenant on HMS *Scimitar*,' he said, 'she was a destroyer – we did six runs at Dunkirk. The first time we had about eighty on board and I said to the captain that I thought we were about fully loaded. Think again – he'd said, think again, and in the end we took across about four-hundred on that trip.'

'Were you being bombed by the Germans?' I asked.

'No – there was a hulk that had been beached – a cargo vessel – and for some reason the Germans targeted it. They wasted a lot of time on that ship and left us alone.'

I knew though, and he undoubtedly did too, that he'd been lucky; the navy had lost six destroyers with a further nineteen seriously damaged at Dunkirk. (120) HMS *Scimitar* was one of only a hand-full that had survived unscathed.

Although doubts had emerged at Jutland, during the First World War, it was the Second World War that had finally disproved the invincibility of the Royal Navy and had hastened the decline of the British Empire – which would have happened anyway, although more slowly. First, in May 1941 the pride of the navy, the battle cruiser HMS *Hood*, known as *The Mighty Hood*, was sunk after only six minutes of battle by the German battleship *Bismark*. Secondly, in December of that same year, the flagship of the Eastern Fleet – the battleship HMS *Prince of Wales* and the battle cruiser HMS *Repulse* were both sunk by Japanese torpedo bombers off Malaya, leaving the Japs the virtual freedom of the Western Pacific. The fall of Malaya and Singapore was then inevitable, and the degradation suffered by 130,000 British Empire fighting men forced into slavery by the Japs finally shattered the invincibility tag of the Empire and lost it its prestige forever. (121)

'I remember when they told us about *Hood*,' Robert said, as if he'd been reading my mind, 'it was such a shock – we couldn't believe it, she was thought of as being invincible, we just couldn't believe it.'

'My father was on *Hood*,' I said, 'during the time of the Spanish Civil War, in 1936,' but Robert didn't response to this, and I felt that maybe it was an opportune moment to both relieve my bladder and give my very clean hand a spot of respite from Blackie's tongue.

'Do you have a toilet?' I asked – a stupid question, but how else do you ask politely?

'Yes, sorry, of course – it's through that door and straight ahead, just to the right.'

'Thanks very much,' I said, hauling myself with some difficulty out of the chair towards the door, whilst simultaneously tugging my licking-hand free from Blackie's tongue. The dog was clearly offended by this and promptly flopped down by the fireplace, pretending to fall asleep.

The walls of the *heads* were covered with framed photographs, this time not of people, but of ships; I noticed *Scimitar* and the aircraft carrier *Bulwark*, and I'd remembered, from my Portsmouth apprenticeship days, that she'd been converted to Britain's first Commando Carrier in 1959. (122) The one exception to the ship photographs was a shot of HMS *Ganges*, the training establishment for boys, which showed the famous triangular mast configuration draped with white-trousered boys, topped with the saluting button boy that I'd seen on TV. Poignant photographs, I thought, are a good way to alleviate the necessary but boring tedium of toilet visitations – something to look forward to in fact – in a small way.

'Interesting photographs in the toilet,' I said, slumping back into the chair; Blackie stirred and raised an eyelid, but I'd obviously deeply hurt his feelings because he slid it shut again apathetically.

'I noticed the *Ganges* mast?'

'Yes, I was captain of *Ganges*.'

'Really! Where was *Ganges* – was it in Falmouth?' I said, thinking I'd read that somewhere on the Internet.

'No, it was in Harwich, the original ship moved from Falmouth in 1899.'

'Oh! – How was the button boy nominated? I bet you had some difficulty in getting volunteers!'

'No actually there was a lot of competition – it was thought of as being very prestigious. There was a lightening conductor up there...' he went on enthusiastically, '...they would grip it between their knees – the button was just less than a foot in diameter, and the button boy at the top was over a hundred and forty feet above the ground – it was the highest mast in the world.' Very dangerous, I thought; the Health and Safety Executive would certainly instantly slap a prohibition notice on it today, or at least an improvement notice until they'd fitted safety nets. 'We used to keep a close eye on the wind speed of course, but I always used to worry – and I was always glad when they came down. I went to a reunion a few years ago with all the past captains and button boys.' Robert's eyes glazed over as he re-lived unspoken events.

I took another sip of the red wine.

'Would you like a top up?' – Robert said, snapping back to the present and quickly whipping the cork out of the bottle.

'Umm – OK, just a small one then please – I've got to drive.' He poured, but it was to the top, and then he struggled to get the cork back into the bottle, missing the neck altogether on the first two attempts. I wanted to help. Then a horrible thought crossed my mind – suppose Robert were to die, with just me here – what would I do, and how suspicious would it appear?

'I noticed the photograph of *Bulwark* too?' I said, dismissing the thought quickly.

'Yes, I was her captain just before I retired in 1961 – I was only forty-nine.' He said. We both took a swig of wine. 'I was lucky then,' he continued, 'I landed a good job taking new ships out on trials. There were two of us; my colleague mostly did Scotland and I did Southampton, Thorneycroft and Newcastle. I was able to live here still, which was good. Did that until I was sixty-one, then I bought a pleasure boat business in Dartmouth – made no money at it though – used to run three boats – met all sorts of people, mostly nice, although you got the occasional funny customer.'

'Strange that you should finish up in Dartmouth when you'd started out at the College,' I said.

'Yes, I joined at thirteen and did four years at the College, then we had to do another four years before we were allowed on our own.'

'What was the College like, was there very strict discipline?'

'Yes, everything was done so quickly – after evening prayers, you had about ten minutes to get back, clean your teeth, wash, fold and lay out your clothes and be ready for bed. Then there was an inspection and if your clothes weren't folded in exactly the proper way, you had to put a tick on a sheet. When you'd accumulated three ticks, you got caned.'

'Where did they cane you?' I asked tentatively.

'On the backside,' Robert said, but I could tell that he didn't want to expand on the subject. Still, I wondered if 'a ticking off', a phrase my Mother was inclined to use frequently, had been derived from the practice he'd described. Anyway, I felt it prudent to change the subject.

'Do you ever get lonely?' I asked with crass stupidly.

'In the mornings for some reason, yes – when I first wake up, but then as the day goes on I start to feel better. I get down into town quite a bit – I've got a little battery powered invalid car that gets me up and down the hill – I lost my wife twelve years ago,' he said, nodding towards the happy photograph of them both that I'd noticed before and which sat centre of the mantle over the fire. His eyes started to glaze again, but then he said sadly – 'Sometimes I wonder why I'm still here.'

'Yes, but you've got all your books...' I said, trying not to sound too patronising, motioning around the room, 'and your memories.' In fact I quite envied him his cosy timeless world and admired him for how he still managed to look after himself – something I was still incapable of. We both sat quietly for a few moments, but timelessness was a luxury I rarely had. It was now just gone eleven and I knew I had a long drive ahead.

'Robert,' I sighed, 'I'm very sorry, and I hope you don't think I'm rude, but I really have to make a move, I have to drive to Plymouth tonight.'

We both got up and so did Blackie, making an immediate beeline for my hand – seeking some final reconciliation. (123)

'I wish I could stay and talk longer,' I said genuinely, 'but I'm a bit worried about the dark roads.'

'It'll be alright when you get onto the A38,' Robert said, leading me to the front door upon which I'd tapped apprehensively just three hours before.

'There's my car,' he said proudly; it was parked up under the car-porch ready to roll down the hill. 'Well you haven't got much out of me!' he said.

I shook his hand and gripped his arm. I really would have liked to have stayed and talked into the early hours but that would mean more wine and I'd be over the limit and would probably fall asleep at the wheel or get stopped for some piffling traffic offence by a bored police-man.

Robert's parting words were incorrect. Although he'd never actually met my Dad, they may just have glimpsed each other all those years ago aboard *Tiger*, before Robert had gone off to the Admiral's cabin for his strawberry tea – it was enough.

◆ ◆ ◆

The road from Dartmouth was as dark, crooked and seemingly endless as I'd feared, but there was little traffic and I only had to dip my head-lights twice before I reached the outskirts of Totnes. Here navigation was tricky, involving a slow tack through the doldrums of thirty-mile-an-hour signs and speed cameras. But after that it was plain sailing with a fair wind, down the A38 – all the way to Plymouth Hoe.

13. Secret Agent Orange Sunhat

'Welcome aboard shipmates,' drawled a white bearded pseudo-sea captain, who looked a bit like Uncle Albert from *Only Fools and Horses*.

I'd arrived at the boat just in time to see a coach party of oldies unload, descend the steps to the jetty and tediously crawl onto it ahead of me. I just managed to shuffle past a few of the more infirm to claim a seat on the upper deck, next to the wheelhouse, before the boat was awash with Zimmer-frames, walking sticks and cups of tea that the oldies wasted no time in procuring and precariously carrying up the steps.

Tiger had spent a fleeting three days in Devonport in June 1927 at No.2 berth and then a further day at No.1 buoy somewhere in Plymouth Sound or in the mouth of the Tamar. I was unable to determine from the ship's log, exactly where, and it was only over breakfast at the Grand Hotel that morning that I'd reflected that Dad would have sailed in *Tiger* up the Tamar to the dockyard – and that I'd do the same.

I'd come well armed for this trip, with a camera *and* a Dictaphone, and took up a strategic position close to the loudspeaker, adjacent to the captain. The disadvantage of this seat though soon became evident as we left the harbour and ploughed into Plymouth Sound – it was the coldest, less sheltered place on the boat.

The commentary started as soon as we left the harbour – '*On our right hand side,*' spieled the captain, in a well rehearsed, west-country brogue, '*the fortress there is the Royal Citadel – that's the home of the twenty-nine Commandoes, Royal Marines – built in the reign of King Charles the Second to protect himself from the people of Plymouth during the civil war. If you walk around the top of the fort, it's exactly one mile long.*' I was pretty sure this captain was a distant relation, if not the brother, of the dark haired, dark skinned, curled West Country tongued captain of *Lorna J* from Weymouth. He wore an earring, which made me think of pirates and of the Jolly Roger.

The boat flew the Cornish flag, which was black and white – the same colours as the Jolly Roger – fluttering out, almost straight, towards the east from a varnished, buttoned pole at the boat's bow. I thought this a bit curious as we'd embarked in Devon, but perhaps the Cornish wouldn't let you tie-up across the border in Saltash if you didn't fly their flag. They're a bit of an insular lot, the Cornish; crossing the Tamar is almost like entering another country, (which is what a lot of them would like it to be). They're very proud of their history and of their flag, which you see everywhere; it's a white cross, instead of the scull and crossbones, on a black background; the black is said to represent the ashes of the tin smelting fires, and the white, the colour of the metal. It's known as St Piran's flag – the patron saint of tin miners, not that there are any active mines left in Cornwall now. St Piran it's said (if you believe the Celts) lived for 200 years, then got drunk one day and died by diving, (or falling), down a well – perhaps inventing the slogan – *Don't drink and dive*! (124)

We passed the red-and-white ringed Smeaton's Tower and skirted starboard of the now abandoned Drake's Island, leaving Plymouth Sound to sail up the Tamar, passing Cremyll Battery on our port side and then the Scott memorial on the starboard.

'...This is where they used to build the old wooden warships,' I next caught the captain explaining, *'look carefully as we go down between pillars on the right hand side, right at the back of the ship – you'll see some of the old figureheads that was on the old wooden warships...'*

There was a planned pause whilst the captain took a sneaky puff on his cigarette and everyone else strained their eyes impossibly to try and see the mythical figureheads. *'...Look up across the old slipway there, you'll see a large granite building with blue windows, coming into view in a few moments...'* Thirteen or so seconds passed... *'There! – Just coming into view now. This is the house where they used to hang the French prisoners of war. It's still fitted with a working trap door and still has a hangman's noose. In that building 147 Frenchmen were hung there – No French out there today is there? I'd hate to think we'd missed any.'* Now, this was a very risqué statement to make I thought, because unless he'd spoken to everyone as they boarded, (which he hadn't), it was quite possible there might well have been some French people on board. At any rate he'd neglected to point out that it was the French officers that had ordered the hangings in order to maintain discipline.

By now we'd reached the dockyard, and it was here that our captain's oration excelled; it appeared he'd developed a more than casual interest in the Royal Navy's nuclear submarines.

'On the right hand side, coming up to A-dock, with the letter A on the side and the next one is' ...wait for it, I thought. *'...B dock. If you look at the top of B dock, where that tanker is, you'll see a black conning tower; that's the nuclear powered submarine, the HMS Courageous...'* Now, not only did I have the Dictaphone running on the seat next to me but I was also snapping away furiously with the camera. *'...Now, she's the sister ship to Conqueror, which was the submarine that sunk the Argentinean cruiser General Belgrano during the Falklands War. The HMS*

Courageous is one of only five nuclear powered submarines in the world to be open to the public ... '

There had been a hell of a debate about the nuclear risks to the City of Plymouth because the Trident fleet was based at Devonport and The Royal Navy had even considered basing the fleet in the United States, which seemed to be an interesting but dangerous development, although maybe appropriate, as the company that runs the dockyard is owned by a company that is owned by a company that is owned by the Republican Vice-President Dick Cheney. (125)

'... Three nuclear submarines here today ... ' our intrepid captain began to spout again, pausing to take another long drag of his cigarette and balancing it carefully back on a ledge by the side of the wheel. *'... The first only came in a couple of weeks ago – HMS Splendid ...converted by the special forces, the SAS and the SBS, she's had her torpedo tubes altered so that the divers can get out with all their equipment.'* Another pause, and another drag taken here. *'... These submarines weigh 4,000 tonnes with three deck levels inside and a crew of 116. She's the first of five to be de-commissioned. The last one to be de-commissioned is due in 2010.'* How the hell does he know all this stuff? Is some of this classified? I thought to myself. Then he astounded me even more by revealing to the oldies why they'd received only a meagre rise in their pensions of late:

'Well, the next two submarines' he continued, *'...the first one is HMS Turbulent. Now the HMS Turbulent has just entered the record books. She's just done the longest ever deployment of a nuclear powered submarine. She's been away from Plymouth for ten months... '* (Peanuts, I thought, Dad used to be away for two-and-a half year stretches). *'...She's travelled 50,000 miles and has just returned from the war in Iraq, where she fired her Tomahawk Cruise missiles at Baghdad. It carries 16 cruise missiles and each Cruise missile has a range of 1,000 nautical miles. Each missile costs £600,000 and during the Iraq war she fired all 16 at Baghdad.'* I did some quick mental arithmetic and made that to be a cool £9.6 million – a very expensive box of fireworks.

Between the submarine anchorages and the approaching bridges at Saltash, our captain took a breather from his narration so I seized an opportunity to ask him about No.1 buoy. I had complete confidence that his vast arsenal of local knowledge would bound to include a nautical *anorak's* mental table of the designations, latitudes and longitudes of twentieth century Admiralty buoys in the Plymouth area – but I was to be disappointed.

'There are buoys E and F, but they're out in the Sound.' He said – and that was *all* he said.

The immense ice-blue-silver tubular latticed structure of the Royal Albert Bridge loomed ahead, shadowing the Tamar suspension bridge that looked almost flimsy by comparison – behind it. The hills of Devon pushed up neatly from the river to sit between it and azure blue sky – beneath the bridges' expanses, whilst their support columns thrust their rippling reflections towards us.

The captain started again. *'...Built in 1859 by Isambard Kingdom Brunel. The main rail link between Cornwall and the rest of the world, the single-track railway bridge was designed to last for one hundred years – you can see that it's lasted a lot longer. Now Izambard was a clever man – the two large sections were floated up the river on barges – then they were jacked up by the tide to their present position. The last major construction job Izambard undertook, he was pushed across the bridge on his deathbed. He died the day before the bridge was opened at the ripe old age of fifty-four... I wont take you under the bridge as I've been told that the trains flush the toilets as they cross the bridge,'* quipped the captain, to chuckles from the oldies.

Instead we headed for a huddle of grey and white buildings wedged almost beneath the bridge on the Cornish side of the river in Saltash, where we moored up to take on passengers for the trip back to Plymouth. Saltash is infamous for the old maritime expression – 'Saltash luck', said to be derived from the many anglers who'd sat on the bridge for hours and caught nothing but colds. (126)

After about ten minutes at Saltash we'd swung out in front of the bridge again, heading for the Devon side of the river for our turn towards Plymouth and I'd just angled my camera to take a close-up of Brunel's enduring structure, when a high pitched lilting Scottish voice sounded over my port shoulder.

'A clever man – Brunel! – He achieved a lot in his fifty-four years.'

'Yes.'

'Are you from around here, or on holiday?'

I glanced to my stern to see, almost on my shoulder, like Long John Silver's parrot, a ruddy-faced Scotsman wearing a bright orange sunhat embellished with black printing that politeness prevented me from reading. The sunhat was pulled down tight over his ears, so that I could imagine the tops of his ears folded down like Freddie Parrot Face Davis's. I vaguely explained that I was combining a holiday with some research for a book I was planning to write.

'Really! What's it going to be called? He asked pointedly.

'Footsteps.'

'Footsteps, why footsteps?' Then I had to relay to him about my Dad and how I was trying to re-visit the places he'd been to.

'Oh, I see…' he paused for a moment and I could hear the gears of his brain crunching slowly around. '…There was a song about that wasn't there?' …And then spontaneously he burst into song, as if someone had lit his blue touch paper.

'I'm following in father's footsteps…' he sang jauntily '…following my dear old Dad.' It seemed that he didn't know any more of the song, because he stopped there. I instantly dismissed the idea of telling him that the song had in fact been sung by the male impersonator, music hall star – Miss Vesta Tilley, (who'd hoped to set her audiences alight by naming herself after a box of matches), because I was hoping for a peaceful, reflective cruise back to Plymouth.

'Did your father spend a lot of time in Plymouth?' he asked.

'No, only about four days.'

'Oh, not very long at all!' he said, obviously unimpressed, which made me feel stupidly obliged to expand further – and before I could stop, I heard myself foolishly saying –

'Next year I'm planning to travel to your neck of the woods.'

'Where would that be?'

'Sorry – I assumed you were from Scotland!'

'Well, actually I've lived for the last eight years in Notting Hill – I'm a Civil Servant. But whereabouts in Scotland will you be going?' he said perking up suddenly with enthusiasm.

'Well, I have to go to the Isle of Arran.'

'Really… that's very close to where I come from in Ayr-shire,' he chortled, 'you'll sail from Ardrossan then.' – he pronounced it *Ard-roosan* – 'You'll actually have to pass through my home town – Stevenston.'

'Oh really,' I said, then shot off my loose tongue again uncontrollably – 'then I have to go to Stornoway.'

'Ah, lovely Stornoway…' he mused and without warning or introduction, he spontaneously combusted into song again:

'Make your way to Stornoway,
On the road to Orinsay,
Where my thoughts return each day,
By lovely Stornoway…'

I thought he'd stop here, but he obviously knew a bit more than the chorus of this one…

'Where the folks are truly kind,
Where you leave the world behind,
Where each cloud is silver lined,
By lovely Stornoway'. (127)

There was no following this – and for a short time all was quiet. We were, by now, approaching the dockyard again, and I pulled the camera out of my pocket and aimed it a submarine.

'Why are you taking a photograph there?' questioned the voice from beneath the bright orange sunhat again. I hesitated; what sort of a question was that!

'I just like to keep a record of the trip,' I said.

'Is that a very expensive camera?'

'No, not *that* expensive,' I said, bemused at where this was taking us.

'They don't seem very big do they – to carry all those weapons – and what did he say – one hundred and twenty men! – But I expect its like an iceberg, with most of it hidden below.'

'I think there's about a third above the surface' I said, 'and I thought he said about one hundred and thirty men.'

It was at about this point that I began to question the apparent innocence of our initial encounter when he'd appeared parrot-like on my shoulder. Had he been watching me all the way to Saltash from somewhere at the back of the boat, observing me clicking away with camera and Dictaphone? I suddenly remembered that the seat behind me had been empty when we'd left Plymouth and that he hadn't boarded at Saltash. There was a period of silence whilst I rustled together these thoughts. During this time I suspected he'd made a mental note of my statement for the MI5 dossier that already contained the notes: *Sallow complexion – un-British looks – possibly of Moroccan origin – suspected membership of Al-Qa'ida*. My misgivings were manifested further as we passed the submarines *Torbay*, *Terrible* and *Turbulent*.

'You know – it would be easy for terrorists to carry out an attack here wouldn't it?' he postulated.

I wanted to tell him that perhaps that possibility had been considered pretty well by the navy and that adequate security measures were no doubt in place – but my mouth somehow wouldn't say the words. Instead, I told him that I knew there were problems in disposing of the nuclear reactors from the subs. This drew no reply from our intrepid Scotsman and I imagined my dossier being annotated accordingly – *anti-nuclear sympathiser*.

As we edged from the Tamar out into the Sound he'd bombarded me with questions about my past, job and my family so that by the time we approached the Hoe, I realised he'd managed to glean a virtual potted history of my life – except that I was careful not to let him know my name. By contrast, all I knew of him was that he was a Scottish Civil Servant, had been born in Ayrshire, now lived in Notting Hill and fancied himself as a bit of a singer.

'Its good to see the Union Jack flying isn't it...!' he said, as we passed the Hoe, in a final test of my patriotism. '...I've seen a few of those down here over the past few days – it's nice to see, don't you think?'

'Yes.'

Definitely not British – I could see the mental note again being made – *Lack of patriotic passion.*

As we disembarked, I glanced back and saw that below the orange sun hat and ruddy face was a tee shirt with Greenwich Observatory emblazoned across it several times. I couldn't see below that because the oldies were obstructing my view, but I imagined he wore almost knee-length khaki shorts.

I slogged it away up the steep Lambhay Hill, around towards the Royal Citadel but, just before I turned the corner, looked back once more and fancied I saw the flash of an orange sunhat. Could it be the MI5 agent was tailing me?

✦ ✦ ✦

I slid into the elevated Walrus Pub, which sits on the corner of Athenaeum Street, to foil my would-be pursuer and downed a very acceptable hot sausage baguette and a lager. The cruise had been enjoyable but I was still no closer to discovering exactly where *Tiger* had been moored. Maybe the library would know. I checked my street map; it was located on the other side of the city centre. I found my way to Armada Way, which, even though it's been around for a while, I still thought impressive – with its fountains, shrubs and statues. Then I arrived at Drake Circus.

Drake was a sponsored pirate, (privateer), who'd followed his profession in the footsteps of Columbus, Cortes, Jean Ribault and John Hawkins. He was a strict disciplinarian; if you got caught stealing on one of his ships your head would be shaved and smeared with a mixture of feathers and boiling oil – a bit more of a deterrent than probation! (128) Anyway, his early piratical exploits obviously fared well on his curriculum vitae, making him ideally suited for a career in the Royal Navy. He originated from Tavistock, fifteen miles up the road from Plymouth, but would no doubt be gratified to learn that the city had not only named a circus after him, but also an island, a park, a hotel, a school, a cinema, an inn, a leisure centre, a bakery, a jewellers and even a nursing home.

The library had a Local & Naval Studies Section, which was excellent. I soon discovered from a current Admiralty chart that No.1 buoy was in Plymouth Sound, at 50° 21.05' N, 4° 8.35' W in a direction ESE of Drake's Island. (130) In layman's terms this meant that if I were to stand on the Hoe by Smeaton's Tower and look due south, it would be about in-line with the southern shore of Drake's island. The only niggling doubt was whether No.1 buoy in 1927 was the very same and in the same location as the current one.

Finding the location of No. 2 berth proved a deal more difficult as the maps of the dockyard only gave, for security reasons, the barest of details. The male assistant, who was perhaps aged around 65, was more than helpful however and wouldn't quit searching every book he could think of, to answer my question. He'd been brought up in Devonport during the war and had a good local knowledge of the area. He was pretty well convinced that No. 2 berth would have been in the South Yard, and pointed it out to me on a three-part foldout map in a book. There had been three separate yards it seems; North, Morice, (once the Gun Wharf) and South, with huddled housing squashed between each like beef burgers in a Double Decker. There had even been a train, with carriages created from converted goods vans, fitted out with bench seating. Trains left every twenty minutes and were still running into the 1960s, linking the three yards. There was a tunnel under the houses, most of which were flattened during the blitz – the area then becoming an Admiralty compound. A lot of South Yard had been destroyed: The Ropery, the Terrace, the Mould Loft, the church and many old mementoes of the dockyard, including a model of HMS *Hood* in No.1 store. (130) So the Germans managed to destroy that great ship twice.

I walked back to the Hoe, stood seaward of Smeaton's Tower and looked out again towards Drake Island, this time with a new perspective, to where No 1 buoy might be and *Tiger* would have been moored. The sky retained a faint tinge of pale blue near its horizon-line with the sea, but otherwise was now a bright white – whilst above, towards the zenith, puffy grey, almost black clouds rolled towards me ominously, promising a spattering shower. The colour of the sea seemed to reflect the bleak pallor of the sky and a suitably grey RFA ship loitered at No.1 buoy. This ship, a speedboat and a white-sailed yacht, gliding silently between the red and green buoys to the west, were the only craft visible inside the breakwater.

Before the war, to reach No.1 buoy, *Tiger* would have had to pass the aptly named Banjo Pier, the fingerboard of which poked out daintily from the Hoe foreshore. Dad might, if he'd managed some shore leave in those three days, have visited this pier, which shortly after his visit ran into financial difficulties that was to be finally resolved (destroyed) by the Germans in 1941. He might have been a spectator at boxing or wrestling matches that the pier hosted or have partaken in a spot of dancing. More likely though I thought, he'd have ended up down Union Street.

My vague plan was to walk to Devonport and then to meander back along the infamous Union Street, and soon after I began this stroll, the first sign of a naval presence appeared. It was a bland one, fixed to a stone wall opposite some tatty looking flats in West Hoe Road. It directed would-be recruits to the Royal Marine and Royal Naval recruiting office with the enticement of: *Good rates of pay*. No mention here of good quarters, beef, pudding and wine – or even of travel, nothing with equivalent interest to tempt a young lad into meeting the modern-day equivalent of Sergeant Grebble.

An acorn on a lamppost and a sign further on along Millbay Road told me that I was on the South-West Peninsular Coastal Path. This was a bit I hadn't walked though; I'd deliberately missed Plymouth, finishing at Turnchapel to the east and re-starting at Cremyll in the west. By this means I'd missed one of the rare breed of bird that resides just past the ferry port along these shores. On the other side of the road, on the corner of Miller Court she perched. The colours were conspicuous – bright red and blue stripes – (the golf umbrella she held like a Victorian lady would have held a parasol). I noticed too that she wore dark trousers and had dark hair, but I wasn't sure of the breed; perhaps she was one, or then again perhaps she was waiting for her boyfriend to pick her up. When I was some way past, I stopped and peeked over the wall, down at the ferry port, then glanced casually back at her – she was kind-of marking time, stepping backwards and forwards. I still wasn't sure as those grey-black clouds now appeared overhead and it began to spot with rain.

Millbay Road runs parallel with and two hundred metres seaward of Union Street. My old friend John from Weymouth wrote me that he'd lived on *The Street*, as it was known locally, before and during the war, next to a house of ill repute, otherwise known as a knocking shop. He wrote: *I thought those ladies who sat on the doorsteps and gave me sweets were great. Those long summer evenings after tea I'd often see those same ladies I knew, strolling on the Hoe with their young men and they'd coax the men to buy us an ice cream from the 'stop me and buy one' Walls ice cream man.* (131) Union Street and its environs was, is and probably always will be the red light area of Plymouth; it was built in 1815, before which it was a marshland link between the three towns of Plymouth, Stonehouse and Devonport, (they weren't officially joined together until 1914). Once, the place had thronged with ladies of leisure parading up and down, but the days when the street was coloured with an interfusion of military uniforms – (and with Scots, Irish and Norwegian trawler-men, their pockets bulging with wads of money – and other things), are long gone. Now it's reported that there are more students than servicemen in the city – and the university has taken over from the navy as the biggest employer. (132)

It's difficult to tell a sailor or marine nowadays anyway, as they all wear civvies when ashore, but I only passed one likely candidate – in fact he was the only person I passed all the way along Millbay Road, Caroline Place and Barrack Place. The shower had been brief, and had only made me slightly damp. By the time I turned left into Durnford Street and reached Stonehouse Royal Marine Barracks, it had stopped.

Almost opposite the barracks was a sign to Admirals Hard, the long sloping stone jetty which would have ferried me across to Cremyll had I chosen to walk this bit of the path thirteen years before. I smiled to myself; there was no apostrophe on the Admirals Hard sign and I thought perhaps he might have strayed down Union Street to get one.

Turning back north, I headed west again over Stonehouse Bridge and up Devonport Hill where I encountered my first alcoholic tramp, dancing down, chuntering away to himself, arms and legs wildly jerking out left and right in a manner that would have instantly landed him a key job at the ministry of funny walks. Just before I steered a wide berth to prevent collision, I noticed the blotched, ruddy face that either comes from the alcohol, sleeping rough, or a combination of both – and then the glazed eyes that apparently couldn't see me at all. I was sure he was going to fall over at any second. Two minutes later came the second blotched red face, this time on the other side of the road, gesturing more wildly, cursing more violently and wearing a dirty white baseball cap.

I followed the stone dockyard walls topped with rolls of barbed wire around to the rusting blue metal Granby Gate. The area inside, (which was apparently only taken into the yard during the war), will – my helpful library assistant had told me – shortly be returned to the people of Devonport. They're going to pull down the wall at last and give the people back its market with its chimney-like clock tower.

Fore Street Gate was and is the main South Yard dockyard gate and it would have been from here that Dad would have emerged in 1927. Then, the Dockyard Chapel, capable of seating 2,000 people, was a dominant feature immediately inside the gate, until it too was bombed to an empty shell in 1941.

To make my way back, I turned down the narrow pedestrian precinct of Marlborough Street and discovered that Drake's descendents had now become bakers. Framed in the doorway of *Marlborough Frames*, sprawling on the floor, were two more alcoholics who'd arranged a social gathering with their bottles and plastic bags. And further along I came across the huge Salvation Army Social Services building that probably accounted for the profusion of vagrants I'd seen.

When I got back to Devonport Hill, I was surprised to see my first alcoholic tramp again, at the bottom, no more than a few metres from where I'd first encountered him. There was a triangle of grass edged by trees and he was sitting upright on the grass, facing the road with his feet on the pavement and the plastic bag by his side.

He called across the road to me, seeing me now it seems when he'd not done so before:

'Excuse me, are there any taxis around here.' There were no slurred words, just I thought, the slight sign of a Scots accent. But it was a polite enough question.

'I don't know mate,' I replied, spreading my arms like Tommy Cooper. Then I saw a taxi crossing at the road junction below. 'There's one,' I pointed futilely.

'They keep going straight past,' he said. I'm not bloody well surprised I thought, and by now that's just what I'd done too – gone straight past. It was only when I reached the junction and crossed the road that I felt a pang of conscience and I remembered the priest and the Levite. Perhaps it'd been a cry for help; he'd wanted me to flag down a taxi for him – to take him back up the hill to the Sally Army – or more likely to an off-licence.

At the roundabout I wondered whether that rare bird would still be there on the corner of Miller Court, so I turned right and re-traced my steps, this time on the other side of the road. A fat old lady, with a cigarette hanging straight-out from her mouth, a bandaged leg and that familiar blotched red face hurried, as best she could, towards me on the opposite side of the road, throwing a stick forward for support as she went. She looked like a retired prostitute. I was just thinking that I must have been wrong about the umbrella bird, and that her boyfriend must have picked her up, when suddenly there she was, still on the same corner! I looked at my watch; an hour exactly had passed since I'd first seen her. Now I knew! Just before I reached her I looked up coyly from my shoes, across at her; she was holding the rolled up umbrella by her side.

'Hi there,' she said. Her face reminded me of a pixie or elf, (but without the pointed ears); she had a wide, cheeky smile and bulging eyes. The smile was accompanied by a little shrug that said – 'I'm a little devil aren't I – you know what I'm doing don't you?'

'Hi,' I said, and by then I'd passed her, (or as The News-of-the-World reporters used to say – I made my excuses.) If only I'd been more adventurous I could at least have eased her boredom by requesting the menu prices, even though I hadn't a penny in my pockets to taste the food. That job's as about as interesting as spotting car numbers I thought and deserves an award – actually, I think the government should present her with a Union Jack umbrella and tee shirt, and designate her an endangered species, (even though police claim there are 80,000 women working in the sex industry in Britain and that 76,000 of them are on hard drugs). Anyway, my rare bird was one of the few traditional remnants I'd observed of Britain's naval past in Plymouth. Her grandmother had probably serviced the fleet before the war in pubs like the Antelope, the Long bar and the Phoenix.

Union Street was where it all used to happen. Old Jack Tars, before the war, used to spin a yarn that they'd downed a pint in every bar in Union Street, but my friend John from Weymouth reckoned that there were so many pubs there then that nobody would ever be able to drink *that* much. In the late 1930s it was reported that there were 32 pubs. (133) In fact most matelots and marines never made it (on their feet anyway) down one side of the street let alone back up the other.

Union Street now lies west of the Pavilion Rink and Pool with its scribed border marked by the plastic tube pedestrian overpass. To survey the street's current establishments I walked its length, gripping my Dictaphone as if it were a mobile phone so that if noticed, I'd appear 'normal'. The eating establishments (mainly takeaways) now outnumbered pubs by far. There were thirteen, including Italian, Turkish, American, Chinese, Korean and Indian. There were now just five pubs, the same count I made of nightclubs and boarded-up properties. No more did this street teem with bodies that at peak hours spilled out from the pubs onto the road – now, at closing time, I crept alone past some dull flats where a stark, stalwart tree ceremonially clung to a patch of earth, prized from uprooted paving slabs, its slim trunk guarded by a stainless steel cage that made the thing it encircled insignificant. Pink tinged streetlights pooled onto the road where a single car flashed past. Across the street stood the skeletal, tall dark corpse of the once Palace Theatre of Varieties, still wearing its last gasp nightclub banners like a wedding dress worn by a widow to her husband's funeral. Opened in 1898 and only saved from demolition by its listed grading, it had seen, in its day, the likes of Charlie Chaplin, Billy Cotton and Danny La Rue.

At the Octagon Roundabout a police car tailed another, at speed, around it – some game perhaps? In their slipstream, an emergency ambulance jerked abruptly to a stop on the roundabout and a fluorescent-jacketed attendant rushed earnestly towards Dillons. I watched in morbid fascination to see the soap unfold – the body being carried out... but it soon transpired that all that would be carried out that night would be a burger; he'd joined the queue.

By the time I made it back to The Two Trees pub, the kids were swaying their way upstream from the new, towards the old – (Union Street), like trout to their spawning ground. They'd spewed out of Kularoos Sports Bar, the Union Rooms and the Australian Bar, and were rolling across the crossings – groups of young girls, bubbling beautifully bulbous boobs from skimpy tops, arm in arm, supporting each other, teetering like a tentative house of cards. The night was just beginning for them as it was ending for me. I reached the paled Victorian grandeur of the Duke of Cornwall Hotel where the tables had already been set and the menus placed for breakfast. Then I was back at The Grand.

✦ ✦ ✦

In the morning I drove slowly over the Tamar suspension bridge and took a brief last peek across the huge tubes of the Royal Albert Bridge down to the waters on which I'd cruised the day before. Then I looked ahead towards the land into which I was travelling – where the inhabitants have for their patron saint a man who's claim to fame was that he'd accidentally mistaken a chunk of tin for coal, had blatantly lied about his age, got blind drunk and ended his days at the bottom of a well.

✦ ✦ ✦

A month later I found out that the Grand Hotel, which had survived the firestorm of the wartime blitz, had caught fire because of faulty electrical wiring. Much of the roof of the Grade II listed building was destroyed and the hotel had to be closed for two years for repairs. (134)

Three months later, I read that two anti-Trident activists had been arrested after breaking into the dockyard, with the intent of taking the nuclear missile submarine HMS *Vanguard* out of service. When I telephoned the Naval Base Museum four months after that to find out if there was a way I could visit No. 2 berth, or at least the museum, to check their nautical charts, I was told that since the break-in, all such visits were no longer possible – except as part of an organised and approved group.

Perhaps MI5 had dusted off and re-read my dossier submitted by secret agent orange sunhat.

14. Psychological Thriller

Some of the main players were already there; others were in the wings waiting to make their entry, whilst still others were not yet inside the theatre. In July 1930, most of the audience wanted to see a romantic comedy, but what was in store for them was a psychological thriller that would make them shiver and sweat. The backdrop that had been bizarrely woven by the Wall Street crash of the previous October, hung in the tatters of recession – the scene was set and the players were soon to take the stage.

Benito was a strange brew – the son of a drunken, womanising blacksmith who only worked intermittently, his mother was a schoolmistress who was the family breadwinner. A former Socialist turned Fascist, his Squadristi had beaten up Bolsheviks even before he'd taken the lead almost eight years before. By 1930, at the age of 46, he was planning ways in which his Imperialist Italian ambitions could be satisfied by the invasion of Yugoslavia, Southern France, and by the annexation of Tunisia, Corsica and French Somaliland. His ultimate goal in Africa was to establish a continuous stretch of colonies all the way from the Indian to the Atlantic Oceans. (135)

In Germany where unemployment had risen 127 percent in a year, it had not been possible to construct a coalition government since March, and in July 1930 a disagreement ensued over fiscal policy between the Reichstag and President Bruning, following which the latter had dissolved the house and fixed new elections. This was the cue for the rise of the National Socialists. Driven by propaganda directed at the farming population and the depression-hit middle class in the towns, they rose to become the second party of the State. They'd increased their vote in a two-year period by a massive 690 percent; Forty-one year old Adolf was soon to be on his way. (136)

Fifty-one year old Joseph had been a red-star performer since Lenin's death in 1924 and by degrees he'd connived to get rid of his main competitor – Trotsky, such that since 1928 the latter had been exiled and was frantically searching for a country to accept him. Germany had already refused him asylum and the UK was soon to follow suit in 1929. (Joseph wasn't quite done though until he finally arranged for Trotsky's assassination via an ice pick in Mexico in 1940). By March 1930 Stalin's other ambition – the implementation of his first five-year plan – had been turned into a bloody civil war that had only ended when the rich farmers (kulaks), were wiped out and transported to Siberia – whilst their properties were turned into collective farms. (137)

Twenty-nine-year-old Hirohito completed the deadly quartet; taking over from his sick father and ascending to the Japanese throne in November1928. He was considered to be immortal – a God, transfused from heavenly and Imperial ancestors.

In Britain, Winston was out of the government and concentrating on his writing, whilst it would be another two years before the 36-year-old Democrat, Franklin D Roosevelt would be elected as President of the US.

When the curtain rose in January 1930, the scene had begun optimistically enough. Britain, the US, France, Italy and Japan were meeting in London to try to agree on limiting the size and number of warships; Ramsay MacDonald had even urged for the abolition of the battleship by the world powers. By April though, it was clear that France and Italy wouldn't agree to the specific terms of the treaty and that the naval limitations would apply to Britain, the US and Japan alone. This turned out to be a farce from Britain's point of view, since she was to be the only country to fully honour any of the naval agreements during the interwar years. (138)

✦ ✦ ✦

The Atlantic Fleet had arrived at Falmouth on the 11th of July 1930, announced by gunfire at Pendennis Castle, amidst the world's uneasy peace, it took refuge for a week from the gestating storm clouds.

The townspeople were delighted at the Admiralty's recognition of the port – as the Fleet usually made it to either Torquay or Weymouth, and it was reported that: *Falmouth entered with the greatest of enthusiasm into the arrangements made to entertain the officers and crews.* (139) Twenty-one ships anchored in the bay off Gyllyngvase beach and in Carrick Roads; the first line, nearest to Pendennis Castle, included *Nelson, Emperor of India* and *Renown.* The Mayor and his entourage soon set off from The Prince of Wales Pier in the harbour master's launch to pay an official visit to the Admiral of the Fleet, Sir Michael Hodges on the quarterdeck of his flagship HMS *Nelson.* The Mayor had said: *We hope in the future you will recognise Falmouth as a port that may be used as a base for some naval purpose. I throw out that suggestion in order that you may use your influence with the Admiralty.* The reply came: *With regard to the naval base, we don't want a war, but if there is one we will see what can be done.* (139) He appeared to honour his word, as when the war eventually came, Carrick Roads was an important anchorage, and in 1944 the docks were a major embarkation point for the D-Day landings. In forfeit though, both the docks and the town of Falmouth were bombed in twelve raids – and 31 people lost their lives.

♦ ♦ ♦

On Friday the 11th of July 1930 Dad was a twenty-six year old marine serving on board his third ship, HMS *Nelson*. He was only three years younger than Hirohito, was junior to Teddy by ten years, to Adolf by fifteen, to Benito by twenty, to Joseph by twenty-five and to Winston by twenty-nine. His mind would not have dwelt too much on the world's power struggles; the only power he'd have been interested in would have been the pulling power of the ship's tug-of-war team at the corporation sport's gala-day planned, for the coming Tuesday.

As it would soon transpire, Dad's old team *Tiger* would beat his new one *Nelson* in the semi-final of the tug-of-war and would go on to win the competition, which must have left him with a strange hollow feeling. At the dance that Tuesday evening I wondered if he'd had any energy left for another pull; the local newspaper reported innocently and maybe even honestly that: *A very happy time was spent.* (140)

♦ ♦ ♦

At the seaward end of Killigrew Street I climbed the one hundred and eleven stone steps known as Jacob's ladder to an anaerobic heaven that melted into Gyllyng Street. From here there were stunning views across the drowned river valleys of Carrick Roads. It was a golden cloudless day; the misty pale blue sky faded hazily into the green-brown meadows above the yellow sliver of sand at Kiln Quay, which seemed then almost to slip lazily into the windless darker blue of the sea. In the foreground I saw, once I'd caught my breath, the floating naked-mast yachts with furled sail rolls clinging cosily to their booms, hugging the harbour like a pack of dogs circling a fire. Further out a dredger lurked purposefully, and in the narrows – between the town and Flushing – a tanker sat motionless, pointing out to sea with a poised strain – feigning departure. Only a couple of sheeted yachts scudded about nervously now and I thought back to that Saturday morning of the 12th of July 1930 when it was reported that: *The sweep of the blue water was patterned with white, as fifty naval boats fought the breeze in sailing races.* (140) Numerous other inquisitive craft, from rowing boats upward, had ventured out into the bay that day to spy on the British Navy, assembled in all its majesty.

The Falmouth Packet newspaper clippings I'd gathered from the Cornish Studies Library in Redruth guided me first to the Wesley Sunday schoolroom. In 1930 it had been turned into a rest room for the naval crews. Over a thousand men were said to have visited it on the Sunday, where the church workers provided refreshments for the day free of charge, and where after the evening service, the sailors took part in community singing. I photographed the building, which was now the Falmouth Amateur Operatic and Dramatic Society house rehearsal room. It was in urgent need of some tender loving care; above its two white-washed church-like windows, either side of an apex-canopied doorway, parts of the stuccoed cement had dropped off.

Falmouth Harbour from Gyllyng Street, looking across to Flushing. August 2003.

I'd noticed a few Wesley halls in these parts. The John Wesley preaching road show had reached Falmouth in 1742 and would, if a police force had existed then, have caused all leave to be cancelled. It's reported that everywhere he went there were riots, stirred up by the clergymen and *gentlemen* who disliked the Methodists' teachings and their unorthodox ways. Wesley linked together spiritual and physical health, and was switched on to all the latest technology. He believed therapeutic electrification was the panacea of numerous disorders; thirty-seven were listed, from blindness to backache and sore throat – to St Anthony's fire – (this affliction incorporated gangrene, and the cure was only claimed if your feet hadn't dropped off first, before you got to see him). Wesley travelled 250,000 miles on horseback, (a pain in the backside in itself), and preached 40,000 sermons, mostly in the open air, not in God's house. In Falmouth, the rioters had attacked the house he was staying in, breaking down the doors, (141) but Wesley could talk his way out of a burning paper bag, and this gift combined with his courage had won the mob over, as it did in many places, such that eventually buildings bearing his name began to spring up all over the country as well as in the US

Dropping down some steep steps onto Arwenack Street I negotiated the long walk out towards the Pendennis headland. Castle Drive curled around endlessly – a one-way motorist route – frequented this day by more joggers than cars, but eventually I reached the Pendennis Head car park, below the coastguard control station and Pendennis Castle.

Old battlements, rose up from the rocks with steps leading up onto concrete platforms that looked like they'd once been gun emplacements. A flagpole mast stood a lonely vigil on the edge of a grassy knoll overlooking jagged rocks, whilst out in the bay sat Black Rock Buoy marking the island where, it is said, the Phoenicians, (meaning redhaired), trafficked with St Piran's children for tin. The Phoenicians originated from the Arabian Peninsula and eventually disseminated to found Tarnish on the coast of Spain and Carthage in North Africa. Their descendants were called Celtiberians, but by the time they'd reached Britain, archaeologists had labelled them *Celts*. (142)

Across the bay on the Roseland Peninsular was St Anthony's Head and the prominent St Anthony lighthouse; whilst to its left were the scattered houses of St Mawes. I skewered the footpath gingerly around Pendennis Point with its layered rocks, and caught above me – a seagull retracting its undercarriage legs; tucking them up neatly into its fuselage body with a smoothness only lamely emulated by an airplane, then it moved its beak from side to side mechanically, in a precise sweeping search for food.

In the bay now – facing Gyllyngvase beach, a lone fishing ship dallied hopefully. Life had become tougher recently for the fishermen of Falmouth. I'd heard on the radio that morning that a fisherman of some thirty-two years, who'd first gone to sea at the age of fifteen, had reluctantly decided to jack it all in because he'd been prosecuted under EU Regulations and fined for unloading illegal catches. He'd thus acquired a criminal record – for trying to earn a living.

Gyllyngvase beach was one of six beaches listed on the back of the free map I'd acquired at the Tourist Information Centre. I couldn't better the description of the beach given in this little gem, produced by Carrick District Council, it read: *A crescent shaped white sandy stretch, ideal for family bathing and water sports*. I remembered then a snippet that had caught my eye in *The Falmouth Packet* circa 1930. In the column next to – *VISIT OF THE FLEET*, the piece affirmed to me how much society has since changed. Sun bathing was only just becoming an acceptable practice, and Lowestoft Town Council had only just scrapped an old bathing byelaw that stated that: *No male bather may approach within one hundred yards of a female bather*. Many authorities had recently: *granted permission and provided facilities for those who desire to bask*

in the sun with the minimum of clothing. (139) It seemed that even prig-
gish, prim and proper, *pixie* Penzance Town Council had finally
succumbed to the modernity of the times, although only after *a lively
discussion,* and had reluctantly agreed to permit organised sun-bathing
on the beach in front of the promenade. Whatever were they thinking of
– Queen Victoria would be turning in her grave, several times!

In 1930 it had been reported that naval men had been seen on the new
miniature golf course and putting green above Gyllyngvase beach; I
imagined the bustle of the small craft that had landed 3,000 men ashore
each day and had ferried more than that number of the general public
from the Prince of Wales pier to inspect the ships. *Jack Tar* – the local
paper again reported – *invariably brings ashore with him a breath of the
salt sea, which does much to savour the spirits of any town.* (139)

The Falmouth hotels along Cliff Road were as Victorian and as magnificent as any at Bournemouth or Brighton, green and cream, with
elegant wrought iron railings, overlooking the dog-turd purged Castle
and Tunnel Beaches. At Gyllyngvase though, the gates to Queen Mary
Gardens were curiously locked, and I could only peer from a distance at
the spiky tropical shrubs. There was no sign of a miniature golf course
or putting green and I turned off inland disappointedly.

I soon reached the stone wall and green corrugated, tin-roofed stand of
Falmouth Rugby Football Club that had in 1930 played host, (as the
Recreation Ground), to the fleet's gala day. To reach it I'd walked down
Penmere Hill and had passed Penmere Halt Station and Penmere Place.
There were a lot of 'Pens' around these parts. 'Pen' is Welsh for 'hill',
from the Celtic again, so the 'Hill' part of 'Penmere Hill' seemed a bit
superfluous – no doubt added later by a Saxon. I quickly circled the perimeter of the ground, in now familiar fashion, to cross Dad's path.
There wasn't much to see apart from the rusty FRFC sign welded to the
tired steel gates and the wooden seats in the tatty stand. There was a
dowdiness about the place that somehow belied the gala day history that
had been made there in July1930, when from those stands the naval men
had shouted themselves hoarse – and from where, when it rained, the
massed bands of the fleet had retired, to strike up with a mixture of sar-
casm, pathos and carelessness – *Happy days are here again.* (143)

Crossing Kimberley Park, I passed a group of young mothers with
their kids, sitting idly behind football pitch goalposts, revealing oceans
of flesh – sunbathing; I tried not to look but thought it a strange place for
such an activity; it wouldn't have happened in 1930. Then I searched for
Brian's house along Trevethan Road.

I didn't know what to expect with Brian; there was no indication from
the letters, of his age – but as he spoke knowledgably about *Tiger* and

Nelson, I assumed he was maybe in his nineties. Even when we spoke on the telephone to arrange a meeting, he seemed careful not to reveal his age, or whether he'd been a mariner. What *did* come across was a strong Cornish accent. Because of the uncertainty over his age, I was half expecting to find him in an old-peoples home, (there was one on his street), but I discovered that in fact he lived in a terraced house, high above the river Fal.

I rang the bell and waited – eventually, when I'd about given up, there was a tapping from a window above; I briefly caught a face in it before the grey grime net curtains flicked back. Then I waited again for what seemed an age until the door opened at first partially, and then fully. Brian was not as old as I'd expected. I stretched my hand and we shook – then I noticed that in his other hand he was gripping a kitchen knife. He beckoned me in, but must have noticed my apprehensive look:

'Oh, don't mind that,' he said, nodding towards the knife, 'It's just old bachelor's ways.' We passed an open door, where I glimpsed a tatty looking three-piece suit. He led the way upstairs, past numerous nautically flavoured pictures, to a room that was not in fact a bedroom – but another lounge where, on a sideboard amongst other model ships were elaborate wooden replicas of the Cutty Sark and Mayflower. I followed Brian to the bay window, where we sat in chairs opposite each other. Binoculars were set up on a tripod in front of the window and on the windowsill sat another pair. There was a clear view across to St Mawes and Flushing.

I looked at him properly for the first time, noticing that his bare arms and hands were mottled with ginger freckles, although now his hair was grey. His face possessed a weathered brown-leather look within which were set thin slit, clear blue eyes. My instant impression was that he was nobody's mug. He wore a bachelor's belt – a rugged worn leather affair that was like one worn by an old uncle I knew as a boy – with the edge curled back in scamp abandon.

As we chatted I gleaned that he was actually only 73 and, although retired now of course, had worked since the age of fifteen as a parks gardener.

'I still do a bit of voluntary work – up on Penmere station, clearing away overgrown blackberries and such. Do you like the view?' He asked, changing the subject suddenly – more as a statement than a question. 'I see all the ship movements from here – there isn't much I miss from this window.'

Then he asked me about Dad and *Nelson* and went off to fetch a photograph album that he talked through as I turned the pages. Suddenly – *there* was the reason that had drawn us together – a wonderful dog-eared black and white photograph of the fleet in 1930 anchored in Falmouth bay; I instantly recognised the triple turrets of *Nelson*, and Brian pointed to where the photograph had probably been taken – at Pendennis Castle. For once, the scene was exactly as I'd imagined it and I savoured the moment – but wished I had that photograph.

I knew from his letters that his big passion was the *Cutty Sark*, but I hadn't realised until he'd told me that she'd spent sixteen years at Falmouth, from 1922 – and so she was there when the Atlantic Fleet had visited in 1930.

'Where was she moored?' I asked.

'Right across there,' he pointed again, 'by Flushing sailing club.' This was obviously the cue he'd been waiting for and had hoped I'd give, because he wasted no time in hurrying away and returning with another album, which he handed me. This, his prized possession, was crammed full with photographs and clippings of *Cutty Sark*.

Launched in 1869, she first carried tea, but later out-sailed all her rivals as a wool clipper. In 1895 she was sold to the Portuguese and re-christened *Maria do Amparo*, sailing between Portugal and her colonies until 1922 when, that autumn, Captain Wilfred Dowman bought her back from the Portuguese and began to restore her to how she'd looked in her China clipper days. Two years after the Captain died, in 1936, his widow presented the *old lady* to the Thames Nautical Training College and she underwent her last sea voyage, towed by tug to Greenhithe. She finished up in Greenwich as an exhibit for the 1951 Festival of Britain.

'Is she privately owned?' I asked Brian, as I closed the album and handed it carefully back to him,

'I wish she were,' he said, 'seeing the sad state she's in now.'

'Have you been up to Greenwich to see her?'

'Yes, a friend took me – we had a day up there.' He said this in a way that conveyed much more than a straight reply to my question. It was as if it had been an ordeal, that he'd been glad to get back to the peace and quiet of Cornwall and that he wished *Cutty* were still sitting over there by Flushing's Carrick shore, in the sea, where she belonged.

I had to go, and Brian followed me down the stairs, this time stopping on the way to point out the significance of the paintings and photographs that hung on the wall. We shook hands at the door – no knife this time. After a few steps I heard the door slam behind me.

The early evening air was still quite warm, but as I turned right down Tresawna Terrace a slight breeze whipped up from the Fal estuary. I thought of *Nelson* then, her stay here had been fairly brief – seven days; she'd left the morning after her obligatory searchlight display, sailing on around the coast to Torquay.

My stay had been even briefer; one complete day, during which I'd walked about eight miles around the place. I wandered off down the hill to where I thought the centre of town and my car would be, thinking again of Dad.

✦ ✦ ✦

I couldn't remember ever having talked to Dad about Mussolini, Hitler, Stalin and Churchill but I remember him once saying that *power* was the thing, not money. John Davison Rockefeller understood this too: *I want to own nothing and control everything*, he once said. But power is finite and in the end Mussolini, was shot by communist partisans trying to sneak across the border into Austria, whilst Hitler blew his brains out via a bizarre angled shot through his mouth, (not wanting to hole his forehead – or was it just his shaky hand)? Stalin's power survived until his brain bled itself to death, taking five hundred people with him as they fought to glimpse his corpse. Hirohito lost his power when he learned that he was no longer a God and that the people had made him mortal – an unhappy state (for him) that he had to endure for another 43 years. His death from cancer on the 7th of January 1989 finally brought the curtain down on the psychological thriller that had begun in 1930.

15. Myths and Legends

As I approached Penzance, the thin strip of Prussian blue that had appeared in the black sky widened and paled to a soft turquoise, which then slowly acquired an orange tinge. It was the most beautiful dawn I'd ever seen – not that I'd seen too many in my life.

Tiger had actually spent one evening and half a night anchored off Penzance on the 7th of June 1927, weighing anchor at 0454 and sailing to Falmouth where the Royal Marines had carried out an emergency landing drill. She'd then sailed to Devonport and Plymouth, before doubling back seven days later, past Penzance and on to St Mary's Roads, Scilly, where she anchored at 1400 hours for a covert operation. (144)

◆ ◆ ◆

At just before 9 o'clock I joined the long queue on South Pier for *Scillonian III*. We checked in through a kind of garden shed, open at each end, but then on the dockside I saw that the luggage was being containerised. Aware that I was holding up the queue, I hastily pulled out from the rucksack things I'd need on the voyage, whilst the tent slipped off, thudding lazily to the floor and somebody behind me clouted the back of my legs with their luggage. It was at that moment, in the midst of the frisson of boarding that the mobile rang. It was Ruth. She asked if I was still going, the answer to which she knew full well. It was her way of making the point again that she objected to my lone travel arrangements. My work had taken me to Plymouth and I'd used its relative proximity to slot-in this visit – but she was not happy.

◆ ◆ ◆

Aboard, there were few spare seats but I managed to acquire one on the lower deck at the stern and to starboard, next to a bespectacled young girl, with her hair in a bandana, who wrote continually in a pocket-sized notebook. Her boyfriend or perhaps brother tried to take a peek at her notes but she shielded the book with her hand coyly. This made *me* determined to sneak a look, which I did by pretending to read my own book; hers was a novel. She wrote with an erudite ease, and the bit I read was actually quite good, doused with a plenitude of adjectives and adverbs mainly with regard to the heroine and her activities – it was obviously a romantic novel and far more likely to be a best seller than anything I might finish up with.

Finally *Scillonian III* got underway and we eased out around Lighthouse Pier and churned away first due south and then southwest where we gathered speed to send rolls of white water skittering away behind us. We trickled down the Cornish coast, hugging the shoreline fairly closely, passing the Minack Open Air Theatre with its auditorium built into the cliff facing the sea, and then we were down past the jagged rocks of Gwennap Head with its funnel near the cliff edge caused by the collapse of a cave. (145) A taped commentary, spoken with a crisp, clear BBC accent, had begun – *Along this stretch of coast towards Lands End are many small coves...*

Feeling 'good' in a Beaufort 4, aboard Scillonian III, on the way to St Mary's.

A boy of about nine appeared on the seat next to the young authoress.

'What's the difference between a myth and a legend?' he suddenly asked his sapient sister out of the blue. Christ, I thought, these Scilly Island holidaymakers are all budding members of Mensa; I'd never have dreamed of asking a question like that at his age. I was quite looking forward to finding out the answer myself, but sis whispered it, (or the fact that she didn't know), in the boy's ear.

Opposite me sat, a young woman with a sallow complexion, wearing white trousers and a matching white fur-lined anorak with a hood edged with the same fur. Her son appeared and thrust some seasickness pills into her hand, then disappeared again into the lounge. Lands End was now behind us to starboard and the sea had started to cut up a bit.

...Beyond the Longships Lighthouse, the commentary continued, *many vessels were wrecked...off Lands End there are the tides and currents of the English Channel to the east, the Bristol Channel to the northeast, St*

Georges Channel to the north, the Bay of Biscay to the south and the majestic Atlantic Ocean to the west. Add to this a strong breeze from any direction and we have a rough sea... The timing of the commentary was perfect; the wind did seem to have picked up.

In 1805, Commander Beaufort had devised a wind force scale, which by 1838 was made mandatory for log entries in all ships of the Royal Navy. (146) The scale ranged from 0 for calm, up to 12 for hurricane, (with accompanying fourteen metre high waves). I reckoned that we were at about 4 on the scale – moderate breeze, with waves of about a metre height. The chops of the channel didn't get its name for nothing; the scend was now noticeable.

A little girl next to me threw up suddenly into a paper bag and immediately the white anorak lady jumped up, grabbed the bag from the girl's father, (who on reflection was maybe her husband), disappeared into the lounge and quickly re-appeared with a new one. Her sallow-skin face had turned a yellowish-grey; she perched her own sick-bag delicately on her white trousers, huddled down into the anorak and slumped her head onto a lifebuoy at the side of the ship. I fretted a bit about whether I'd get seasick, especially as I'd forgotten to pack a hammock, but relocated myself amidships on the buttoned top of a white ventilator. Everything seemed all right.

✦ ✦ ✦

As we approached St Mary's I deduced, by consulting the little Scilly guidebook, that it must be high tide, because we took the northern approach route, first coming across the scattered Eastern Islands, then St Martin's and Tresco away to starboard as we slowed and entered the calmer waters of St Mary's Roads. This was where HMS *Tiger* had anchored for almost twenty-seven hours in 1927 – although I didn't know precisely where. The log recorded that the marines' party had left the ship at 14.50 and had landed ashore – somewhere? – (I didn't know this either) – at 15.20. The party returned on board at 17.45, which meant that Dad had probably only spent about two hours ashore. (147) Had it been a covert operation?

In Redruth, I'd spent a good portion of a morning at the Cornish Studies Library scanning copies of *The Cornishman*, (including all its regional variations), and had laboriously and carefully checked them all without finding a single reference to the visit of *Tiger*. I'd written to The Isles Of Scilly Museum Association and to the editor of *The Scillonian Magazine* and had drawn blanks there as well. That's what I mean by covert operation; nowhere could I find out anything about this visit – it had either disappeared from all records or wasn't recorded in the first place. Surely the visit of a 704 ft long battle cruiser sprouting eight 13.5

inch and twelve 6-inch guns couldn't have been an everyday occurrence for the islanders!

There was plenty of time to make these reflections as we slowly cruised down the roadstead and into the quay at St Mary's. By now virtually everyone was standing and most had crowded to the port side to get their first look at Hugh Town, so that the ship was noticeably listing; if she'd been a smaller craft we'd all have been swimming ashore. The midday sun was strong, glinting on the calm, rippling sea of the bay as we slowly edged in. An assortment of baseball caps, sun hats and sea captain's hats shielded eyes from the sun, whilst I first squinted and then used a hand to try and catch sight of my rucksack as it vanishing from the container into a Land Rover, to be driven off across the island without me to Garrison Campsite. This was an arrangement I didn't much like.

The quay is built on Rat Island, so named apparently because once, if you had left your horse tied up on it for more than a few moments, you'd return to find it a skeleton. (148) We all paraded from the quay into Hugh Street, clogging it – before dispersing like sparks from a firework into the hinterland.

Climbing rutted, slab-paved Garrison Hill, I encountered a man wearing a lilac flower in his buttonhole, and for a moment thought that this was some sort of Scilly Islander custom. Perhaps all the men on St Mary's wore lilac flowers, perhaps those on St Agnes wore yellow and those on St Martin's wore pink – but then, after I'd passed through the bell-hung Doric-like arched entrance of Garrison Gate into the walled grounds of Star Castle – at the Star Castle Hotel, I noticed a wedding party, that gave explanation to the lilac flower!

Star Castle had been built in haste; completed in just eighteen months, under the orders of Queen Elizabeth, just after the Spanish Armada had been sighted rendezvoused at Scilly. On the 19th of July 1588, the great Spanish crescent was sighted from there and Raleigh's beacons flared down the coast. (149)

Passing Star Castle and rounding Newman House I looked back, and down over a sea of green ferns to the cobalt sea of the roadstead below, where spume circled the rocks of Rat Island and to where, below the white walled pastel grey roofs of the buildings on the quay, *Scillonian III* was still moored.

At the Garrison Campsite, the office-come shop was closed and there was no sign either of my rucksack or of anyone to release it from wherever it was being held prisoner. So I retreated reluctantly back towards the isthmus of Hugh Town with my pockets stuffed with the essentials I'd retrieved from it on South Pier at Penzance.

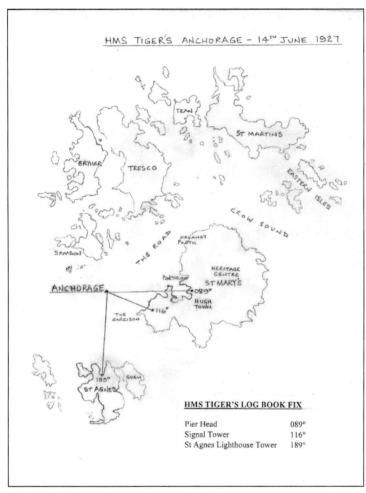

HMS TIGER'S ANCHORAGE - 14TH JUNE 1927

HMS TIGER'S LOG BOOK FIX

Pier Head	089°
Signal Tower	116°
St Agnes Lighthouse Tower	189°

The Isles of Scilly showing achorage co-ordinates of HMS Tiger on 14th June 1927.

A dusty narrow footpath dropped down in looping undulations and bent towards the sea doubling back west. The path opened out at various battery points around the headland. The most picturesque of these was Woolpack Battery with its paved promontory, cropped daisy lawn and neatly cradled cannons. The air was warm, now with little breeze, and the sky had assumed a hazy grey amalgam through which the sun tried to peer in desperation. If it were to rain it would be a long walk back to the campsite to free the rucksack and retrieve the mac (that I'd anyway actually forgotten to pack). It didn't take long to circumnavigate the small peninsular and come again upon Garrison Gate, but this time I headed down the hill back towards Hugh Town.

The guidebook map showed that there were six beaches facing St Mary's Roadstead and I had no idea which one Dad would have set foot upon as a member of the marine's landing party, at 15.20hours on the 14th of June 1927. The only thing I could do was to traverse the shoreline of each beach from Town beach, Hugh Town in the south to Bar Point in the north. I missed Town beach on the outward trek by following the road out past the school where a sandy footpath edged off left through marram grass down to Portmellon beach. Both these beaches seemed too close to the dinted harbour to be suitable landing sites for the marines, and I began to speculate on the nature of *Tiger's* seemingly unreported visit to Scilly.

Perhaps this exercise was part of a new role envisaged by Admiral Sir Charles Madden, later to become First Sea Lord, whose committee had recommended in 1924 that the Corps of Marines should, amongst other duties, provide a strike force to seize advanced bases and attack enemy lines of communication. This was the concept that would form the basis of the Mobile Naval Base Defence Organisation to which Dad would eventually be attached in December 1940. Perhaps the ship had, at Plymouth, been loaded up with a Hathi (elephant) tractor and scaffolding in order to land heavy guns on Scilly. Perhaps beach inclines, tidal state and the structure of landing craft for concentrated loads had all been studied. (150) Or perhaps the local press had just been inept and had simply missed the visit. Perhaps the marines had merely route marched off across St Mary's for an hour and route marched back again?

From Portmellon I hopped gingerly over slippery rocks to Porthloo beach, its white sands strewn with trails of seaweed. The tide was out, revealing a mass of irregularly sized, green pyromorhite-colour tinged rocks and stones that would surely aggravate any amphibious landing. There seemed no alternative but to climb up onto a road by Juliet's Garden Café and follow an island tour bus along for a while like the tortoise and the hare. I was the tortoise and the bus the hare, stopping at intervals whilst the driver spieled his commentary into a microphone. Finally, somewhere near the golf club I overtook it, like the tortoise I was, for the last time and hacked off seaward along a narrow overgrown footpath, down onto rocks – heading for Carn Morval Point. At Halangy Porth families had gathered on the sands putting the final touches to impressive looking sand castles that were about to be judged, and from there I followed a footpath along the shoreline, north to Pendrathen.

Somewhere near the Innisdgen bronze-age tombs I flopped down on a wooden seat dedicated to one Vi Whitticar, where I complied with its inlayed message – and rested to enjoy the view. Out past a foreground carpet of ferns Crow Rock reared up from the sea that stretched away across to Tresco and St Martin's. Something stirred then in the back of my mind. I wasn't sure what it was, but as I looked across at Tresco a half-thought suddenly flitted into my head and straight out again before I could capture it or bring it into focus – it was like a rare butterfly that you see in a mere flash as it darts past you on a footpath.

The air had a balmy, aromatic smell to it, redolent of the Greek islands. I took in a deep breath. Then I walked back along the path, turned inland and followed a crooked little lane back south past a cottage where a basket of bulbs sat by a gate with a sign describing their unpronounceable species together with a price tag and an honesty box. Such rustic delights still exist on Scilly.

Back at Juliet's Café again, I took stock: Of the six beaches, (five of which I'd now crossed), Porthloo below the Café seemed to be the most likely upon which a marines' landing party could have alighted; even allowing for its stony bottom at low tide, its location somehow seemed right – and I had a feeling about it. I crossed Town beach just in case though, then climbed up onto Hugh Street and selected the Atlantic Hotel for a pint.

◆ ◆ ◆

At the campsite my rucksack had been let out on parole, and in less than two hours I was back at the Atlantic Hotel.

Even though it was early evening, the place was packed. I ordered the Monkfish on a Bed of Saffron Rice, but the abruptness with which my order was taken left me with the distinct feeling that a person alone using up a table set for two was just a nuisance and of course lost revenue. I'd seen a sign advertising a film show about shipwrecks, to be held at the Methodist Church Hall and was hoping for a quick meal in order to catch it. But in the bar I waited, like a shipwrecked sailor, for almost an hour to be called to a table. It was excellent though.

I made it to the drab Methodist Church Hall at about twenty past eight, five minutes past the start time for the film show, the doors were locked and there was no sign of life. No noise came from within. It was a *Scilly* mystery. I decided to go on a pub-crawl instead.

The Porthcressa Inn was empty apart from a man with a greying beard and bald patch spreading from the back of his head who sat alone with a pint of Guinness smoking cigarettes he'd rolled himself. He wore a blue shirt and blue serge trousers like the navy's number eights and he looked like a fisherman.

The Bishop & Wolfe pub was busier. It's named after Bishop's Rock and Wolf Rock (or their lighthouses) – two features of the Scillies that have contributed to about 900 shipwrecks and the loss of 2,500 sailors over the years. The rocks are why a triangle of lighthouses and lightships now surround the islands. The corners of the base of the triangle comprise Seven Stones to the northeast and Wolf Rock to the southeast. Round Island is to the north between Tresco and St Martin's, whilst Peninnis sits on Peninnis Head on the southern tip of St Mary's. At the western tip of the triangle on the outermost rock in the archipelago is the tallest lighthouse in the British Isles – Bishop's Rock. The Scillies would be like a floodlight football pitch if the beams of all the lighthouses were to shine inwards towards the islands at the same time.

I spent some time in the pub observing folk, and then as the evening wore on noticed that the fisherman had migrated there too – now maybe on his fifth pint of Guinness. I'd also consumed a fair amount of alcohol and, through the haze that crept slowly over me like a shroud, I began to puzzle again the thought that had flitted in and out of my mind back on Vi Whitticar's seat at Pendrathen. It was no use, I was too drunk and now had to tackle Garrison Hill for the third time that day.

Weaving my way around to Garrison Gate and then up past Star Castle, the way ahead was pitch black; there was no light pollution and few stars. I was totally alone and there was no sound apart from a gentle breeze. There was a quarter of a mile to walk to the campsite in the vacuum blackness…then suddenly, ahead and slightly from the right, the great lightening glare of the beam of Bishop's Rock light swooped swiftly and unexpectedly anti-clockwise, blinding me temporarily so that I staggered and almost fell. Further up the hill the light of Peninnis joined in, like spotlights on a stage. The Bishop's Rock light emits two white flashes every 15 seconds, the Peninnis one white flash every ten seconds so, as I made my way up Garrison Hill, they danced spectacularly. (151)

The footpath to the campsite led off southwest to the centre of the Garrison peninsular and I knew that beyond this, again in a southwesterly direction, was the smaller island of St Agnes whilst beyond this again was the dreaded Western Rocks. Here lays the Gilstone Ledge, below which somewhere is the remains of the wreck of Rear Admiral Sir Cloudesly Shovell's flagship the *Association*, that foundered there in 1707, a small part of its treasure unyielding still to the divers. Further out, on Tearing Ledge – south of Bishop's Rock, what little remains of *Eagle*, another of Shovell's ships, is scattered on coral ridges and sandbanks.

In ancient days people believed that the Scilly Isles were cursed and that to the west of the Western Rocks the sea ran into gargantuan falls at the end of the world. Sirens here lured hapless sailors onto the rocks with phantasmic and charming songs. It's said that sailor's prayers turned the sirens into a flock of seagulls that still keep watch over the reefs. Images of old ships have been seen moving through storms, packed to the gunwales with crews of sea zombies and, if ever the Scillies are in great danger, they say that the ghost wreck of the *Association* will be seen off St Mary's under full sail. The line between myth and legend, it seemed to me, was getting thinner in this secret place that hid its secrets well from mainlanders. (152)

Neither of the lighthouse beams flashed at the campsite, which was in complete darkness and in total silence. I tugged at the tent zipper, then at the flysheet zipper and crawled inside; it was so dark I couldn't see my hands in front of my face. I snuggled down into the sleeping bag and was very soon having a strange dream about a rare butterfly flitting across an unknown beach where dozens of lilac buttonholed Scillonian clones of the grey bearded balding fisherman had gathered at a wedding gripping pints of Guinness. Then a phantom detachment of Royal Marines appeared from across the sea; but the wedding party ignored them, as if they hadn't seen them. So the marines turned around and waded back out under the waves. I followed them then, in the dream... deep into Davy Jones's locker.

✦ ✦ ✦

I unzipped a corner of the tent flap and peered out wearily and warily. A thick, early morning mist veiled the site and the outside of the tent was wet. A notice on the door of the camp shop gave instructions for those leaving that day. Luggage was to be labelled and deposited at the camp office-come shop by 9 a.m. so that it could be taken down in the Land Rover for the 4.30 p.m. ferry. This meant that the things I'd carried around with me yesterday, I'd have to carry around again today. Nice organisation.

I was still no nearer to solving the mystery of which beach Dad had come ashore on, so the first port of call was to be the library on Garrison Lane. In fact it was closed until 11 a.m. this particular day; it only opened for fourteen hours a week anyway, so statistically I had as much chance of finding it open as Aldershot have of winning the FA Cup, (sorry Aldershot). Instead, I climbed the narrow wooden staircase of the museum in Church Street.

It was a tidy little museum with the usual bronze-age artefacts, pottery and taxidermic bird rarities that are found in most local museums, but I almost caused a major discomposure of it by knocking over a wooden dolphin that swam on a shelf by the side of a full size, fully rigged pilot gig built in 1877. At any rate I just managed to avoid the disaster by catching it as it started to take a dive. I followed this performance with a few camera flashes in a vain attempt to capture artefacts from the wreck of Sir Cloudesley Shovell's *Association* and a map of the wreck sites – but I could see that the cabinet glass had created a glare problem – and a photograph of me taking a photograph of it.

After my riotous tour, I asked the genial grey-haired gent at the desk if by chance the museum held local newspapers dating back to the 1920s.

'No – sorry, we don't,' he said with a smile, 'have you tried the library?'

'They're not open yet, and I don't have a lot of time I'm afraid,' I said.

'Then your best chance is probably the Heritage Centre, I know they used to keep old newspapers up there – not sure if they'd go back that far though – but it'll be worth a try.'

'Thanks – whereabouts is the Heritage Centre?' I asked.

'At the bottom of the stairs, turn left and keep going for about a mile or so. There's a turning off to your right – I think its signposted.'

'Thanks.'

It was a pleasant walk; the balmy scent of narcissi drifted around me lazily; the mist, having long since cleared, had left a blanket of thin high cloud which had not yet dissipated – but it was still a warm day and warmer still after I'd walked for a while. A family of novice cyclists passed, having obviously just collected their machines from the hire shop; the adults struggled with the effort required to make it up a hill, their childhood memories of the experience having somehow been mysteriously erased when they'd made the rash decision to hire the bikes. Motorised traffic was delightfully sparse, although there are supposed to be 800 vehicles for the nine miles of road, few passed me; it was a fact I found hard to believe. (153) A dusty, gravel and shingle track led past a run-down farm, and an amazing field full of blue flowers (that might have been wild agapanthus). Unbelievably, after such a short walk, I was now in the centre of the island and had reached Longstone Heritage Centre.

The woman at the desk was typically very helpful; people were always helpful where local history was concerned. She told me that local newspapers used to be kept at the Heritage Centre until ten years ago, but that the man who'd owned them had then gone to live in Truro and had taken them with him; now apparently he charged extortionate prices for copies.

'You could try *The Cornishman*,' she suggested enthusiastically, 'they're in Penzance – then there's *Scilly-up-to-Date*; I think they publish from the Porthmellon Industrial Estate – or *The Scillonian Magazine* – ask for Clive Mumford at the Paper Shop – it's at the far end of the Strand.'

I thanked her. But of course I'd already checked out *The Cornishman* at Redruth and I'd written to Clive at the Paper Shop – both without result.

Back in Hugh Town I couldn't find the newspaper office on Porthmellon Industrial Estate but to cheer myself up spent a little time browsing in the Man of War antique shop on The Strand, where some of the coins salvaged from *Association* still reside and can be purchased.

At Mumford's paper shop I briefly spoke to Clive, author of several books relating to the Isles. I'd followed all the leads he'd given me (in a letter he'd written almost a year before) without success – except for the one about talking with two venerable Scillonians who were both in their nineties and might just have remembered the brief visit of *Tiger* seventy-six years before. There were a number of reasons I didn't pursue this avenue of discussion with Clive – firstly, the shop was busy and I hadn't made an appointment to see him, secondly, the chances seemed so slim that I almost felt embarrassed to ask again, thirdly either or both of the ancients might since have passed on, and lastly I'd just remembered that the letter in which he'd named them was in my rucksack which was probably at that moment trundling its way down Garrison Hill in the Land Rover heading for Rat Island. In the event I mumbled something semi-incoherent and left in embarrassment.

With a couple of hours left until the ferry was due to sail, I returned to Porthloo beach – the most likely one I thought, upon which Dad would have landed – and sat on a bench just above the shore on sandy scrubland. I stared for some time out between Newford Island and Taylor's Island and imagined one of *Tiger's* small craft negotiating a coarse between the two. Would it have been the ten-foot skiff dinghy or one of the thirty-foot gigs I wondered? A gig would have been the most appropriate craft for Scilly. Then there was that remote possibility that there had been some clandestine operation with elephant tractors, scaffolding and landing craft that the Admiralty had requested the local press not to report.

The red and pink keels of several rowing boats pointing skyward were squashed amongst the marram grass, and beyond these a road twisted away up to white walled grey roofed houses, then higher still to a large dormer bungalow.

I must have dozed a while in the hazy sunshine and when I woke... a black dinghy was heading towards the shore. I heard footsteps, and down the road came a dark haired middle-aged woman wearing striped purple pantaloons and a green shirt. She breezed behind me and then dropped down onto the beach, where she loosened and rolled up the pantaloons to her knees and waded out to the two men in the dinghy. I must have dozed again but then was aware of her close to me again, shuffling past, and I watched still dazed, as she walked slowly back up the track onto a tarmac road, laden with nautical artefacts – maybe fishing gear, maybe diving gear – I couldn't tell. She was heading up to the dormer bungalow from where I now realised she'd been watching earlier, through binoculars, the progress to shore of the black dinghy. I wondered if the bungalow had been built before 1927? Then I hoped she hadn't been looking at me through the glasses at the moment I'd shoved my hand down my trousers to ease a particularly virulent itch.

✦ ✦ ✦

I chose the same seat on *Scillonian III* that I'd occupied for the outward trip. We got under way and moved out around The Garrison Peninsular; it must be low tide I thought – we're taking the southern route back around the island.

Then suddenly it happened…a butterfly darted past my eyes in a flash on the sea breeze…and the half-thought that I'd not been able to capture on Vi Whitticar's seat returned – but this time the blurred focus set. What a bloody fool I'd been – all along I'd been thinking vertically, but not laterally… All the time, because the ship's log had said that *Tiger* had anchored in St Mary's Road I'd assumed, through association, that the marines had landed on a beach on St Mary's – why couldn't they have landed on the other side of The Road, on one of the other islands? There were lots of possibilities I hadn't even considered. I pulled out the Scilly guidebook map – they could have landed on St Martin's flats, on a beach on Tean, St Helen's, Tresco, Brhyer, Samson or even St Agnes. And now, as we rounded The Garrison, past Bartholomew Ledges, with the island of Gugh off the starboard bough, it was too late; I'd never ever return to Scilly and unless somebody could verify that Dad *had* landed on St Mary's I'd never actually be completely sure that I'd trodden the ground. Edward de Bono – forgive me!

A flock of seagulls followed *Scillonian III* for some while, then gradually one by one they peeled off and returned back to the Isles. All except for one cheeky fellow, who gently eased himself down onto the top of the flagpole and settled there for the ride. I thought he was a siren in disguise that'd come to escort me from the Isles so that their secrets could be preserved. Why was there no film show at the Methodist Church Hall? Where did Dad land? Why are there no records of the visit of *Tiger*? Why had the anchorage position been entered by an officer who'd maybe been on the gin? How many lilac flowers does it take to make a wedding party on St Mary's? Myths and legends are safe on Scilly – into perpetuity and beyond.

As Lands End came clearly into view ahead and to port, the seagull finally departed the flagpole, veering away gracefully high up into the wind. Then for some reason I thought of today's date. It was Friday the twenty-second of August. I remembered this fact just at the instant I saw an article whilst flicking through the Scilly Guide Book. The piece read: *Shipwrecks in Scilly – One of a series of four slideshows held in the Methodist Church hall at 20.15, except for the third Thursday of the month when the show is held on the Tuesday of that week.* That's why the place had been deserted – it had been the third Thursday. One secret had been uncovered at least.

I made sure I was safely on the A30, had cleared the Penzance traffic – and my head, before I rang Ruth on the mobile.

'Hello – it's me,' I said, 'I've just got off the ferry at Penzance.'

'I suppose you've done what you wanted then?'

There was an inordinate pause whilst I pondered the ambiguity of her question.

'Mmm...Sort of,' I replied finally, but by this time she'd already hung up. (154)

16. Mistaken Identity

A singular serenity always seemed to overcome Ruth when she crossed the border into her native Wales; the restoration of her Celtic spirit perhaps. Albeit that this time we were not heading for her hometown in the south, but to the north-west of the country, where, as she'd say, they talk through their noses and never in English, especially when those dastardly infidels happen to be around – unless that is, they actually want some fact to be known. Still, I felt a change occur in her as we drove on through Welshpool and the rain, (which I pretended not to notice and made sure I didn't comment on), began to spatter the windscreen.

When we re-emerged outside, having partaken of a pub lunch in a place that it required the production of phlegm from the depths of the throat to pronounce correctly, the clouds had thickened and the proper stuff, (*curlaw* – pelting rain, in Welsh), was descending unmercifully. Surprisingly, unlike the Eskimos, (who apparently have sixteen words to describe different forms of snow and ice), the Welsh are unimaginative or in denial – either that or I have a crap English / Welsh dictionary, because apparently there are only two Welsh words to describe rain – *bwrw glaw* and *curlaw*.

I'd been driven to take this damp trip to the village of Llanystumdwy because I was intrigued by the elusive man who as Prime Minister had affected the transportation of my Dad to (almost) face the Turks at Chanak – David Lloyd George (Zorba). Like Napoleon, he'd subsequently invented his own deep liberalised mythology, but anyway, I was hoping to find clues to his pro-Hellenic predispositions at his shrine in Llanystumdwy. To round off the trip I planned to swing up to the Menai Strait and take a sneak preview of Bangor, which the log of HMS *Tiger* had told me she'd visited for five days in July 1928.

✦ ✦ ✦

Two old ladies preceded me at the entrance to the Lloyd George museum; they were engaged in a long and (probably) interesting discussion with the young man behind the counter. They were of course speaking in Welsh and I caught the instant change in his disposition when I was miserably unable to answer whatever question he'd asked me in that tongue. If he'd asked me if it was still raining I might have been able recognise the word and answer him in English. It was one of the few words I'd managed to learn from my Welsh-speaking wife, who'd unfortunately no appetite for the museum and had decided to remain in the car.

It was a good little museum, interestingly chronicling the life of the man, commencing with his youth spent in the small house in the village where he'd lived with his mother and brother. I compliantly followed the directed clockwise route around the museum, so that his life unwound like a spring: In 1880, aged seventeen he'd been articled to a firm of Portmadog solicitors; ten years later, having gained a reputation locally for opposing landowners and championing the cause of Welsh nonconformity, he'd narrowly beaten the Conservative candidate at a by-election to become MP for the Caernarvon Boroughs. By 1900 he'd became a well-known public figure as a Liberal radical with his outspoken opposition to the Boer War, notably by attacking Joseph Chamberlain and alleging that his family were making money from government contracts to supply the troops. This stance had however put him in some personal danger but had also helped to ensure his selection to the Liberal Cabinet of Campbell-Bannerman in 1905, following the demise of the Tory government. (155)

Half way around the museum, I sat patiently alone in the little theatre, waiting for the two old ladies to appear, for the dark to creep in and for the jerky black-and-white footage to splatter forth. The video fortified the exhibits and photographs of the museum admirably, exalting his achievements – which were numerous.

Before the First World War, as Chancellor of the Exchequer, he introduced old age pensions, (but only because Asquith, who'd preceded him in that role before becoming Prime Minister, had already prepared the legislation). And it was Lloyd George who'd been responsible for National Insurance, which at the time had been resented by most working people. Then as war was declared, he first became Minister of Munitions, (where his innovations had dramatically increased production); next he succeeded the ill-fated Kitchener at the War Office, and in December 1916 he finally became Prime Minister.

In this latter role he saw Britain eventually scrape through to victory and himself emerge, like a butterfly from a surprised chrysalis, to become known as – 'the man who won the war'. It was in the last year of that war that the coalition government he headed passed legislation that allowed women of over thirty to vote and that same government who raised the school leaving age to fourteen, (although by this time Dad, who was then fifteen, had already been working as a farm labourer for two years). Finally, in 1919, after the war, he'd brokered the Government of Ireland Bill, which gave the Irish home rule, but kept Ulster within the Union.

The other side of Lloyd George, perhaps understandably, was unapparent from a tour of the museum – but I already knew that his changes of stance by the 1920s had stigmatised him as untrustworthy and unprincipled, and that the split-up of the Liberal Party had ultimately been brought about by his proposal for a War Cabinet in 1916, (which would exclude Asquith). There was no mention either of course of his womanising and probable affairs with the wives of other Liberal MPs – or that he'd kept a mistress for thirty years – or that he'd admired Hitler in the 1930s – or that the coalfields of South Wales had turned their backs on him after he'd sold-out to the Tories and had prepared the way for the return of the mines to the private sector in 1921.

The big omission for me though was that there was no reference at all, anywhere in the museum to his aggressive stance over Chanak where he threatened the Turks with war in what was believed to be an attempt to whip up a patriotic storm and force the Tories into agreeing to fight another election and form another coalition government under his leadership. (156) There's nothing like a war to pull people together, but the threat has to be real, otherwise the reverse can be the outcome. And so it proved for Lloyd George – the Tories dumped him following Chanak and he was finally repaid for having fractionalized the Liberals in 1916. The museum seemed for me to leave the man gloriously at his zenith in 1919 – and then jump to his death and funeral at Llanystumdwy in March 1945.

Ruth had no interest in venturing into the drizzle, (an equivalent word of which there doesn't appear to be in Welsh), so I wandered alone up the lane to the grave, surrounded by palisade fencing and sitting on a mound high above the banks of the rushing Dwyfor, in which the man had once fished. I threw off the hood of my anorak and stood there alone for several minutes, pondering his ambivalence. It was an impressive resting place for him, with the river's wild and complex gushings through the rocks below, and above, the peace of his grave. It seemed to mirror his life. Then I reflected that if General Harrington had done what this man had ordered I might not have been here at all.

✦ ✦ ✦

Something was not quite right about Bangor; I couldn't put my finger on it, but as we drove in, I felt the place emanate a strange incongruence. It didn't have the feel of a place that the fleet would have frequented.

We parked awkwardly and illegally not far from the tourist information centre and I ran in. The bespectacled, middle-aged man behind the desk was counting the day's takings – or maybe his winnings on the races. It was just gone 5 o'clock and he was about to close up. It would have been a good time to commit a robbery I thought, and felt that maybe he thought that too and felt uneasy. I made polite conversation about the weather, (as it had now finally stopped raining), helped myself to a free brochure, which contained a map of the place, and sneaked quietly out the door.

The map showed Bangor pier poking flimsily out into the Afon Menai Straight, and I remembered the folk song, a one-hit wonder by Fiddler's Dram that had made it into the pop charts back in 1979 – *Day Trip to Bangor*. A line in the song referred to the pier and so on impulse I decided to take a quick peek at it and swung the car around at its entrance. Here, the incongruence I'd felt as we'd first driven in stiffened into disquiet and doubt – the straight was tidal! The tide was out, revealing mud flats with a narrow and definitely shallow channel of water winding through them. A huge warship such as *Tiger* wouldn't have been able to anchor there. Had I got the right place? Was there another Bangor? From the back of my mind, like a gnawing answer to one of those *Who Wants to be a Millionaire* questions, I half recalled that there was another Bangor – near Belfast in Northern Ireland.

At home later, I checked back through my scant notes from the PRO visit and found that I'd been somewhat remiss in not copying the latitude and longitude of Bangor from the ship's log. However, I *had* recorded the anchorage coordinates and one of these, (RUYC flagstaff – 149°), gave me a clue. I quickly zipped the initials into 'Google' on the PC, and up popped a description of the Royal Ulster Yacht Club. Final proof was found from a record of HMS *Nelson's* visit to Bangor in a copy of *Globe & Laurel* which made reference to a dance held on board and to the *enticing colleens* – a quick dictionary search confirmed things – colleen – Irish – a young girl or woman. So there it was. Not only had I got the wrong Bangor, but also the wrong country.

17. Follow that Dream

Suffering from the onslaught of decrepitude, my teeth were beginning to fall out from gum disease and I'd recently been obliged to have a plate fitted, which I detested, with three upper false teeth attached to it but which, if I didn't wear it left me looking like a gapped goof if I smiled or more especially laughed. At home I always took the thing out and hid it behind a photograph that sat on a bookcase in my study. On the morning of my planned departure – my falsies mysteriously went missing.

'So where are my teeth Ruth?'

'I don't know – you must have left them somewhere!'

'Yes I did – I left them behind the photograph – here look – where I always leave them. So where are they now?'

'I don't know – you're going senile, they're probably still in your mouth.'

'It's not funny Ruth – I'm already late – I have to catch the ferry – it's pre-booked and sails at two-forty-five!'

A year had passed since the visit to Wales until I was finally able make the trip to Ulster, and from there up into Scotland. The trouble with Ruth had started about a month before, and it reached a frenzied state of war as the date drew nearer. It occurred because I'd told her I wanted to travel alone again.

◆ ◆ ◆

The bus diverted right, up into the Kilcooley estate and along Drumhirk Drive where, for reasons known only to the Ulster Volunteer Force, a booby trap bomb had blown a car and its protestant driver into small pieces at the height of the troubles in 1997. (157) This was, (I assumed) a protestant area, evidenced by a Presbyterian church and murals painted on the ends of buildings – one commemorating the 1914-18 War and another emblazoned RED HAND COMMANDO.

'Excuse me,' I said, turning to the elderly woman in the seat behind me, 'but could you tell me – um – when we get into the centre of Bangor please.'

She looked at me as if I'd just landed from an alien planet, which didn't seem far from the truth.

'You'll not be going any further,' she said with a chuckle, 'the bus finishes at the terminal in Bangor.'

I thanked her, feeling altogether stupid, but also somewhat relieved.

Bangor Main Street was a disappointment. Sitting on a wooden bench rummaging through the rucksack for the address of the B & B, I felt depressed after the ten-hour journey – and very alone. The place was uninspiring; it could have been in any high street in England; the only thing missing was the ubiquitous pedestrian precinct. I walked towards the sea and then south, around the bay. The tourist office was of course closed, so I skirted back around the modern marina and up a hill to Princetown Road.

My room was small but comfortable enough, overlooking a small car park bordered by a neatly trimmed hedge and trees. Beyond, the view spread out to church spires, pied houses and grey rooftops, below which were the streets of Bangor where Dad had in all probability walked, whilst eyeing up the enticing colleens, almost seventy-six years before – they were the streets I had yet to explore.

✦ ✦ ✦

Bangor Bay Inn was actually a hotel converted from two nineteenth century houses. It was busy but, as I stepped inside, a young man dressed in a black silk shirt and black trousers immediately offered me a menu and a welcoming smile – that was, until he realised that not only had I (stupidly) failed to make a booking, but also that I was alone. Then he quickly lost interest and disappeared in an efficient flurry to attend to more important clients. I decided to have a pint anyway, partly because there was an elevated television set in the raised dining area showing the opening game of Euro 2004, which had just kicked off.

Still searching for somewhere to eat I headed north around the bay, scouting inland up Albert Street for a likely establishment. Instead, I came upon the raucous, bubbling Ormedu Arms. Euro 2004 football was on the TV here too and the place was packed out, mainly with men, groups of them overflowing around the entrance and out into the street. I had to push and weave my way through to the bar like a wayward fly trying to make it through a morass of his mates to get to the faeces. I ordered a pint but noticed that everyone else was ordering pitchers from which pint glasses were topped-up – it was cheaper.

A young man next to me on the barstool seemed to be watching me, and after a near miss on goal, he finally asked – 'Are you English?' I wasn't sure what I'd be letting myself in for.

'Yes.'

'I thought so – I'm a Liverpool supporter.'

' I support Portsmouth,' I said, almost defensively.

'Really!' he smiled. Then he rattled off a string of facts about Pompey that I, a supporter for just about fifty years, didn't know.

'I'm Brian,' he said, offering his hand.

'Mike,' I said, and we shook.

'How do you think England will do?' He asked.

'Not very well actually, but I think they'll probably make it through the group stage.'

'They could make it all the way to the final,' he said optimistically, and then raved on for the next five minutes about Michael Owen and Stephen Gerrard.

'I think that Wayne Rooney might actually be the – uh – guy to shine in this tournament,' I said tentatively. Now here I'd inadvertently struck a discord, because Rooney at that time played for Everton, and they were a Catholic team by tradition. Grudgingly he agreed – and then declared his allegiance to William of Orange.

'My father is German – so I'm going to find it very difficult to know whether to support Germany or Holland,' he said 'they play against each other in Group D on Tuesday night... Are you working over here?' he asked. So then I had to relay the reason for my visit.

'You should come over just for a holiday,' he said, 'you know, in Spain I met some English people who'd never been to Northern Ireland. When they thought of it, all they thought about were the troubles. We feel very close to England over here...' he said, letting this statement hang in the air. 'There's some wonderful scenery over here you know, you'd be surprised – and there's the Giants Causeway of course.'

'Where *is* that actually?' I asked ashamedly.

'Its up in County Antrim.' Now here I really could have shown my ignorance, because I wasn't sure where that was either, but I kept quiet...

'The troubles seemed to have quietened down now!' I said, instead.

'Yes, but there's still a mad fringe element – although most people just want to live peacefully.'

I hadn't noticed until he shuffled off the barstool and hobbled his way slowly to the Gents, but Brian was disabled. He explained that he'd left school when he was nineteen but had only managed to get a job within the last two years. He was now thirty-one. I bought him a drink and told him about the troubles with Ruth and this unaccompanied visit – and how much the trip meant to me.

'You have to do it if it's your dream,' Brian said, 'you *have* to! My dream is to find somebody who wants me for *me* and doesn't pity me for being disabled.' His dream somehow seemed more honourable and less histrionic than mine. We talked for what seemed like an age, but the referee blew up for half time, which meant it was only about 8.30.

'Brian,' I said 'I'm going to have to go. I've not eaten yet...' I held out my hand, and we shook again, this time holding longer.

'It's been really good meeting you,' I said.

'Will you be here tomorrow – for the England game?' he asked, looking a little disappointed.

'Yes, definitely.'

'OK, I'll be here too – my Dad brings me down – I'll see you tomorrow then.'

At the bottom of Albert Street, I passed the Rose & Chandlers pub and noticed that the gigantically rotund doorman was dressed in a similar black silk shirt and black trousers to the young man in the Bangor Bay Inn. I wondered if this was some sort of secret Bangor uniform with a hidden, perhaps sectarian, significance – and plucking up Dutch (or maybe Catholic) courage asked him...

'The same guy owns both places,' the doorman said – with a huge grin the size of his torso.

◆ ◆ ◆

HMS Tiger, under the command of Captain Lake, arrived in Bangor on Tuesday afternoon and anchored about a mile from shore. The approach of the magnificent vessel was watched with keen interest by large crowds from vantage points on the shore. (158)

I read this report from *The County Down Spectator* in my room, and decided to spend the day tracking down and visiting the trio of ship anchorage co-ordinates to ascertain exactly where the ship had been anchored in the bay. I'd read that she'd been about a mile from shore, but that didn't pinpoint her. The first co-ordinate was Bangor Church Spire at 178°, and I set off brightly down towards Main Street feeling good, with belly full of an Ulster fry-up.

There were two contenders for the spire in question – St Comgall's and the First Presbyterian Church. As I approached the former, a single peal began from its belfry at two-second intervals, as if someone had died. In order to determine which spire the officer on the bridge of *Tiger* would have selected as the more prominent. I walked down to Queens Parade and looked back over the nouveau block paved path, edged by washed out purple and grey walls, past the clinically cool focal fountains, bordered by their manicured shrubs, to the town beyond. The spire on the left – St Comgall's, was marginally the taller. St Comgall's, the Anglican spire, would have been the one, but it didn't matter much anyway as the two were only about a hundred yards apart.

The harbour was a total transformation from how Dad would have remembered it but the vast changes had only happened since the nineteen-eighties. Now, where there had once been an open shoreline and a sandy beach, the corral-like extended concrete tentacles of North and Pickie piers captured a sheltered harbour and marina basin. Dad would probably have landed on the old wooden pier, which had been replaced by a concrete one as early as 1932, or maybe the tender berthed at the New pier, as photographic evidence showed that *Renown* had done in the 1920s? (159) I walked all the piers anyway. The place would really have been bustling then; the *Princess Margaret*, (a steamer that sailed during summer from Stranraer to Bangor), alone carried around a thousand passengers; Dad would have probably seen her – the ship that is, not Princess Margaret.

I knew that I had some time on my hands before the tourist office, which I wanted to visit, would open, so I wandered west through Pickie Family Fun Park with its swan pedal boats, miniature railway, jack-in-the-box and crooked cottage. There was some high cloud, but it was getting warm and the sun soon began to squint cautiously through. There was little breeze and families were already out enjoying the weather and the park. Grown men were playing with radio-controlled boats on the man-made lake and my first unfavourable impressions of Banger were changing dramatically, (which just goes to show how dangerous these can sometimes be). I climbed a path to peek through the tall slim trees down at the gaily-coloured plastic kid's paradise of Pickie Fun Park where, until its sad closure in 1991, the famous Pickie Pool had stood. When Dad had been here in 1928 the new Pickie Pool and high diving boards, that were to stand here for the next sixty years, were still three years away from opening. But still, I thought that Dad might well have swum here in the cold seawaters, maybe practicing his underwater hand-stands that were to later so impress me as a boy.

It was in a field beside Pickie Pool that between 15,000 and 20,000 Orangemen had gathered on 12th July 1867, (177 years after the Battle of the Boyne), in defiance of the Party Processions Act which had become law in 1850. The organiser, William Johnson, spent a month in jail for this contempt before being elected as a member of parliament the following year, where he went on to campaign for the repeal of the Act that had imprisoned him – an event that finally materialized in 1872. (160)

History and religion seemed to pop up in the most unlikely of places here. The theatrical director, Sir Tyrone Guthrie said that: *With the possible exceptions of Jerusalem and Mecca, Belfast must be the most religious conscious city in the world.* (161) I reckon Tyrone must have popped down the road to Bangor too. Next to the miniature railway was the message: CHRIST DIED FOR THE UNGODLY; I'd thought a ride on a miniature railway to be quite an innocent activity until then, but maybe they hand out cocaine to the kids! Further along the path towards Crawfordsburn, topping a low white wall which skirted a cropped grass playing field, was a neatly overlapping vertical-slatted fence and on it, overlooking the centre of a small keyhole-shaped seaweed-flung pebble beach, was a large sign displaying an extract from Psalm 95:

The LORD is a great God, and a great King above all gods
In whose hand are the depths of the earth: the peaks of
the mountains are His also. The sea is His, for it was He
who made it: and His hands formed the dry land.
Come, let us worship and bow down:
Let us kneel before the LORD our maker.

Can you imagine this sign being sited in Blackpool or Skegness? But there it was, undamaged and spotless. I hadn't yet undertaken an extensive survey, but wouldn't have been at all surprised if the toilet graffiti in Bangor was religious instead of obscene.

In a tree-surrounded dip in the tarmac track I rested on a wooden seat to snatch a peaceful interlude before the stroll back to Bangor Bay and the tourist office. I sat relaxing and people-watching the Sunday walkers, but even here religion conspired to befall me. Behind the seat a starched face with a grey King George V style beard stared up at me from a soggy, yellowing pamphlet. It'd been distributed by the Irish Christian Mission and propagated the work of American evangelist Dr. R.A.Torrey. I flitted through it but it didn't *save* me I'm afraid, so I returned it to its secretly planted position behind the bench and started the walk back to Bangor Bay; a sign along the way warned that fast ferries can cause unexpected waves along Lough shore – a spontaneous Irish way, no doubt, to be baptised into Pentecostalism!

The tourist office had opened an hour before; I nosed around it a bit and then, expecting a dolefully negative reply, hesitantly asked the assistant if she knew where one of my anchorage co-ordinates might be – Grey Point. She surprised me by producing a leaflet with a map of Crawfordsburn Country Park that pinpointed it exactly.

'There's a fort there,' she said perkily, pointing to it on the map, 'it's a wartime battery – you can go around it if you want – there's a museum too!' I thanked her, it was quite a long walk though, back the way I'd just come, and then a good deal further on again.

The second anchorage co-ordinate – RUYC flagstaff at 149°, was the one that had drawn me to Ireland. The prominent three-storey red-brick clubhouse with its chimney-stacked square tower and Tudor-style half timbered gables stood behind a stone wall, across a wide, rising dandelion and daisy mantled lawn, from which steps guarded by white balustrades climbed up past two seaward pointing cannons.

Tiger had arrived at Bangor on the 10th of July 1928, three days before the Royal Ulster Yacht Club's annual regatta was due to start. The scene from the clubhouse had been one: *Full of life and colour. The bat-*

tle cruiser Tiger and HMS Selkirk were gay with bunting and the big yachts, with their great spread of canvas, towered above the smaller craft which were dotted over the water. An auspicious send-off was given to the regatta by the race yachts exceeding 21 metres rating in which His majesty's Britannia, Sir Thomas Lipton's Shamrock (sailed by the veteran Captain Sycamore, with the owner on board), Lord Waring's White Heather II and Sir William Berry's Cambria competed. (162)

I took a photograph of the Club, crossed the road to the sea wall, pulled the compass from the rucksack, gently turned it until the green pointer settled on north, then locked it and looked out to sea trying to project the ship's location. Bangor Church spire at 178° would have been almost due south from *Tiger*, so she'd have been almost due north from *it*. I imagined the officer on *Tiger* finding this famous flagstaff at 149°, then the spire slightly further west. Grey Point 269° would have been at the far western tip of the concave sweep of the coastline. I needed to make that long walk then; I needed to mentally string a line across the sea from there and join the three convergences in my mind's eye so that the beautiful *Tiger* would re-materialize.

Until then I'd been so engrossed in this nautical notion that I'd failed to notice a gathering of around a hundred people below sharp black crags, stained sepia, nearer the shoreline. In a small rocky cove to my right they stood, crowded mostly on a sea-pocked niche of flat rocks. All were facing the sea. Opposite them, in the water up to their waists and fully clothed were half-a-dozen men. Something was happening and I didn't know what it was, (Bob Dylan's voice echoed somewhere in my brain). Those on the shore were mainly young, with just a sprinkling of the middle-aged and children. Those in the sea, facing them, were older men; some bearded. More people were picking their way carefully across the rocks and I followed their ant trail back; they were coming across the road – from The Kings Fellowship. I checked my watch; it was just past midday. Then suddenly one of those on the shore, a teenage girl dressed in tee shirt and jeans, waded out to two of the bearded ones. A conversation ensued and then she turned to face the shore, the bearded ones each holding her arms. There was a hesitation, but then within a moment all had become clear – holding onto their arms, the girl was swung swiftly backwards and downwards, then upright again – she was being baptised. As she emerged, pushing her hair away from her face and wiping the salt from her eyes, there was applause from those on the shore and someone took a photograph. I strolled up past the large, modern, Kings Fellowship building – JESUS GIVES YOU THE POWER TO CHANGE, declared a sign; there was even a website address. Religion had roared into the twenty-first century in Northern Ireland young and vibrant.

Walking back towards the centre of Bangor, along Seacliff Road, a sign warned that shellfish found on the shores of Belfast Lough would be contaminated by raw sewage and that typhoid fever would likely result if they were consumed. Apparently only forty-five percent of Northern Ireland's beaches comply with European law and unfortunately Bangor still had no sewage treatment plant for its 60,000 population. (163) I thought about those recently baptised as *born again Christians* and hoped they'd remembered to close their mouths and nostrils. I also made a mental note not to sample any locally caught fish.

The remainder of the afternoon quickly melted away. Several watering and feeding stations on the walk through Bangor punctuated the slow progress I made towards Grey point. The afternoon had become sunny, warm and humid, so that the sweat had soon sopped my shirt collar and the front of my shirt had begun to glue itself to my chest.

I passed again the spots I'd visited that morning: Pickie Family Fun Park, Psalm 95 wall and Torrey's seat, before breaking new ground. On a gatepost at the entrance to Crawfordsburn Country Park was a NO CYCLING sign below which had been affixed a smaller sign that said simply – St John 3:7. Could it be that the charismatic Christians had been out spreading the Gospel this far west? I looked up the verse later, it read: *Marvel not that I said unto thee, Ye must be born again.* They had it seemed got this far!

As Crawfordsburn beach appeared, spread out in the distance before me, I caught sight of an ice-cream van and suddenly fancied an iced-lolly. Children chuckled excitedly and paddled in the brown waters of a stream that trickled down towards the beach.

'They'll be coming out in a rash soon,' I overheard a woman say as I crossed the little bridge to walk above the beach and below the grass banks upon which it appeared half the population of Belfast had descended. There were picnicking families spanning several generations, groups of noisy youths cavorting, and courting couples canoodling. Small fires had been lit and barbeque smells wafted lazily towards the sea. The smell emanating from other people's barbeques somehow always seems more distinctive and appealing than from your own, perhaps because it creeps up on you unexpectedly. When I finally reached the ice-cream van, a long queue of people were trailing away from it and my desire suddenly waned. I decided I'd buy one on the way back.

Ashamed that I am to admit, but I never did make it to Grey Point. I made it instead to Quarry Port, which from east of Crawfordsburn Beach had looked to be the far western tip of the concave sweep. Ahead though the path dropped down to Helen's Bay beach, climbing up again beyond to the promontory of Grey Point – a walk of maybe a mile. I managed to cobble together in my mind some reasons not to do the walk: Firstly, the ship's anchorage co-ordinate for Grey Point had been 269°, almost due west, which meant that I'd be looking due east from there and I argued to myself that looking east from Quarry Port wouldn't be too different from looking east from Grey Point. Secondly there was that waiting iced-lolly, and thirdly the most important reason – France was playing England in the opening group-B-game of Euro 2004 that night. The kick-off was at a quarter to eight and, working back the times in my mind I knew that I'd be pushed to make the walk *and* catch the start of the game.

Instead, I scrambled over the rocks and set up my compass on a tufted mound at Quarry Port. A couple watched me inquisitively. Looking east I could see Bangor, and beyond the rocky outcrop of Ballymacormick Point. Now I could visualise *Tiger's* position. She would have been north from Bangor and on a line from Quarry Port to Ballymacormick Point, at a position where Bangor Bay meets Belfast Lough. Feeling vindicated, I snapped shut the compass and began walking back towards Crawfordsburn Beach. As the view down to the beach emerged, I couldn't believe it – the ice-cream van had gone!

✦ ✦ ✦

Sunday night was a deal quieter than Saturday night in the Ormedu Arms. I made my way to the bar unimpeded, ordered a pitcher and looked around for Brian – of which there was no sign.

I'd walked swiftly back from Quarry Port, pausing only at an off-licence to purchase half a bottle of McKibbin's rum. I'd never heard of this spirit until the previous evening when I noticed it behind the bar of the Bangor Bay Inn. It was locally produced and, being a rum sort of person, I thought I'd give it a try. I'd quickly showered, changed, gobbled a chicken-burger-meal sluiced down with an ice cream and a Coke at the banal Kentucky Fried Chicken place in town and had made it to the pub with all of five minutes to spare before kick-off.

In a moment I was joined at the bar by two fellow England supporters, both from Ulster, one sporting a Manchester United tee-shirt – which led me to accept without question Brian's claim of the previous evening that virtually everyone around here would be supporting England.

England had played a tough warm-up game for Euro 2004 against the mighty Iceland – a country whose population England exceeded by a factor of about two hundred to one, and who would have only stood a chance if the game had been played on skates. The score didn't finish up 200-1 though, but 6-1. Still, Eriksson kept the same midfield quartet to deal with the paltry French, who even had the audacity to start strongly. But Wayne Rooney soon proved to be outstanding.

'Sounds Irish doesn't he – Rooney? That's Irish isn't it?' the Man U man asked his mate. Bound to be I thought, but Catholic too probably. Still, the Man U man raved on about him, so I felt it imprudent to comment. Beckham got a free kick not long before half time and whipped a cross over to Lampard, who headed in the first goal – 1-0, no problem! A cheer went up from the three of us at the bar, and what seemed to be the rest of the pub. Great.

Into the second half and Rooney rampaged forward again to be chopped down like a demolished chimney by Mikael Silvestre, (a United player); the Man U man next to me didn't know whether to laugh or cry. Penalty – and up stepped Mr Beckham – surely this would be an England victory now! ...But...unbelievably that Man U reject keeper, baldy Barthez had the audacity to save the spot kick. The Man U man blew a mouthful of beer across the bar, just missing the barman. Of course Barthez knew Beckham well and which way to dive. He'd probably have saved it if he'd been blindfolded.

Now, with fourteen minutes to go Eriksson played his trump card and took off Rooney to preserve Anglo-French diplomatic relations, and keep his options open in case the French might offer him a job in the future. He brought on Heskey who obviously felt that the game needed a little zap and a bit of an edge, so he immediately fouled on the edge of the area. By now, we three at the bar were all smiling into our glasses; I'd timed the emptying of my pitcher to the ninetieth minute of the game – England had won hadn't they! But then Zidane curled the free kick past James and suddenly in the ninety-first minute it was 1-1.

At this moment I realised that all in the bar were *not* supporting England because as the ball hit the back of the net a roar went up from, it seemed, almost everyone else in the bar except us three – the bar was full of Catholics or anti-English Protestants! (Brian had been wrong). Either that or they'd all put a bet on France to win at Corrals.

There was worse to come; in the ninety-third minute Gerrard played a back-pass to James but under-weighted it and as Henry pounced on the loose ball. James pulled him down and it was a penalty. Zidane put it away tidily and another huge roar went up. Unbelievably now E-N-G-A-L-A-N-D had suddenly lost. The Catholic, anti-English gamblers noisily celebrated, but at the bar not a word was said; glasses were drained in silence and I disappeared quickly and angrily out onto Albert Street and into the night.

On Crosby Street a black-silk-shirted gorilla outside a pub joked across the street to another that England had blown it, and they both laughed. At that moment a flock of pigeons took fright and flew noisily from the rooftops of buildings. It was a strange ending to the evening – perhaps even an omen?

I finished the night gloomily in my room. First I tried Ruth on the mobile, but as usual there was no reply, so I asked the machine to tell her to ring me. Then I broke into the McKibbin's.

✦ ✦ ✦

Unless it happens to be a Bank Holiday, Monday is not a good day to visit the Heritage Centre in Bangor – because it's closed. Perhaps the centre has some recondite connection with Chinese restaurants, which also seem to pick that day to close, but more likely it has something to do with William III, who thought Mondays to be unlucky. It was unlucky for me as well in terms of my aspirations to visit it, because this was to be my last day in Bangor. It *did* mean though that I'd have more time to do less – a luxury I rarely seemed to possess.

From Castle Street I meandered down Park Drive to the public library on Hamilton Road, named after Sir James Hamilton, the founder of modern Bangor, who'd been given lands by James I. (164) It seemed almost a sin to spend time cooped up inside on such a sunny morning in the Province and if I'd been a Catholic, it would surely have warranted a couple of Hail Mary's. But the local history section was well stocked, offering a balanced religious view of Irish History that surprised me. When Dad had been here 76 years before Britain's union with the whole of Ireland had just been split, six years before – to the south then had been the Irish Free State. I wanted to try and understand the history that had led up to that event and spent the next two hours in there, scanning 180 years of Anglo-Irish history that terminated with the Battle of the Boyne. There was still 300 years left when the library's locked toilet door and desperation drove me out.

I emerged into the squint-inducing, bright *orange* sunlight that fused fuzzily with the *shamrock-green* grass and headed in earnest to Ballyholme Bay. I took lunch lazily at a sun-shaded table outside the only pub I could find in Groomsport whilst the sun blazed in a cloudless sky, before returning north into the National Trust land, to Ballymacormick Point.

I chose a spot behind a rock, above a small patch of pebbles, not too far from the sea, and shielded from the freshening north-westerly wind, stripped to the waist and lay down to let the sun soak into my pores. For the first time in perhaps a year I felt totally relaxed. The only sounds, during the two hours I spent there were the waves, an occasional bird and the wind gently buffing my eardrums. On one occasion a collie dog, bounding into view below on the pooled rocks, startling me by splattering pebbles, it was followed a few moments later by its lady owner – but otherwise it seemed I was the only human on earth. For a long while I watched a heron picking about in the rocks, lazily looking around then carefully making its slow stately stilted-leg steps before picking again. Out to sea I caught sight of the grey outline of a ship – it looked like a naval ship, slowly slipping into Belfast Lough from the west. It wasn't *Tiger*, unless I'd been subliminally filled with something by the Kings Fellowship and was witnessing a vision. But it did look like a Royal Naval ship; it was too distant to tell. I watched it until it's stern vanished past the headland of Grey Point – then I headed back to the public library on Hamilton Road.

✦ ✦ ✦

There are probably a dozen prodigious facets of Bangor nightlife that I shall never experience, because my last evening in Bangor was spent sipping McKibbin's in my room and attempting to understand the complexities of Northern Ireland politics from a television program.

The results of the European elections had just been declared and representatives of the major parties were being jointly interviewed. Jim Allister of the Democratic Unionist Party (DUP), Ian Paisley's party, had won with 31.9 percent of the vote from Sinn Fein's Bairbre de Brun with 26.3 percent. Jim Nicholson, representing David Trimble's Ulster Unionist Party (UUP), had just beaten the Catholic Social Democratic and Labour Party (SDLP) candidate for the third elected position after second and third counts had gradually transferred votes. It was all confusing. There were antagonistic debates – the DUP accused the UUP of deceit whilst also demanding of a smiling, (or was it smirking), Bairbre de Brun that the Good Friday agreement be implemented in its entirely – including disarmament. Not a lot seemed to have changed since Dad had been here 76 years before.

I felt myself beginning to nod off, but as I reached for the remote control to switch off, a news item flashed up on the screen – there'd been a bomb attack at a golf club somewhere and a British soldier, gun slung over his shoulder, was walking slowly away from the scene. The item didn't invade my dreams though; they were of the halcyon tranquillity of the spot behind the rock at Ballymacormick Point. And anyway, Bangor, Northern Ireland and most of its people seemed far too good for many more bad things to happen to them.

✦ ✦ ✦

I'd carefully tucked the half-empty, half bottle of McKibbin's into the centre of the rucksack, cushioned erect between clothes, but the X-ray machine had somehow detected it so that the rucksack was hauled from the conveyor and the bottle held up and inspected at eye level as if it was the timing mechanism of a bomb.

'You know Sir that you're not allowed to carry this on board don't you?'

'No – I didn't – no! What can I do then? – You're not going to confiscate it are you?'

He looked at me with a cheerless intensity for a moment, then, recognising my embarrassment, but still not smiling, his face suddenly turned softer.

'You'll not be drinking this on the ship will you Sir?'

'No,' I said, not at all sure if this was a question or an order.

'OK then,' he said, gently jiggling the bottle snugly back into its niche and closing my rucksack.

The Royal Ulster Yacht Club, Bangor, Northern Ireland.

18. Midge Meadow

It was after five o'clock when I pulled into the car park on the dockside at Ardrossan. The last sailing of the day was at six and I passed the time quietly reading in the bright modern terminal building.

The sailing to Brodick was pleasant enough on the Caledonian MacBrayne motor vessel *Caledonian Isles*. But seconds after they pulled up the gangplank I remembered that the mobile phone was still sitting snugly in its holster in the car being uselessly charged-up on the dockside. It would, come night, be the object of a smash-and-grab that would be a major source of entertainment for the bored youth of Ardrossan. It surely wouldn't be there when I got back two days later. Worst of all, I couldn't make the call to Ruth that I'd promised her in Bangor.

As we approached Brodick, I slung the backpack awkwardly onto my back whilst still in my seat and climbed up quickly to the port deck. The forested hills were layered with pale yellow-green fields interspersed between a patchwork quilt of bright green trees, whilst in the background the darker myrtle-green conifers prevailed. Beyond these again purple tinted hills were etched into a backdrop of blue sky upon which floated a matrix of cirrus clouds. Two orange tungsten-halogen lights glared over the ship's side from forked white tubular booms on the deck; they were directed to the stern and into the cobalt sea, for a reason I was unable to figure out. Slowly Brodick crept closer; the white, grey and red buildings dotted between the green emerged slowly as specks then grew into recognisable forms, whilst in the foreground the little jetties and the pier, to which we were heading, threaded out gingerly from the sandy beach.

A woman next to me was describing the scene excitedly on a mobile phone to somebody in Bradford, Crawley, Milton Keynes or somewhere else down in England. Her description somehow heightened my own expectations. It *did* look alluring. Arran means peaked island in Gaelic. It's dissected by the Highland Boundary Fault, that makes the north rugged and hilly whilst the south is gentler and low-lying, that's why it's clichéd as Scotland in miniature. The village of Brodick is in the middle of the island on its east coast. It's named from the Norse *breda-vick* meaning broad bay, and into this bay once sailed Viking galleys, much as *Caledonian Isles* was doing now. (165)

Dad probably never saw Brodick Bay. Although submarines known as the Perishers would come to the Clyde from around the world to train

---

and even had their own social centre in the Douglas Hotel in Brodick, the Royal Naval fleet always anchored off Lamlash, three miles to the south. I'd known about Dad's visits to Lamlash before I'd opened the ships' logs at the PRO, because in the old brown case I'd found three sepia-faded postcards, (the only UK postcards in the whole case). Two were identical, because Dad, having visited the place three times, (twice on *Tiger* in 1927 and 1928, and once on *Nelson* in 1931), had obviously forgotten he'd purchased a postcard of the same scene on a previous visit. He'd spent a total of ten days at Lamlash – the ships were anchored between the village of Lamlash itself and the shelter afforded by Holy Island, which straddles the centre of Lamlash bay.

I knew I wouldn't get to see Lamlash that night because the campsite was, (as I then thought), in Brodick. Anyway, it seemed more appropriate to savour the excitement of seeing the place for the first time on the morrow – this, a place that Dad must have *really* liked in order to have spent his wages on postcards.

I walked down the ship's gangway onto Brodick pier just ahead of a young backpacking couple.

'Do you know where the tourist information centre is?' I asked, turning to the longhaired, dark skinned lad.

'No,' he said, shrugging his shoulders and spreading the palms of his hands upwards, which made me think he was French.

'There's supposed to be a campsite not far from Brodick, isn't there?' I continued, feeling a kind of bonding with them, as they were the only other passengers lumbering along with backpacks and a guitar case, containing, I supposed, a guitar – or else enough dope to raise that old devil Aleister Crowley from his grave in Brighton and spirit him to the island that very night.

'We are intending to wild camp,' he answered, with a pleasant smile and in an accent that confirmed my first assessment.

'Ah, I think you might have a few problems there,' I said in an inadvertently patronising way that I instantly regretted. He smiled again, with a *couldn't-care-less* expression.

The tourist information centre, situated just off the pier, was amazingly still open. I'd expected it to close its doors the instant the ferry moored up as appears the norm with integrated services in the Union. Bus timetable creators it seems attend a special school to learn how to arrange things so that you always *just* miss your connection from a train, after a frenetic rush – and then have to wait around several hours in a drab, dank little waiting room. The young man behind the counter explained quickly that the campsite was over two miles out of Brodick to the north.

'You can catch a bus to take you part way – from outside here,' he pointed, 'number 322.'

I thanked him and made-way for the French couple to ask him about wild camping – and the half-a-dozen or so other passengers who'd formed a snaky queue behind them. Then I remembered that I needed to eat somewhere and waited impatiently for the queue to slowly melt from the counter into the hinterland of Arran, during which time the number 322 bus disappeared away up the road.

'No, there won't be anywhere up at Glen Rosa,' he said with a smile, (or was it a smirk?), 'your best bet is to eat on the way – as you pass through Brodick.'

Brodick is one of those places that didn't appear to have a centre. The main road, which looped around Brodick Bay, was dotted on its land-ward side with a few houses, B & Bs, guesthouses, hotels and shops and that was it. Not many people or vehicles were about – most of the 1,000 inhabitants, (twenty-two percent of the population of Arran), were no doubt sitting comfortably in front of the TV watching some English or American soap! I trudged on famished, along Shore Road, fearing that not only would I have no breakfast next morning and no evening meal that night, but also I'd have to put-up that wretched tent in the dark – a feat which would be more difficult than usual given that I'd neglected to undertake a practice erection (oops!) before I'd left home.

It was then, in that moment of deepest despair that I stumbled upon Stalkers, a no frills Scottish eating house that I didn't approach at all stealthily having read the inclusion of a most reasonably priced fish & chips on the menu displayed outside. Stalkers is said to be the oldest building in Invercloy, (a part of the village), built around 1809. (166) I didn't know this of course at the time, nor did I care!

'A table for one please?' I inquired hopefully.

'You can sit anywhere,' replied the obese but cheerfully affable young waitress. Then, as soon as I'd struggled out of my backpack and propped it up dangerously against a table leg she was back scribbling down my order and within ten minutes she'd returned again with a wonderfully huge plate of haddock and chips; the best I'd tasted in years.

As I finished, the waitress scrambled around my backpack with two cups of tea for a couple behind me. I tried to move the pack, but she chuckled and smiled.

'I'm used to climbing over things, we've got two boxer dogs upstairs,' she said as she collected my empty plate.

'That was great,' I said, 'and I was grateful for the speed of service – I've got to get to the campsite and put the tent up yet.'

'Where's the campsite?'

'Glen Rosa.'

'Oh! You've got a couple of hours yet, before it gets dark,' she said, then added 'I hope you've got lots of midge repellent?'

'I've got absolutely nothing,' I said despairingly.

'Ah! What you'll need then is a damp towel.'

'A damp towel?'

'Yes – trust me – a damp towel! Then wrap it around like this.' she mimed a demonstration of wrapping a towel around her podgy arm. 'It'll do the trick – trust me.' For that tip, I left her one too, and started out again to cover the remaining two miles.

The main road twisted on past the Heritage Museum to a fork where it branched right up around the coast, past Brodick Castle that was stormed by Robert the Bruce in 1307. I took the alternative left branch, inland on the String Road, built in 1817 by the prolific, Scottish civil engineer Thomas Telford. The String Road shot off across Arran to Machrie and Shiskine on the west side of the island, but soon I turned off it, right – onto a surfaced lane which very shortly disintegrated into a stoned and then earthen track that began to climb up steeply through the glen. (167)

A sign by a cottage, (apparently a farmhouse), at the side of the track informed me, after about a ten minute climb, that I was at Glen Rosa. I knocked on the green door that was eventually opened by a frail, grey-haired old lady who asked me, after making sure she'd first secured the camping fee, if I had any midge repellent – and then disappeared for several minutes trying unsuccessfully to locate some. Now I really did fear the worst.

The charge for the night exceeded my expectations but the campsite didn't. Firstly, it was a further half-mile up the track – in fact I began to wonder if I'd somehow missed it, or if there was some sort of Scottish Island scam being pulled. Then... I saw it below me on a plateau, with the little river Rosa winding past on its eastern side, and beyond – a fern engulfed rise (ideal midge breeding ground) climbed up to a pine forest that swept north to the foothills of the 2,866 foot high Goatfell. Six small tents were dotted across the plateau; one and two occupant affairs, like mine – not at all related to the flash aluminium framed kind seen on civilised sites. This was almost wild camping. Almost, because at the southern end of the site on a slight rise, stood a bleak looking flat-roofed, whitewashed toilet block.

Bleak was, I soon discovered, a very appropriate description; the gents comprised a urinal and two cubicles, one of which was missing a door. There were no such luxuries as electric lights, a shower or even hot water, and actually only one of the cold taps emitted any water. The two sinks were supported by a flimsy looking retrofitted piece of pipe which

I accidentally knocked away the next morning and thought the whole caboodle was going to finish up on the floor. I conjectured that someone trapped in the trap in the dark might well explain the missing door. The only notable asset was the presence of toilet paper. A past visitor, a veritable master of understatement, had reported on the Internet that it was: *a bit basic*. (168) One thing was certain – Telford hadn't built this delight.

It didn't take too long for the midges to discover a new arrival. I'd just spread out the outer tent on the ground when the first wave dive-bombed and, although I was already in a sweat, I quickly threw on a jumper to cover my arms in lieu of the availability of an immediate damp towel. Apparently there are 37 different types of midges in Scotland, five of which bite humans. (169) Worldwide there are, it seems, 1,400 haematophagous species, (miniature vampires); so the Scottish should think them-selves lucky they've only got 37 – (no they shouldn't)! Not wishing to appear to be unselective towards midges, but the little devils all looked the same to me. It appears they're attracted by sweat and the carbon dioxide breathed out by people. This I can verify; the more I huffed and puffed to get the tent up, the more I was invaded. If I'd pissed myself I'd have attracted even more it seems, because they like the smell of urine too. It's the females that do the damage – as always (oops – another politically incorrect statement!), and a paper produced by the University of Aberdeen submitted that their biting in swarm proportions might be related to *strong host defence reactions* (what does that mean, me thrashing about wildly like a helicopter about to crash?) and *the midge survival strategy of safety in numbers*. They say that if you kill one, a thousand come to the funeral. (170) What they needed on this campsite was one of those midge magnets that gives off carbon dioxide and sucks the little devils into a bag – that would soon sort out their safety in numbers strategy.

The one condition that the midge and I both found agreeable was that the ground was on the boggy side, which meant I didn't need a hammer to knock in the tent pegs. And whilst I slid home the pegs, I developed a survival strategy of my own. Once I'd clipped the inner tent to the outer, I stuffed everything else into the rucksack and, in one speedy operation, unzipped the inner tent, threw in the rucksack, dived in headfirst after it and re-zipped the inner tent. Rolling onto my back I gazed up at the fine roof mesh of the inner tent to ensure that the midges were either outside the tent or hovering in the space between the inner and outer tents. There was no way any could have got in the inner tent in the split second it'd taken me to dive in…but no…! Somehow a small gang of cowboy midges had managed to rustle themselves in and were bobbling around *inside* the mesh in the roof of the tent, so that I spent the next ten minutes squashing them in murderous fashion without any guilt... well maybe just a midge's smidge; they might not all have been of the biting variety.

It remained light enough to read until almost 10.30 p.m. – at which time, having drained the remainder of the McKibbin's, I zipped up and tried to sleep. At the cottage there was a sign that warned – LATE NOISE, LITTER AND DRUNKENNESS WILL NOT BE TOLERATED. By whom I wondered? – The cottage was half a mile distant and I couldn't imagine the frail, grey-haired old lady doing the rounds. So instead of sleeping, I lay listening to the clear sounds emanating from the other tents carrying across the field.

The French couple were here somewhere, (almost wild-camping) – although I hadn't realised it until I'd heard the longhaired, dark skinned lad begin to play the guitar and she sing in accompaniment; they were good too, she sounded a bit like Jacqui McShee, of Pentangle. I was sorry when they stopped and got into the dope. In another tent two Scottish girls were holding a loud conversation interspersed with a more than ample abundance of *foocking* adjectives. It was well after *foocking* midnight before they drifted into *foocking* sleep, punctuated then by loud *foocking* snoring from one, and by the other, a persistent hacking cough:

'Ah cah, ah cah.' I thought I managed to hear the occasional *foocking* fart in there as well...it went on and on...

'Ah cah, ah cah...' the coughing continued, whilst I turned first from one uncomfortable position on my back, to another on my left side, then to my right side and so on.

'Ah cah, ah cah...' Finally, at 3.45 a.m., (I'd clicked on the torch to check my watch for about the twentieth time), the people noises were joined by those of the birds – the lead singer first, soon followed by the chorus.

I gave in then – and went to sleep.

◆ ◆ ◆

A fine rain was falling lightly on the tent as I crawled out in the morning to unzip it apprehensively and take a quick look out. It didn't seem to be much – a fine mizzle that quickly, but almost imperceptibly, soaks you. The midges were there too, darting around madly in a swirling swarm, artfully dodging the drizzle droplets and planning their next raid.

Nobody else had yet emerged as I trudged up the slope, with dripping anorak-draped hood, to luxuriate in the facilities of the toilet block. The French were fondling, the Scots were snoring and everyone else had unzipped their tent, looked out, and crawled back into cosy warm sleeping bags – sometimes even their own.

Inside the whitewashed eighteenth-century crofter's farm that houses the
Arran Heritage Museum, the ticket lady gave me directions to a cluttered
little office littered with computers, box files and papers where a retired
old gentleman told me that Stuart would be in later. Stuart had written
me a long letter in reply to my inquiry of almost three years previous.
The furnished Victorian cottage and old smithy provided interesting
enough diversions whilst I awaited his arrival.

Then I spotted four framed documents (one labelled SECRET) displayed on a wall. The Lamlash naval base was to be closed down and
there was a proposal that the target repair and towing organisation
should be retained by the Admiralty and remain at Lamlash, administered from Marine House. (171)

Marine House struck a chord somewhere from within the dim cre-
vasses of my mind. One of the faded postcards I'd found in the old
brown case showed Marine House from the Brodick Road and now I'd
just discovered its significance. It was likely, I thought, that Dad had for
some reason paid at least one visit to the place, maybe to collect incom-
ing mail which was processed through there. Outgoing mail, Stuart had
written me, was brought ashore by the ships' pursers by the sack-load,
all of which had to be hand-franked at Lamlash post office, (sometimes
they'd had to get someone over from Ardrossan to help out). I knew that
Dad had once been a ship's postman, (a role typically assigned to a
Royal), but I was pretty sure this wasn't until much later, when he'd
been promoted to corporal. Still, I was certain he'd been to Marine
House.

Stuart was as helpful as he could be, given that he didn't really know
what the hell I was looking for, but couldn't add much to what he'd already told me in his letter. The ships, he'd written, would have been
moored in the deepwater sheltered anchorage of Lamlash Bay – in fact I
already had an exact anchorage from the log of *Tiger*. The fleet, he said,
had visited Lamlash for many years; he'd recently come across a photograph in the archives that showed eleven warships (sailing ships) in
Lamlash Bay, as far back as 1888. (172) Shore leave would probably
have been spent drinking at the Lamlash Hotel, that he said was now
called the Pier Head Tavern – which had changed little since the 1920s.

✦ ✦ ✦

It was early afternoon when I emerged from the museum. The rain had
stopped and large patches of blue were squeezing through the clouds that
somehow appeared to be decomposing. All now seemed to bode well for
the six-mile walk to Lamlash. The road was single carriageway without
pavements, a long stretch of it straight but undulating. The occasional

car roared past, one cutting-in dangerously close. I looked back once, surprised to see between the trees, a clear view of Goatfell, rising to its flattening peak, mauve and majestic.

I began to get excited, anticipating my first view of Lamlash bay from the Brodick Road, seen in a way that totally contrasted with how Dad would first have seen it as *Tiger* rounded Holy Isle. (But perhaps I thought, he'd marched this way on a day trip to Brodick)? My first view was of the mound of Holy Isle, but it still came unexpectedly as I crested a long shallow hill. It had taken me a day and a half to reach this spot and look down to the bay, seen through trees, a sea of ferns and a profusion of tall bright violet-belled lupins. Telegraph poles lurched through the foliage towards the village, and I followed them then, down the hill to the village.

Marine House was at the bottom of Brodick Road and I wanted a photograph of it from the exact spot as the postcard in the case. A glimpse of sea at the bottom of the road and a road junction off to the right, suggested a match, which could be guessed from the postcard. All else had changed – the rugged low stone wall had been replaced by fence panelling. Properties, now mature houses, had long ago been built to line the Brodick Road which, together with the foliage of mature trees, now totally obscured the once clear view that could be had from this point of Marine House, Holy Isle and the bay beyond. I took the photograph and walked down to the shore and towards Margnaheglish to get a better view of the house that had now become a hotel, part converted into self-catering apartments and advertised on a board that simultaneously declared they had all been taken.

Across the millpond waters of Lamlash Bay a trace of white smoke crept from behind trees beyond two terraced whitewashed cottages that snuggled down on the shore of an otherwise baron green and purple-sloped Holy Isle, which rose to over a thousand feet at Mullach Mor.

Where in the bay had *Tiger* been moored? I pulled from the rucksack my compass and *Tiger's* anchorage co-ordinates – *Church spire 272°, Pier head 297°, Hamilton Lts. 042°.* (173) Behind me stood the old church of St George's on a low wildly overgrown rise. The last service had been held there in 1947 but now its lower windows and door were boarded up. From the cavities and ledges of its steeple, bushes resembling small trees skulked. At first I thought this was 'my' spire, but the compass showed it to be closer to 360° than to 270°. The spire I sought must be further around the bay to the southwest, so I moved off in that direction.

Drifting into the Drift Inn, I ordered pâté and oatcakes and sat outside at a picnic table worrying about the gloomy sky. The blue patches had begun to lose their battle with the high white cloud canopy that was beginning to close in again. The view was over the pub lawn to Lamlash Bay, where in 1548 the ship carrying the five-year-old Mary Queen of Scots from Dumbarton to France had once sheltered – and where on occasions several hundred Royal Navy sailing ships had anchored. (174) Now it was liberally dotted with yachts and motor craft. I was alone outside, apart from a large seagull that cheekily stalked up to within a metre of my table and cocked his head to one side, eyeing my oatcakes. I grudgingly tossed him a morsel, which he quickly gulped – a reward for his cheekiness; it was a prize for the glutinous gull with most gall.

Further south around the bay, by the pier, I poked around for a while in a yachtsman's haunt coincidentally enough called Seagull, in which were shelved an assortment of nautical books, then wandered onto the short concrete pier from where boat trips ran to Holy Isle. Originally called Eilean Molaise after the Irish Saint who'd preached there around 680AD, the Isle was now a Buddhist retreat. (175) To cross that stretch of water to it would be the closest I could get to Dad's anchorages. Numerous rabbits populate the island, and dogs, alcohol and fires are supposedly all banned, (although judging from the traces of white smoke I'd seen earlier, someone was busy violating this last rule). The price of the boat trip was seventy percent higher, mile for mile, than the Portsmouth to Ryde ferry, (reportedly the most expensive in the UK), and although I wanted to make the trip, for me the price would have had to include getting drunk, setting fire to a few rabbits and sending my Jack Russell, off after them to put out the flames.

The pier was different to the one that Dad would have seen; in those days it was a long slim wooden affair that protruded well out into the bay for the steamers to access. It had been the lifeblood of Lamlash, and the steamer traffic between May and September swelled the population of the village by seven-fold. It fell into a state of disrepair in 1947 when the Duke of Montrose exerted pressure for it to be shut down to mitigate his expenditure for its repair. (176) But it struggled on and remained in use by the ferry companies until 1954, being finally demolished sometime in the 1960s. (177) It was to this now vanished pier that Dad would have disembarked for shore leave in the 1920s and 30s, and it was the head of this pier that would have been seen at bearing 297° from the ship's bridge. Stuart, at the Heritage Museum, had told me that the old pier had been a few yards south of the new one, so I was close to the first co-ordinate.

Dad's second visit on *Tiger* was in July 1928, when two destroyers and 15 submarines of the H class accompanied her, (more submarines than the whole Royal Navy fleet now possesses). Their visit was quintessentially recorded in the local press as:

One, sailing through the bay in a pleasure steamer, was struck by the fierce-looking, shark-like shape of the undersea type of warship. The 'Tiger's band discoursed fine music at the two crowded dances given in the Public Hall during its visit. (178)

So now I made for the Public Hall, which was just inland of the Church of Scotland, the spire of which at bearing 272° from the ship, (my second co-ordinate), would have stuck up like a stout reddish-brown pencil behind whitewashed houses. I could only guess what it had been like when Dad had maybe waltzed around the floors of the Public Hall, but now – it was a grey-roofed, horizontally timbered, maroon-painted building with boarded windows, behind a stone wall, surrounded by trees. It reminded me of an abandoned scout headquarters.

A few things remained. The second sepia postcard that the case had yielded was labelled: *Lamlash showing Goatfell in distance*. This had been taken from high ground to the South of the bay, so I headed there, passing a caravan and camping park that, being by the sea, was probably midge-less and a much more desirable abode than Glen Rosa. I tried unsuccessfully to hug the shoreline but was forced inland by the mouth of a bridgeless stream – tracking seaward again at the first opportunity. A dog barked threateningly at my confused prowling on each of the four occasions I approached its master's property, until its lady owner dragged him inside. A dirt track headed up through trees; it afforded only a few brief squints to the bay below as it rose, and at each of these I pulled out the old postcard and tried to match it to the present view – but then I kept climbing when the views didn't seem to match. Finally, I emerged onto a road – the main road to Whiting Bay, and still I was climbing – now fearing that the view, like that of Marine House, had dematerialised. At a clearing, opposite a house, the view and the postcard seemed finally to correspond. Was I standing on the exact spot of the photographer who'd taken the view depicted in the postcard of the 1920s? It seemed so. In the house opposite I thought I saw some movement and imagined an old lady dialling 999 as she watched this lunatic holding up a postcard and peering around it into the distance. (179)

Back at sea level I slouched on a bench seat, stared out across the bay at the two anchorage co-ordinates I'd visited, (the pier, and the steeple of the Church of Scotland), and pulled out a map of Arran. With the compass pointing north towards the northern tip of the main island and Clauchlands Point, the co-ordinate of 042° Hamilton Lts. seemed to match that of Hamilton Rock. This rock is apparently the only place on Arran named after a Hamilton, whose family owned the island since

James IV of Scotland gave the Earldom of Arran to his cousin James in 1503. But naming a rock after the Hamiltons is about as complimentary as naming faeces after Thomas Crapper. (175) I puzzled over the Lts. Part of the co-ordinate – there never had been a lighthouse on the rock, but the three co-ordinates on the map seemed to tally and this placed *Tiger* at a position midway between the Church and Holy Isle.

It began to rain as I took refuge in the Pier Head Tavern where I was sure Dad would have spent more than a few hours and pounds over seventy years before. It was just after 6 p.m. and on the TV, Greece and Spain were playing in Euro 2004. The barman noticed my interest in the football.

'What they can't stand around here,' he said, 'are the commentators – they're *so* biased! They ran a sweep in here on Sunday to guess in which minute of the game somebody would mention 1966.'

'How long did it take?' I chuckled.

'It wasn't until the eighty-third minute – nobody won – so it's a roll-over for tomorrow night!'

'Are you staying in Lamlash?' he asked.

'No, unfortunately not,' I said.

'Pity – it's a folk night here tonight – in the room next door there,' he said.

I stripped off my dripping, shiny anorak, stuffed it into the bottom compartment of the rucksack and decided to attempt to break my record for the longest stay in a pub ever. It was dry at least and was better than an evening in the tent on midge meadow.

I ordered a chicken curry, and ear wigged in on Davie, a loquacious local, who was putting the world of Lamlash to rights to an audience of two of his ruddy-faced cronies. They were talking about fishing; I caught snippets of Davie's deliverance, like occasional words heard in a howling wind: 'That line of buoys, they're muscle ropes,' I heard him say – then, a little later: '...exported to the Far East'. What I couldn't figure out was whether he was pro, anti or neutral the fishing debate. The lobby being put forward by COAST – the Community Of Arran Seabed Trust, was to section off a no-take zone at the northern end of the bay and a less stringent marine protection area to the south. These areas would then be monitored and compared to the status quo area outside the bay. Scallop dredging has, over the years since the 1970s, stripped the seabed bare of natural aquatic species and the plan is to allow them to re-colonise. (180)

The curry came, with two large pompodoms that covered and hung over my plate, obscuring what was below; it was very hot – akin to a Madras. The Davie brigade, with a last bemoan about the loss of the

White House, (once a hunting lodge) wandered off, away to their homes to see what the wife had laid-on for tea. Their departure was the start of an atmospheric metamorphose of the place – something I'd never witnessed in a pub before – gradually the evening clientele – the folkies – arrived.

The band drifted in from 9 p.m. onwards and people took their drinks through to the room next to the bar. They were the usual mix I'd expected, hippy types, disguised behind beards, glasses and long hair. It was almost exactly as I'd remembered such nights way back in the sixties, except that now most of the audience were in their fifties and sixties. The music was good with the usual cries of 'Yes' at the end of numbers before the onset of applause. It was *so* good that the bus deadline to Brodick I'd set passed without my realising it. It was gone eleven then before I finally convinced myself to leave the comfy ambience of the music and tackle the six-mile hike back.

◆ ◆ ◆

The rain was intermittent; I zipped the anorak right up as I passed the pier, but as I turned inland up the hill on Brodick Road past Marine House, it stopped again. At the top of the hill, I turned slowly to take a last melancholic look back at Lamlash, before breaking into a gentle jog down the hill. The lights of Troon and Irvine on the mainland glowed orange, far away across the Firth of Clyde down to my right. It was a damp but beautiful night.

At midnight it was dusk when I reached midge meadow, and as I passed the green door of the cottage at the top of the rise, I suddenly felt the hot Madras curry rumbling down to the lower reaches and knew I'd not make it to the tent without an urgent detour to the 'palatial' whitewashed toilet block. Not blessed with lights, the place was, as Dylan Thomas had eloquently put it, bog-black (or perhaps it was bible-black)! Anyway in this case bog-black was more appropriate. I selected the trap with the missing door, which was just as well given the urgent nature of the situation.

Somewhat relieved, I slithered down the slippery path to the tent, unzipped it, threw in the rucksack, crawled in myself, zipped up the tent again without worrying about the midges, pulled off my shoes and climbed into the sleeping bag in my clothes. Sleep came within two shakes of a happy lamb with a short tail.

◆ ◆ ◆

'Aaaaaaagh!' – What strange creature was this! I thought, unzipping the sleeping bag and crawling out.

'Aaaaaaagh!' – There it was again, from somewhere high up!

Ten minutes later, after I'd hauled my way back up the even-more slippery path in the rain to the toilet block, I understood what the cry had been. It had been the shocked lamentation of two sleepy Scotsman upon discovering – in the trap with the missing door – within the vicinity of the toilet bowl, but not actually in it – a messy mass of brownish-black excrement.

In posh hotels they provide a card and an envelope so that guests can convey to the management their thoughts on improvements to the facilities. The card I slipped through the letterbox of the cottage's green door read – BUY A BLOODY GENERATOR.

A breakfasted, slightly stouter Sassenach stumbled slowly out of Stalkers on his way to catch the ferry back to the mainland. Then he began to worry about the broken car window and how he would contact his wife if the mobile phone had been stolen.

Lamlash, with Goatfell in the distance – June 2004.

19.   The Spirit Of Scotland

In 1940, the war was going badly for Britain. In June, France had capitulated and the Italians had joined in on the side of Germany; Mussolini had his greedy eye on Yugoslavia, Tunisia, Corsica, Egypt and Greece – and Hitler had promised to leave him a free hand in the Mediterranean. (181) Mussolini had, as long before as 1923, tried to steal a piece of Greek territory by landing on Corfu. Then in August 1940 – as a prelude to a declaration of war – Italy had sunk the little Greek cruiser *Helle* while the ship was engaged in religious celebrations off the island of Tinos.

There was a beneficial knock-on effect to Britain as the Greeks were dragged into the war – because now she would allow Britain to use Suda Bay in Crete without protest. (182) Greece had received a British guarantee of support in April 1939, so Suda Bay was set to play its part as an advanced naval base for ships taking part in the Greek campaign; its defences were to be built up so that it could be used as a naval fuelling depot. The Royal Marines – MNBDO 1 were to be sent to defend the base; their task, in Churchill's words, was to turn Suda Bay into an island fortress – a second Scapa Flow. (183)

Dad was still a Corporal in January1941 when the First RM Group MNBDO 1 were issued their kit, so I doubt he knew his destination as he caught the train at Portsmouth's Fratton station on the 31st of that month. I wondered how he'd broken the news to my Mum and where he'd told her he was being posted. He might have been slightly bemused to find that included in his personal baggage, along with one sea-kit bag plus drawers, were khaki shirts and two pairs of khaki shorts – especially when the train was heading north to Glasgow – now I know the Scots wear kilts, but khaki shorts in Scotland in the middle of winter! Dress for the journey had also been stipulated in detail and issued as:

K.S.D. or battle dress, cap F.S. trousers, boots, marching order complete with rifle or revolver, water bottles filled, greatcoat worn, knife lanyards will be worn, A.G respirator heavy position, A.G. equipment rolled, helmet W.P. in bag slung on pommel of bayonet. (184)

◆ ◆ ◆

I anxiously peered over the rail of *Caledonian Isles* to the car park at Ardrossan and tried, in vain, to pick out my car. Was it still there and if so, had it been broken into?

The mobile was unbelievably still nestled in its holder. Among its numerous recorded calls was the one from Ruth I'd been expecting, asking why I hadn't called her as I'd promised.

As I drove out through the town and headed north towards Largs, I called her and tried to explain. Unusually, I was able to complete an explanation without sentences being truncated by interruptions and from this, I concluded that she wasn't alone.

'So where are you now?'

'I just explained,' I said, 'I've come off the ferry from Arran – I'm in Ardrossan.'

'Where the hell's that?'

'It's in Scotland.'

'Huh – I gathered that – where are you off to now?'

'Glasgow.'

'What the hell are you going there for?'

'I'm going to the King George V Dock, It was where Dad sailed from, to go to the middle-east – during the war.'

♦ ♦ ♦

At Gourack I parked up and looked out across the steely, blue-grey water of the Firth of Clyde to Kilcreggan and beyond, through the wandering lochs to the dark mountains with rolling grey clouds descending over them like a mantle. Half-a-dozen grey motor-torpedo boats were scudding forlornly up the Firth towards Glasgow – and I thought then of the convoy of about 60 ships that had sailed in the opposite direction on Saturday the 10th of February 1941. The convoy was carrying the 267 officers and 4,909 other ranks of MNBDO 1 – one of whom was my Dad. (185)

Two troop ships (code-named H1 and H12) had set out from King George V Dock at 1000hrs that morning, joined at Gourack by a third – (H6); two of the ships were originally of the Glen line, converted to troop transports. (184) One of these was the *Rangitata* – a second was the SS *Almanzora*, (185) whilst the third was probably the *Rangitiki*.

The *Rangitata* was a passenger and cargo vessel built by John Brown & Company at Clydebank and was delivered to the New Zealand Shipping Company in 1929; she was one of three sister-vessels that had previously been on a four-weekly service between England and New Zealand; she'd transferred to the Federal Line in 1936 and survived until 1962 when, at the ripe age of 33, she was finally scrapped. I was convinced (a gut feeling) that Dad had sailed out to Egypt on this ship.(186)

I'd written to the Clydeport Authority the previous month and had been given permission to visit the King George V Dock, but my appointment wasn't until the following day, which meant I had the afternoon free to visit the Clydebuilt Museum. It was located on a site that was also occupied by The Braehead Shopping Centre; one of those dreadful shopping complexes – stereotypical of those in Britain, Europe, America and probably now almost the entire world. Built at a cost of £285 million, on land that until 1999 was agricultural and on which few feet had trodden – now it was overlain with the usual plastic-concrete-steel structure, and the land trodden by the entire populace of Glasgow – not to mention foreigners like myself.

The Centre stood where the basins of the Shieldhall docks scheme should have been. In 1911 the first proposal had been for five great tidal basins to be built on land purchased by the Clyde Navigation Trustees. Work had started on the site in 1924 but, because of the depression, the King George V dock was the only enterprise to be completed.

The KGV dock was opened on the 10th of July 1931, at the height of the depression, by – guess who? King George V accompanied by Queen Mary. A twenty-one gun Royal salute was fired as they sailed into the dock aboard the new turbine steamer called – guess what? *King George V* to break the ribbon stretched across its entrance. On their last visit to Glasgow in 1927, the King had opened the King George V Bridge – I bet the workforce didn't run a sweep on what they thought the new dock would be called! (187)

King George V dock, Glasgow.

♦ ♦ ♦

Once a country house with farm buildings, the hotel, situated by the 'beautiful' refinery town of Grangemouth, had been extended. A new block had been built, and it had been thoroughly modernised.

The bar was spacious but crowded. Unusually, for a large hotel it stocked ginger beer, so I ordered a bottle to accompany my double dark rum that made a Caribbean drink known as a dark and stormy. I couldn't see the brand of rum and caught a mere flash of the label as the barman whisked it away onto a high shelf.

Most of the seats around the tables were taken up by little knots of oil industry businessmen sipping their pints and talking shop, only occasionally glancing up at a huge screen showing Euro 2004, whilst a mile away the porcupine orange flares of the refineries burnt away with a beauty that contrasted sharply with their consummate cat-cracker ugliness. I leant against the bar to face the screen. England had earlier cruised to a 3-0 win over Switzerland and now Croatia was taking on France.

In the corner of my eye I saw her approaching – a dark haired woman in her late thirties; she made to walk around me to a space at the bar, but clipped my foot and gripped my arm as if she'd almost tripped over it.

'Sorry,' we both said simultaneously and smiled.

'If it's Scotland – I can't see them crying,' she said in a deep masculine English, accent-less voice, nodding towards the screen.

'No,' I said, not able to find an instant witty response. She was obviously ignorant of the tournament, and anyway the only Scotsman in the place was the barman. She ordered a half a pint of bitter and, whilst it was poured, I sneaked a sideways squint at her. She looked Hispanic, wearing large gypsy-ringed earrings, which somehow matched her long Roman nose. She was small breasted, tightly clad in jeans and was in no way attractive, but had an interesting lived-in face.

She was definitely looking for a man for the night – any man, and I was pretty sure that the stumble had not been accidental. But already she'd given up on me and I watched as her slender form slipped away from the bar and weaved amongst the tables like a mantis searching its prey in ruminative unobtrusiveness. She reminded me a bit of a witch, and she targeted three middle-aged men seated around a table, slithering, apparently unseen by them, into a vacant seat on the adjacent table. I watched her, spellbound then, as for the next ten minutes she tried to emerge stealthily from her mantis camouflage and vamp into conversation with a fat, balding man seated closest to her. But each time, after a brief exchange, he returned to chat with his associates or sloped a look up at the screen. Eventually her attentions faltered and becoming bored and frustrated she began to sip nervously at the bitter whilst her eyes roamed around the room for other possible victims. Then, after five minutes she gave up, rose quietly from her seat and slid away around the tables out towards reception. There would be no male mate to eat tonight.

The game finished within five minutes, so I drained my dark and stormy of unknown brand, left the bar, strolled past reception, swung open the door into the corridor and headed for my room. Suddenly, ten metres ahead, I caught sight of the tight, slender, jean-sheathed arse of Mantis dawdling, whilst I, at my natural walking speed, approached her at the comparative speed of a missile. Before I reached her, the missile guidance system luckily veered me right, up a staircase to my room on the first floor, but at my door I had some, not uncommon, key-fumbling trouble opening it and, looking down the corridor, saw (in a mad glimpse of the apocalypse), Mantis, (who'd obviously climbed another staircase), fast approaching. Before she came down on me, I succeeded in executing entry, and then heard myself make an absurd, inane and instantly regrettable remark as she passed me:

'I was sure this was my room!' I said, and closing the door, heard hers close the instant after – she was in the room next to mine; it was the last room in the wing.

I took a last look out the window at the sweet orange refinery flares away in the distance, untied the cords of the long heavy curtains, pulled them closed and switched on the television. After a quarter of an hour I heard Mantis next door apparently on the telephone and, why I don't know, but I had this sudden urge to eavesdrop. On the desk was a bottle of Scottish spring water and two glasses facing down, one of which I snatched up and squeezed gently, in a rolling motion, to the wall. The glass didn't help much; I could hear her deep masculine voice, but could only catch snatches of conversation – although it became apparent she was talking to a man. But there was another sound though – it was a kind of multifarious whispering that seemed to come from the walls, as if someone were tapping messages through the heating pipes, but in whispers. The Mantis conversation went on for some time and I got bored, so flopped back on the bed and watched a programme on TV. When it ended, I went to sleep.

✦ ✦ ✦

Through closed eyelids I sensed something and, opening my eyes, saw an intense white light radiating from the wall opposite me, where earlier I'd pressed the glass. An instant later, and for no more than a few seconds, the figure of a woman moved from the spot where the light had appeared towards the drawn-curtained window. She was dressed in a full, long black, nineteenth century dress that, below the bodice, spread over a bustled frame and flowed heavy to the ground – except that she moved above the ground. On her head she wore a black bonnet or caleche and she seemed to be looking at me as she moved, but with expressionless eyes – and then, at the curtains, she was gone. I didn't feel frightened or threatened, but knew that I'd just seen something I hadn't believed in until that moment – a ghost!

I switched on the light – it was four-fifteen in the morning.

When I was a boy I'd asked Dad if he believed in ghosts, he'd replied without hesitation that he didn't and I remember that I'd pressed him for the reason. He'd said it was because he'd never seen one. It was a scepticism I'd shared with him ever since – until that moment in the hotel room…now I knew I'd seen one; it wasn't a dream – the clarity and detail belied that possibility, but still I started to doubt what I'd seen.

How, if the room was dark, I asked myself, did I see the crisp detail of the black costume she wore; its gathered muslin frilled little bonnet and the black silk pleats on the dress? I couldn't explain it! Was it a mourning dress? Was she a widow? Had her husband died close by? I switched off the light again; it was still dark outside, but a chink of moonlight shone through onto the wall – not at the point where the intense white light had appeared; but still, I questioned whether this could have been what had awakened me. No! This was the real thing, or as near as an apparition can be to it – I had just seen a ghost! I switched on the light again and began to reflect on the events of the previous evening – was this something to do with the mysteriously branded rum I'd drunk at the bar? Was it something to do with Mantis?

Then I thought of what I'd done – of the glass that I'd slid to the wall – of the whispering – and I remembered that thirty years before in another hotel I'd been one of five young men who'd dabbled with a hastily constructed ouija board that had scared the shit out of us all. Now, I knew I had just seen a ghost; there was no doubt – so, I thought, something must exist after death. But does this mean there is life after death? And if so has God got anything to do with it?

Later I wrote to the hotel, enclosed a stamped, addressed envelope and asked if they'd heard any other reports of ghosts frequenting the place. But recognising a mad Englishman when they heard from one, or perhaps not wishing to frighten off the clientele, they took great care not to reply – but I bet they steamed off the stamp!

❖ ❖ ❖

I gave the guard in the security cabin the name of my contact at Clydeport and he, surprisingly and without any fuss, directed me through the cobbled dock roads to their office which, although I didn't realise it at the time, was directly opposite the very dock I'd travelled to see.

I'd written to Peter, the Operations Manager, who'd passed me down the line to Alastair, who'd passed me down the line to Donald, a tall well built, grey haired man of about my age. Without pre-amble we donned hardhats and made for the dock. In the brief time I'd spent in the offices a heavy shower had ensued but now, as we walked the few metres to the dock, it began to ease and clear to a wispy-white-cloud blue sky.

The deepwater dock was just a dock, known as 'the wonder dock' when it opened in 1931 at a cost of £2 million; it's now the last dock still in use in Glasgow harbour. (188) More fascinating was the remains of the railway platform where around 5,000 troops had de-trained in February 1941. The railway tracks were still there, rooted within the puddle-pooled uneven cobble road and now filled with rainwater. The end of the platform revealed that its edge, nearest the track, had been constructed upon layers of bricks, which were dislodged and crumbling, whilst the remainder consisted of cast concrete slabs with tall rusting lampposts stabbing it at intervals. An oppressive encroachment of tree foliage emerged from the rear of the platform and ran along its length, patched with areas of slimy moss and weeds growing up through cracks. I wondered why they'd never got around to demolishing it, as it'd obviously not been used for years.

✦ ✦ ✦

When Dad had been here, waiting to embark ship, things had been chaotic. The Luftwaffe had made a reconnaissance of the Clyde shipyards and docks as early as 1939 and had made their first daytime raid on Glasgow on the 19th of July 1940, so there was an inevitable air of uncertainty about everything. (189) I wondered how Dad had got on; one anti-aircraft battery had apparently spent over 48 hours on the train and in a transit camp, followed by a six-hour wait in river lighters, before embarking ship. (190)

It took until the 10th of February 1941 to get the convoy fully assembled and ready to sail, which it finally did – out past Greenock, south down the Firth of Clyde, skirting around Arran and Kintyre, before turning a course north into the Atlantic to steam anti-clockwise around Ireland and head (the long way around) to the Mediterranean. The convoy reached Freetown in Sierra Leone on the 2nd of March, where it paused for six days before sailing on down to Durban, where after another six-day stopover, (which included a march past at the town hall and a church parade), MNBDO 1 joined another convoy bound for Egypt – to arrive at Tahal Camp on the 23rd of April. (184) Egypt was to be merely a staging post for the marines; the target all along had been

Crete – to fulfil Winston Churchill's vision of it as an island fortress, from which the Royal Navy could control the Mediterranean.

Mussolini had, against German wishes, invaded Greece in October 1940, expecting an easy victory against the despised, 'racially inferior Levantine Greeks', and a country one-sixth its size. But, assisted by Mussolini's ill planning the Greeks pushed the invading army back into Albania and pinned them there for three months. (191) In March 1941, the Italian Navy was also soundly defeated by the British off Cape Matapan near Crete and, to repair the damage to the united fascist front from these two events, the Germans came to Italy's aid by declaring war on Greece in April. By the 27th of that month the swastika was flying over the Acropolis – and the British, new Zealanders and Australians were all pouring out of Greece and onto Crete.

Fortunately for Dad, there was only enough shipping to take about 38 percent of MNBDO 1 from Egypt over to Crete where they landed on the 4th of May. Coastal and anti-aircraft batteries were sent, but it had been decided to keep the Land Defence Force in Egypt. (192) But the Germans invaded Crete too quickly for the British and soon took the island. Of the 38 percent of marines that arrived on Crete, 57 percent of these finished up as casualties, with 900 being taken as prisoners-of-war. (193)

Dad was to stay in Egypt for around eleven months, finding himself eventually in the plotting room at Abu Qir (Kanopus), near Alexandria. (194) From there he was moved to Ceylon, before eventually making it back to Britain in April 1944 in time for the Normandy landings; he'd not seen my Mum for three years and three months.

✦ ✦ ✦

Donald gave me the full tour; he'd spent his life in shipping and knew a great deal about the work of Clydeport. We tramped up to the Clyde where he pointed out the various shipyards and ex-shipyards across and up the river. I spotted the huge hammerhead crane across the water and he told me it was called a Goliath. I told him I'd worked for three weeks at the top of a similar crane in Portsmouth dockyard, (but didn't tell him that I'd been spotted by the charge-hand trying to break the 'peeing from the top of a crane' world record).

We crunched over broken glass, called cullet – an unwelcome cargo to handle; Donald said: 'Not many shipping companies want to handle that stuff – you see those piles of scrap over there,' he continued, 'that's all going off the Santander to be made into cars – then it'll all be on its way back over here again. – 'Over there,' he pointed, 'waste paper going to Turkey, to be made into toilet rolls.' He seemed to know every cargo –

Boiler tubes made at Babcocks going to Michigan in the States; sand collected from Oban; cement from Port Talbot.

'A lot of the crews never want to leave the sea,' Donald said, as we started to walk back, 'they have a thing we used to call tankeritus – I had it too – went from one tanker to the next, very rarely got home.'

'Where was home?' I asked.

'I'm from the Outer Hebrides – at the Butt of Lewis – right at the top. I go back once a year to see the family – I'm actually going in a few days time for a week.' He said.

'Really, I've got to go there in a few days too – to Stornoway,' I said.

'What days will you be there?'

'Monday and Tuesday.'

'Well, when you're there, look into the Carlton – it's a pub on Francis Street – chances are I'll be in there.'

'OK, I will.'

We were walking back now, along the length of the KGV dock towards the Clydeport offices.

'Each building along there was once a berth,' said Donald, 'there were originally nine berths – there are ten now – but in the past, ships would have been double moored all along there.' Now, the dock was empty except for a Norwegian frigate.

'There's a big NATO exercise on in a few days time – they'll all be coming in for a couple of days to get drunk before going out on the exercise,' he smiled, 'fifty percent of the crews are women now though – all except for the US ships.' Donald was now in full flow – 'the Americans don't even want you to know they've got a ship in now,' he laughed, 'but everybody knows – including the ladies of the night. They're totally paranoid since September the 11th.'

Back at the offices Donald scribbled down his phone number.

'Give me a ring if you want to know anything else,' he said handing me the slip of paper, 'if anything springs to mind – and don't forget – the Carlton on Francis Street.'

We shook hands and I drove off to get horrendously lost in Glasgow for the next hour, trying to find my way onto the M8. I was attempting to head east, back ten years in Dad's life to October 1931 – to South Queensferry.

✦ ✦ ✦

You'd have got pretty good odds at the bookies against Margaret – who'd been born in Hungary in 1045 – donating her name to a small Scottish town; but this was what she managed. At the age of 12 she arrived at the English court of Edward the Confessor, but after the Battle of Hastings had fled to Scotland where she was welcomed and known as

'The Exile'. Here she was married off, against her will, to King Malcolm Canmore, but must have warmed to him a bit because she bore him six sons and two daughters. Then she set about trying to civilise him... but didn't completely succeed at this task – because he invaded England five times. (195) She was none the less a very devout woman – and it was because she regularly crossed the Forth to visit the shrine of St. Andrew in Fife that the place of her crossing became known as The Queens Ferry. (196)

I became entangled in the traffic that followed in Margaret's footsteps, crawling its way down towards the Forth Road Bridge which, when opened in 1964 was the longest suspension bridge in Europe, but at the sign for South Queensferry I swung off right and then turned left to drive through Port Edgar.

From a grassy terrace above a small outcrop of rocks, opposite the entrance to Hopetoun House, described in the tourist brochures as: *Scotland's finest stately home*, (which on blue moons is apparently used by members of the Royal Family), I clambered down to a small sand and pebble beach. Looking north across the Forth I glimpsed Rosyth Dockyard and the flat grey top of what looked like a factory building.

Dad had only been to Rosyth twice. In 1935 he'd arrived at the railway station, as a newly promoted corporal, to join HMS *Effingham*, just before she'd cast off to sail down to Spithead (and then on to Sandown Bay) for the Silver Jubilee Review by King George V. His second visit was aboard the light cruiser HMS *Danae* in 1939, immediately after the review of the reserve fleet in Weymouth Bay by King George VI. She'd moored at No.14 buoy off Rosyth in-between sea exercises and would soon return to Portsmouth to prepare to sail to the South Atlantic.

There were no grey warships over at Rosyth now, just a listless tanker and a red-and-white *Superfast Ferry* butting out to sea then down towards Zeebrugge. The river was the colour of cold pewter under a matching gunmetal sky; the weather had changed yet again that day.

To the east were the two bridges – juxtaposed and entwined in perspective as if they were one. Dad's other visit to the area was on HMS *Nelson* when, according to the ship's log, she'd anchored directly under the Forth railway bridge – the more distant of the two bridges from my viewpoint – off South Queensferry (the road bridge had not been there then of course). Shore leave had been granted by Captain Watson, (one of 17 captains *Nelson* had seen during her 20 year history), which (again according to the log) started and finished at Port Edgar.

Port Edgar was a naval base until it was closed in1928. Ten years later the ex- destroyer barracks was converted into hospital buildings; but on the outbreak of war the base was again re-opened, remaining so until

1975, where it functioned variously as a school and training establishment. (197) Now – I felt as if I were trespassing as I stepped out along the jetty, (on which Dad would *not* have come ashore, as it was far too new). It was part of a marina and yacht club that exuded an air of exclusivity – with its chandlery and its yacht club café that advertised it was OPEN TO MEMBERS AND GUESTS.

I drove on hurriedly, parking in the cobbled centre of South Queensferry itself, and walked down to the massive rust-red columns and girders of the great railway bridge. At a stall by the side of the bridge I bought a hotdog and wondered, squinting up through the drizzle at a train rumbling across it far above, exactly where under this magnificent, huge Victorian structure *Nelson* had been anchored.

The autumn of 1931 had been a peculiar time for the flagship of the Atlantic Fleet – she'd made an eight-day 'softening-up' stopover at South Queensferry, (with the delights of Edinburgh only ten miles away). King George V had himself ordered it. Here, the newly appointed Commander-in-Chief of the Atlantic Fleet: Admiral John Darby Kelly had gone from ship to ship addressing the men; he'd made jokes about the Admiralty which at that time – following recent strange events further north – especially endeared him to the men. (198) Then, *Nelson* and the Fleet had sailed to the place that had been the focus of those strange events – to continue the sea exercises that had been terminated by them. It was the place I was to travel to next – Invergordon.

20.   A Mutiny of Royals

At Perth it began to rain, and as I drove through the Grampians along the A9 the temperature dropped to 4°C. It was mid June. Dirty marshmallow clouds clung around the mountains where traces of snow still clung on desperately – resisting the fleeting June sunshine. The clouds flopped down into the valleys, hanging motionless like a sea fog. It was so cold I switched on the car heater.

In a lay-by on the bridge over the Cromarty Firth I strolled across the A9 and looked out seaward through the murk – past a string of oilrigs that now scarred the centre of the Firth, (some claim they're pretty at night), to where I thought Invergordon would be – just around the bend in the shoreline. It was still raining hard, with gloomy black clouds overhead and no sign of a break in any direction. I retreated quickly to the car.

The turning off the A9 to Invergordon at Tomich was confusing – it pointed inland. That was the reason I missed it, but I supposed that most tourists unless they'd arrived by ship, might do the same – especially as the guidebook more or less suggested that this was a good idea: *The A9 bypasses Invergordon, 14 miles northeast of Dingwall*, it read, *and unless you have a reason to stop off, don't bother.* (199) At Kildary Milton, five miles further on along the A9, I headed back, in the direction from which I'd come, but now along a B-road that first hugged the Nigg Sands and then the deep water of the Firth as it trickled back towards Invergordon. But this approach coincidentally proved the most appropriate because it ghosted the coastline that *Nelson* would have taken into the port.

Dad had visited Invergordon four times on HMS *Nelson*, I had the anchorage co-ordinates from the ship's log, (though some were illegible – the officers needed to take handwriting lessons; somebody should have told them that they were writing for posterity!); the visit that really mattered for posterity was Dad's third one. On that occasion the flagship had moored up at No.22 buoy in seven fathoms, secured by six shackles, astern of HMS *Malaya* – just off the Nigg Sands. It was 7.35 p.m. on the evening of Sunday the 13th of September 1931 and most of the rest of the Atlantic Fleet were already anchored in two lines, north and south; *Nelson* anchored at the eastern end of the northern line. (200)

A long thin pier now clawed its way out into the Firth, like an emancipated centipede – this was the smelter pier, built by the British Aluminium Co. Ltd. in the early 1980s, it terminated at a jetty upon which was mounted an orange crane. The crane, or perhaps between it and an oilrig slightly out from it, was where I reckoned *Nelson* had moored at No.22 buoy in 1931. I passed the unpretentious black-on-white INVERGORDON sign and parked up.

In between the spatters of rain and with great gulps of the muddy smell, I left the comfortable warmth of the car to take a photograph of the pier and the small rocky foreland from which a lone wader-clad fisherman stood, on this dismal Saturday morning in June. All was a dull silvery grey – the Firth, the sky – everything. If ever there was a place to mutiny, this was it, especially in autumn when the damned Admiralty have just cut your pay by a quarter!

◆ ◆ ◆

Nelson had been late in leaving Portsmouth for Invergordon because the Commander-in-Chief – Admiral Sir Michael Hodges – had been taken ill on returning to the ship on the 7th of September and had been carted off to Haslar Hospital with pleurisy, or thrombosis, depending on which account you read (maybe he had both). (201) *Nelson* dawdled around in Pompey waiting for the C-in-C to recover but finally gave up and weighed anchor at 12.13 p.m. on Friday the 11th of September.

Philip Snowden, the ex-Labour Chancellor, now in the National Government, had announced his budget in the Commons the previous day – Thursday 10th, whilst the rest of the Fleet were conveniently all at sea. A letter detailing the cuts, had been sent to Hodges aboard *Nelson*, but Rear Admiral Tomkinson, (who'd taken over command of the Fleet from Hodges when it sailed for Invergordon on the 8th), apparently knew *sweet F.A.* although it's been said it was likely he'd read of the cuts on board *Nelson* on Monday the 7th. (202) The crew of *Nelson* had however found out about the cuts from the *Portsmouth Evening News* that Friday night, before they'd unhappily sailed for Invergordon, stewing in their own juice all the way on the voyage up north.

To Dad, who'd engaged in 1921 and was on the 1919 pay scale, the budget would mean a cut from four shillings to three shillings a day, dragging him back in line with men who'd enlisted after October 1925 when the pay rates for newly enlisted men had been reduced – by the then Conservative Government.

I wondered if he'd attended the meetings that were held in the men's smoking room on the forecastle, (addressed by Able Seaman John Everson, known as Red Admiral) – probably not, because he was a marine and they were not altogether trusted by the seamen. (203)

The marines' barracks was traditionally positioned between the officers' wardroom and the seamens' mess because in the days of the press gangs the marines were there, (it was joked – or maybe not!) 'to stop the seamen from eating the officers'. (204) In most other ways though the marines were much the same as the seamen, (although mentally they assumed a closer affinity to the stokers); they were on the same pay rates as the seamen and carried out many of the same duties.

As *Nelson* sailed into Cromarty Firth on the evening of Sunday the 13th of September, her crew weren't to know that the rest of the fleet had learnt officially that very day of the cuts via an Admiralty Fleet Order posted on the ships' notice boards (all sixteen printed pages of it). The sending of the Fleet Order had somehow been delayed by two days. (205) The seamen and marines of *Nelson* soon found out that they weren't alone in their disquiet, as cheers, (not whistles – which had been banned aboard HM ships after the Nore mutiny of 1797), greeted them from the other ships as they anchored. Slips of paper later came aboard telling the men of the meeting that the crew had held that afternoon ashore, in the canteen. (206)

◆ ◆ ◆

Back inside the car I noticed that one of my fingers, (the wedding one funnily enough), had lost all feeling and had turned white. To make matters worse I was bursting for a pee. The map I had of Invergordon town centre seemed to show a toilet by the Arts Centre in the High Street, so I drove into the town, parked and, in the rain, searched for it in vain where I thought the map showed it – on the corner of the High Street and Castle Street.

Libraries usually have toilets so, as I'd planned to spend a few hours there looking at the local papers of September 1931, I hurried on desperately in an eldritch crossed-leg scurry. The library doors were shut; I pushed them in indignant disbelief – shut! When I'd telephoned the librarian the day before, saying I wanted to visit the next day – a Saturday, the librarian definitely told me that their opening hours were 9 a.m. to 5 p.m., so I read the board outside with some incredulity:

Tuesdays – 12 to 5 p.m.
Wednesday – 10 a.m. to 12, and 2 p.m. to 5 p.m.
Thursday – 10 a.m. to 12, and 2 p.m. to 5 p.m.
Friday – 2 p.m. to 8 p.m.
Saturday / Sunday – Closed.

Perhaps it was the accent that'd done it – was she a Jacobite sympathiser who still bore a grudge over Culloden?

Still busting, I walked on in soaked hooded anorak to both ends of the bleak and almost deserted High Street in search of a loo, or a shop that might sell incontinence pants, then I pulled the map out my pocket again and this time noticed in the bottom right hand corner:

*FACILITIES: TOILETS – LOCATED **IN** ARTS CENTRE IN HIGH STREET.*

The word 'in' wasn't in fact in bold letters, but it should have been, to accommodate blind old incontinent sods like me.

The Arts Centre was situated in the long High Street, which stretches the length of Invergordon town. The original settlement here was known as Inverbreakie, but in the 18th Century the estate was purchased by Sir William Gordon of Embo, hence the name.

At the west end of the High Street at its junction with Shore Road, amid the dense undergrowth of a shrubbery, neatly pebbled at its borders with a closely mowed lawn stood a huge rusting anchor. It had been positioned in front of a crescent of concrete that acted as a nautical sightscreen, whilst in the foreground stood a wooden framed notice proclaiming:

WELCOME TO INVERGORDON.

Below this was a conspectus of the port's associations with the Royal Navy.

Daniel Defoe, then an English agent sent to Scotland just prior to the Act of Union in 1707 was the first person to advocate in print the naval potential of the Cromarty Firth, but Royal Naval ships first began to sail these waters whilst searching for Jacobites during the rebellion of 1745, (pity they hadn't found the librarian). HMS *Glasgow* was the first ship to be stationed in the Firth, but it took until 1912 before the Firth was formed into an official strategic naval base... and then it was only classified as second class.

The notice majored on the events that occurred here in December 1915 when the cruiser HMS *Natal* blew up and sank within five minutes, resulting in the loss of around 400 lives – both locals and navy personnel. The wreck used to lie in what the navy called the fairway, and as ships passed the spot they would sound the 'Still', but in 1931, when Dad had sailed in, the wreck was being slowly cut up and taken away piecemeal – like ants carting away a chunk of bread. (207)

I stood dripping wet, and took a photograph, then read the notice again – there was no mention of the mutiny; Invergordon seemed to be in denial.

✦ ✦ ✦

On the morning of Monday 14th aboard *Nelson*, Captain Watson had addressed the crew about the cuts. I wondered how he'd couched in his speech the fact that the Board of Admiralty had broken its pledge that had been given to the men about the1919 rates – that their pay wouldn't be cut back in line with those of 1925, something that would also affect their pensions? Watson told the crew that the ship would be sailing on exercise the next morning. He must have known that something serious was afoot when a torpedo-man spoke up that it wouldn't. (208)

The reasons for the pay cuts were complex: Dad – when I was a boy – had voted Conservative; this was unheard of for the dockyard area we lived in, which bordered the slums of Portsea where everyone voted Labour. I'd always puzzled why he'd voted this way as we were certainly working class – and one day I asked him:

'The Labour party cut our pay,' was all he'd said – no elaboration, no details, nothing about a mutiny, just that. Half a century later I discovered some of the things that had rightly or wrongly shaped his view.

Britain's second Labour Government came to power in the summer of 1929, led for the second time by Ramsey MacDonald, the illegitimate son of a maidservant, Ann Ramsey. But in 1929 the Labour Party again had no clear majority and had to rely once again upon the support of Lloyd George and his Liberals to hold onto power. MacDonald's election pledge was to reduce unemployment, (which stood at over a million, though still under 10 percent), but here he'd picked up the *shitty* end of the stick because five months later the New York stock exchange collapsed and, as everyone had depended on American loans, (which were now no longer forthcoming), the rest of the world too was then plunged into depression.

By December 1930, unemployment had risen to 2½ million. The Chancellor, Philip Snowden, having already inherited a weak position from Churchill, now found that whilst his yield from taxes had gone down, his expenditure on unemployment had gone up, and by February 1931 he was eagerly grasping at the straw of a Liberal proposal for the appointment of an Economy Committee – against the wishes of many of his own party. (209)

Sir George May, who'd come from the Prudential Insurance Company, chaired the committee (the man from the Pru). Four of its members were also leading capitalists. Its report, published on July 31st, concluded that Britain had an immediate deficit of £120 million, (or £170 million in a full year), only £24 million of which they, the capitalists, reckoned could be recouped through taxation. The rest of the money, they recommended had to be obtained by cutting unemployment relief and by salary cuts for police, teachers and the armed forces.

Whilst the May Committee had been deliberating, the Board of the Admiralty had sent it a memorandum in which they stated that:

All the departments agreed that men entering the services in 1919, or who had since entered, had a moral claim up to a point and in certain cases...there would have been a contractual obligation had it not been for the Crown's privilege.

The references of 'up to a point' and 'the Crown's privilege' gave the Committee a loophole through which they gratefully fired off their arrows. The First Lord of the Admiralty A.V. Alexander told the Labour Cabinet:

I think the personnel of the Navy as a whole will loyally accept the sacrifice that is demanded of them in pay if equivalent reductions are made throughout the Public Service and if the unemployment rates are reduced. (210)

The Admiralty's view was that, as there was no apparent difficulty in recruiting or retaining men, the 1925 pay scales must be OK for everyone. (211) They conveniently forgot that there were 2½ million on the dole – and they were either ignorant or uncaring about the predicament of the likes of an able seaman aged under twenty-five, (who was thus ineligible for marriage allowance), and who was on the 1925 scale. For this poor devil the weekly cost of the sum of the rent, light, cooking, coal, insurance, food, clothes, and hire purchase instalments on the sticks of furniture in the home he tried to keep, actually exceeded his weekly pay. (212)

MacDonald and those who supported him were viewed as traitors to the Labour Party and on the 31st of August the Party in Hampstead, where MacDonald lived, expelled him. But Snowden, who'd come across to the new National Government with MacDonald, pushed through his budget just the same; he made all the usual tax increases – beer, petrol, tobacco and income tax, but the economy cuts were imposed on top of these; all those persons paid by the state, including the armed forces and the unemployed were cut by 10 per cent, except for the police who were let out of jail with a 5 per cent reduction. The teachers were taught a lesson – they were given a 15 per cent cut.

The cuts the navy were to suffer varied; a Lieutenant Commander would only lose 3.7 per cent, whilst an Able Seaman would lose the later notorious 25 per cent. Dad, I'm sure, believed what he'd told me, when he'd said – 'The Labour party cut our pay,' but in truth the blame could be shared by any number of people – politicians of all three parties, the bankers, the businessmen, and not least by the Board of the Admiralty. Dad had made an indelible connection between James Ramsey Mac-Donald, the Labour Party and the cuts – and it had stuck forever, even though in 1936 MacDonald had joined Stanley Baldwin's Conservative Cabinet.

It wasn't just ghosts Dad had been wrong about!

✦ ✦ ✦

I walked from the anchor back up into town, intent on savouring a visit to the Admiralty Pier until last. The buildings were, an assortment of colours; redbrick, white, but mostly grey and shabby, (although the gloomy weather may have unduly influenced my judgement), except for a neat row of terraced cottages on Joss Street. The flats were grey too, festooned with satellite dishes that must be a necessity in a place like Invergordon. Behind Joss Street, between the Church of Scotland and the community centre sat the town's tanks – they looked like oil storage tanks; I didn't inspect them too closely, so they could I suppose have been gasometers. At any rate they were imposing if not impressive.

In Carol's Café I spotted two rare breed tourists, the only ones frequenting this place apart from myself – (and even I was of doubtful classification). To escape the rain, they'd migrated to the warmth of the café where they sat sullenly facing each other across a Formica topped table, huddled over cups of tea that they'd resolved to last as long as possible. My thoughts returned briefly to the Isle of Wight – and then I decided to find a place for lunch.

I plumped for The Marine. It was the second nautical name I'd spotted – the first being Nelson Photography – (I didn't know Horatio had developed a blind eye for photography!). The Marine had to be a place frequented by the seamen, stokers and marines in 1931 – it *had* to be, because it was one of the few drinking establishments around; Invergordon was apparently a most difficult place to be bad in, especially as – in general – shore leave was only until 8 p.m. (213) Because of the fear of mixing high explosives with drink, the government, during the First World War, took control of licensed premises throughout, (amongst other places), the Cromarty Firth area. Well actually it was our old friend Lloyd (Zorba) George, whose famous quotation had been that Britain were: *Fighting Germans, Austrians and drink, and as far as I can see the greatest of these foes is drink.* (214) It was even suspected that the government watered down the beer. (215) Most men, it was said, went to the canteen.

A sign on the wall of the pub amused me whilst I ate a macaroni cheese lunch – ANY ONE REPEATEDLY SWEARING WILL BE ASKED TO LEAVE THE LOUNGE. The word 'repeatedly', qualified things a bit, obviously the odd 'fuck' here and there would be tolerated, but you'd be in big trouble if you switched into Billy Connolly mode – and how would they cope if the man himself appeared on one of his world tour stop-offs?

Returning to the rusty anchor, this time I turned left onto Shore Road towards the harbour, to reach Natal Garden. Constructed by volunteers, it was opened in 2001 by the gardening expert Charlie Dimmock whose help it could have done with at that moment. A little plaque in the garden explained *some* of the history of Invergordon. I say some of the history because although mentioning the roles that both Admiral Jackie Fisher and Winston Churchill had both played in developing Invergordon as a naval base for the Atlantic Fleet, the plaque never mentioned the role of the lower deck at Invergordon in changing the history of Britain in 1931 and in changing the Royal Navy forever.

Invergordon was still in denial it seemed. But the plaque did clear up one thing – the tanks *were* oil tanks, constructed to feed the oil fired boilers of the dreadnought battleships of the First World War; the first five were constructed in 1912 and at one time, if not now, there were as many as two-hundred (216).

The naval base itself finally closed in 1993, (it had been run on a care and maintenance basis since 1957). It had been a base then for just 81 years. In the halcyon days, the Invergordon Highland Games would be organised to coincide with the fleet's autumn cruise and the prostitutes would arrive from all over Britain. Each day then the Royal Marine band had marched through the streets, leading the men to the playing fields. (217)

The Admiralty Pier was still there, but signs indicated that Ballerman Transport now occupied the area that had once been the naval dockyard. The last naval vessel had in fact sailed out on the 30th of March 1993. There was nobody around so I nosed about a bit and, at the mouth of the pier, took some photographs, expecting to be barked-at at any moment by some dork in a peaked cap. It was a concrete pier, modern looking – so I doubted it was the 1931 version; in fact I learned later that the pier had been rebuilt in 1952-3. (218) Now, plashy and silvery pooled with rain along its length, lined on its western side by Armco barrier, a white control tower marked its seaward end and a talc sky puffed over the pale green hills beyond. A steel-grey becalmed sea circumfused it and a sign mounted on a lamppost at its entrance said:

NO ENTRY
PRIVATE FACILITY
UNAUTHORISED PERSONS
DO SO AT THEIR OWN RISK

Normally this wouldn't have bothered me; I wanted to walk to the end of the pier and look seaward, up the Firth to picture the Fleet there, (*Rodney* and *Hood* were anchored almost immediately out from the pier), but for some reason I hesitated – perhaps there might be somebody in the control tower – I don't know why, but at any rate I didn't do it. Instead I simply stood there, imagining the events that had taken place over 72 years before…

Aerial view of Invergordon harbour and town, circa 1928
[Photo from Invergordon Image Library – by Park School History Publications].

On the evening of Sunday 13th of September 1931, after Able Seaman Wincott and others had climbed on tables in the canteen to make their impromptu speeches, the men had walked on down through the town singing *The Red Flag*, to arrive at the pier, where a few more speeches had been made before they'd noisily boarded the liberty boats to return to their ships. On several ships they remained on the forecastles, making speeches, cheering and singing until a late hour. (219)

The following afternoon, Monday, up to 6,000 of the 12,000 men of the Atlantic Fleet took shore leave – 600 of them from *Nelson*, 100 of which may have been Royal Marines. Maybe one of those was Dad – the odds were less than 50/50, it depended which watch he'd been on. The starboard watch were given leave from *Nelson* that afternoon but the liberty-men were warned, (so the ship's log reflected), that the ship was under sailing orders. (220) It was to be the second night that a meeting would take place in the canteen, and the ship's company of HMS *Nelson* were particularly bitter about the reductions in pay and took a large part in the meeting. Some of the officers at Invergordon thought in fact that the mutiny might have been averted if it hadn't been for the subversive influence of a large number of the men from *Nelson*. (220)

✦ ✦ ✦

Mutiny had been sporadic in the Royal Navy since the days of James I and in almost all cases it was due either to the badness or insufficiency of provisions, or to some or all of the seamen's meagre pay being with-held. Except for the period of the Commonwealth, which paid and treated them very fairly, things continued much the same through the eighteenth century until by 1783 they reached a pitch when the ships' companies of *Ganges*, *Janus* and *Proselyte* threatened to run their ships on shore and destroy them unless their wages were paid instantly. (221)

The captain of *Janus* was ashore at the time of the mutiny and the crew refused to hoist out the long-boat to bring him back on board, suggesting that the boat should be manned out with marines – this was done. The marines would not join in the mutiny and thereafter were employed to keep the peace and guard the town of Portsmouth.

At the Spithead mutiny of 1797 the demands of the seamen for a pay rise, for better food and for the removal of sadistic and bullying officers were all fair enough, and the fact that they'd received no acknowledgement for about two months that their grievances had even been received let alone considered didn't help much. So it was that on the 15th of April the Channel Fleet refused to sail. On *Robust* the Captain of Marines had applied to the captain of the ship for authority to act, but he, like every other captain, had dared not order his marine detachment to fire on the mutineers without an order from the Admiralty – though they surely would have done so if ordered. On *London*, the First Lieutenant did actually order the marines to fire and five men were killed. In general though the mutiny was so sudden that the marines had no time to get to their arms. (222)

Later that same year things got a might nastier in the mutiny of the Nore at Sheerness. Here the mutineers tied officers to their beds, added weights and hoisted them by their feet to the yard arm by a block and tackle before letting it go, to plummet them into the sea where they left them until they'd almost, but not quite…drowned. The marines here too supported the officers, such that one lieutenant of the marines was sentenced by the ringleaders to be hanged, having the noose actually placed around his neck beneath a hoisted bloody-red flag, before they changed their minds. (222)

The mutiny that outdid even the Nore occurred again at almost the same time, in South African waters aboard HMS *Hermione*; this time the captain's affinity for the cat attributed to the cause. His batting average over a 38-week period was 2.2 floggings and 36.6 lashings a week. The captain, whose name was Pigot, paid no regard at all to the lives of his crew, which was his final undoing as the tortured men could stand it no more and mutinied by clobbering the marine guarding his cabin and feeding Pigot, eight of his officers and a midshipman to the fishes. Unfortunately, the mutineers upset the navy big style by sailing the ship to the Spanish Main and handing it over to the Spanish. Such that the Royal Navy persisted for nine years in hunting down the 33 mutineers and hanging every last one of them. All of the marines remained loyal and served as witnesses in the long series of court-martials. (223)

✦ ✦ ✦

This was the historical baggage that the marines carried to Invergordon; remember, they were sworn men, who still sometimes jokingly referring to the seamen as 'pressed men' – and this allowed them a feeling of superiority over the seamen. How they would react to the situation was unknown both to the officers and the seamen. Admiral Tomkinson himself admitted in his report to the Board of the Admiralty that: *The position with regard to the Royal Marines was uncertain.* (219) Able Seaman Fred Copeman, who like Wincott was serving on *Norfolk*, had recognised the unique and important position of the marines. He was a member of the starboard watch that had been given shore leave on that Monday evening of the 14th of September.

The story of what happened inside that long, low army hut of a canteen, (aside from the game of crown and anchor), depends upon whose report you believe. The officer of the shore patrol, Lieutenant Elkins, who'd entered the canteen to try to stop the meeting, claimed that a glass was thrown and then the men around him linked arms and ushered him towards the door. Seaman Wincott however claimed that, when the glass shattered, Elkins made a dash for the entrance. What *everyone* agreed was that because of overcrowding in the canteen, the meeting had to be moved on to Black Park, a football ground a bit further from the pier, (now Invergordon football field). Here, from the roof of a pavilion, men addressed the crowd. Some wanted everyone to stay ashore – but then one chap advised them it was more sensible to go back on board where it was more comfortable and they'd at least be fed. (224) It was from this roof that Able Seaman Fred Copeman had made his speech, at the end of which he emphasised the importance of the marines – 'There must be no question of splitting one section from another,' he'd said, 'the marines must enter this fight with us from the beginning.' Back on *Norfolk* later that Monday night the marines were asked point blank: *Are you with us – Yes or no?' They'd shouted – 'Yes, we're in.* (225)

I could find no reports of what happened aboard *Nelson* that night or how soundly the marines on her had slept – but they all knew that, when reveille would sound at six o'clock the next morning, something extraordinary would probably occur.

✦ ✦ ✦

Crossing Shore Road, I climbed inland up a trim grassed hillock skirted by a concrete-posted wire fence and stood above an old sea-mine painted bright claret mounted on a plinth. It overlooked a diversification of buildings, all of which had the common features of white walls and grey roofs; they themselves overlooked the Admiralty Pier from which I'd just come. At the top of the hillock was Hayes Hall in which was housed a delightful little museum.

As I squeezed money through the slot of a small cylindrical box, I learned that the museum had only been open for two weeks. It was *so* new that large areas of floor space were still vacant, not yet occupied by glass cabinets. The cabinets that *were* there were stuffed with interesting local history and bits of naval history. There was the HMS *Natal* incident, some snippets about the loss of the matelots' rum tot and a list of traditional Royal Navy toasts for each day of the week, the most amusing being Saturday – *To Sweethearts and wives, may they never meet.*

The mutiny was featured in the same glass cabinet, (at last recognition!), next to the HMS *Natal* incident, with conservatively phrased headlines from *The Daily Express* for Wednesday the 16th of September that declared: *Unrest in the Navy – The senior officer Atlantic Fleet has reported that the promulgation of the reduced rates of Naval pay has led to unrest among a proportion of the lower ratings...*

✦ ✦ ✦

In fact, on Tuesday morning of the 15th of September: The overwhelming majority of the lower-deck personnel of the Atlantic Fleet refused to take their ships to sea or to contribute any activity toward raising steam or weighing anchor. (226) *Warspite* and *Malaya* were already out at sea, they'd been carrying out sub-calibre shooting, whilst *Repulse*, anchored just off Cromarty at the mouth of the Firth, and remote from the rest of the Fleet, had sailed as planned at 6.30 a.m. But on *Valiant* – almost everyone stayed in bed, including a good proportion of the marines; the Captain of Marines had in fact been refused permission by the Captain to parade his men (armed) at 6.00 a.m. But it was the stokers who'd actually prevented her from sailing. On *Norfolk*, the marines, (who'd feared being called out one-by-one by their name and number and given an order, which as sworn men they'd be unable to refuse), had asked the seamen for, and had been given protection from, the officers; they too refused to obey orders to turn to and later barricaded themselves in their barracks. (227) On none of the other ships had the marines been asked to join in the strike, (it was considered a strike by the lower deck, not a mutiny, perhaps because if it were deemed to be a mutiny, Kings Rules and Admiralty Instructions stipulated that every person subject to the Act: *Shall suffer death or such punishment as is hereinafter mentioned.*) (228) On *Adventurer*, the Captain of the Marines wanted to fix bayonets, so the seamen took no chances and battened down the hatch to the marines' mess deck. On *York* an officer threatened to use the marines to clear the forecastle, but was advised that this was extremely unwise.

On Dad's ship, *Nelson*, the ship's log recorded at 0600: *Hands fall in – prepare for sea*, as if nothing was happening, but at 1000 it noted that: *Hands employed – part of ship*. (200) There had been a fear that the officers would attempt to put to sea themselves, so the forecastle party lashed up the anchor cable during the dogwatches. The perpetrator of this 'crime' was later earmarked by the special intelligence service as being one: *William J. Pigg, AB; a very bad character who would preach sedition on the flimsiest excuse*. (202) Commander Lake, who was much respected by the men, confined to his cabin one rash officer who'd reacted to this by threatening to call out the marines; he'd have had a job to find them anyway, because most had hidden themselves in lockers. (229) (Perhaps Dad had never told me about the mutiny because he didn't want to admit that he'd spent most of it hiding in a locker)!

At 7.a.m. when the breakfast hour had begun, large numbers of men gathered on the forecastles of eight of the thirteen ships that were anchored at Invergordon and from 8.00 a.m. a strange form of dissent began – cheering – which was followed by the order to fall in for work at 8.30 generally being disobeyed. At about 9.30 Tomkinson, realising he was on a loser, cancelled the exercises and recalled to port those ships that were out at sea. (230) This included *Malaya*, where it was reported that the marines, from their turret, had jokingly (maybe) suggested their guns be trained on Ramsey MacDonald's house near Lossiemouth. (231)

Aboard *Rodney* the men attached ropes to a piano and hauled it up onto the forecastle where it was played for the next two days solid as a signal to the rest of the Fleet that the strike was still on. The locals over in Invergordon could hear it: *They were giving it laldy most of the night,* one had written to me. (224) The voices of hundreds of men drifted across the water as they shouted from ship to ship.

On Wednesday the 16th the men got hold of the morning papers and read those *Daily Express* headlines, now newly displayed in the museum, that: *The reduced rates of Naval pay has led to unrest among a proportion of the lower ratings...* (Editors of newspapers had been asked to avoid using the word 'mutiny') This political understatement only served to get the men's backs up further, and nobody quite knew what would happen next...

What perhaps only a few of those on board ship at Invergordon knew or suspected was that some of their Lords of the Admiralty had suggested sending in armed boarding parties, (this had been the action taken against the Chilean Navy who'd mutinied three days before for similar reasons), whilst still others actually proposed that the fleet should be bombarded by heavy howitzers from the hills around the Cromarty Firth. Almost unbelievably, the Cabinet were apparently prepared to sanction this idea, and its acceptance was only narrowly averted by the First Sea Lord – Admiral Field, who urged that the ships be returned to their home ports, thus curtailing a planned eight-week stay to only five days. (232) Just after 3 p.m. Tomkinson, aboard *Hood*, received a signal instructing him to this effect; it was a signal that split the lower deck, such that the officers weren't sure, until the very last minute, how their orders to set sail would be received and acted upon. On *Valiant* the use of force was seriously considered, whilst on *Nelson* the officers considered parting the cable if the men refused to unmoor the ship... (233)

Just before midnight Tomkinson sent a signal to the Admiralty that all the ships had sailed.

✦ ✦ ✦

I camped that night near Dornoch, and next morning after a good greasy café breakfast next to a greasy garage, returned to Invergordon. Approaching it along the Saltburn road, the clouds lifted, a pallid sun peeked warily through, and I saw in the distance a huge multi-decked, sparkling white cruise ship alongside Admiralty Pier. I was about to witness the transmogrification of Invergordon from the dismal, damp, grey, deserted place it had been yesterday to a sunny vibrant hothouse of Sunday tourism full of Americans and Japanese. The places that had been drably closed yesterday were today open, with music pouring softly from their doors – the expensive souvenir shops and the store next to Admiralty Pier. But nobody had apparently told poor Carol that the cruise ship *Royal Princess* was arriving that day; Carol must have been the Invergordon pariah – either that or she was a religious nut who was opposed to Sunday opening, or perhaps she was just too idle to get out of bed. Whichever it was, the doors to her café remained firmly shut.

I was annoyed with myself for not walking to the end of Admiralty Pier the day before, for not 'treading the ground' – breaking my second ground rule, so I decided to re-address the situation. But now, sitting on a low wall by a red-and-white barber-pole barrier at the pier's entrance, sat a stocky security guard equipped with a short-wave radio. He was not old but had a shock of long straight grey hair. Passengers on their way back to the ship were flashing some sort of pass at him.

'I'm not with the ship,' I said naively, but with honesty, 'but could I just walk to the end of the pier and back again?'

'No.'

'Would it make any difference if I tell you the reason why?' I said, crouching down level with him.

'No.'

So I told him anyway, but knew I was wasting my time – this jobs-worth cretin wasn't going to budge. 'You can come back tomorrow and go to the end,' he said condescendingly.

'I won't be here tomorrow,' I said, turning away abruptly to avoid an otherwise close inspection of the cell in Invergordon's nick; he was too fat to have chased me to the end of the pier, but would definitely have radioed for the local bobbies – which would have at least brightened up their day.

Giving up on the pier, I turned my attention to the canteen where the lower deck meetings had been held in 1931. But I had no idea of where it was or had been; for some reason I'd imagined it to be in the compound by the docks. I drove around in a perplexed, somewhat dazed state – there was nobody about in the back streets of the town – it *was* a Sunday after all. But then in one of those unexplainable kismet moments, at the east end of Joss Street I saw him on a corner. He was old of course, perhaps in his eighties, with grey hair balding at the crown, wild bushy eyebrows, (like Dennis Healey's), and a ruddy face that clashed with his mauve pullover. For some reason that I never discovered, he was bending over a low garden fence as I lowered the passenger window and asked him if he knew where the Royal Naval recreation grounds had been. He walked over slowly to the car and I leant across and pushed my map of Invergordon through the window to him.

'I'm interested in the mutiny,' I said, 'I'm trying to find the canteen where they held the meetings.'

'Ah! I remember it,' he said, 'I was born in 1921 – I think I was about twelve or thirteen at the time.'(He'd actually been ten). 'They were all sat out there on the football pitch in Black Park, each man with one or two pint mugs of NAAFI beer. They were saying we're not going back on board. There was a lot of noise amongst them all, but no trouble for the locals. The police had just had a pay rise and they'd had a cut,' he said, looking skyward to visualise the scene of seventy-three years ago. 'You could see them all up on deck – there were piano's playing, lots of noise. The marine band marched at funerals.' He said, beginning to ramble a bit.

I got out of the car; it had begun to rain slightly again.

'What about the pubs?' I asked, 'have they all gone?'

'No, they're all still here, just as they were – you know, the locals had pint sized glass jugs for their milk for some time.' (224)

'And what about the canteen?' I asked, 'where is the canteen?'

'Ah! The canteen – yes, it was up there.' He pointed north, towards the oil storage tanks. 'If you go back up the road to the church and on up Academy Road over there – it was up there,' he said, pointing again.

'Thanks very much, that's brilliant,' I said, and went to shake his hand
– but he had an empty china mug in his right hand that he had to awkwardly transfer to his left before this could happen.

'By the way,' I said, as I climbed back into to car, 'what's your name?'

'Davie,' he said, bending back over the garden fence with his mug.

I photographed things and trod the ground – but the significance or not
of that trodden ground, I didn't learn until later. (234)

✦ ✦ ✦

In the aftermath of the mutiny, various things had transpired…The Government agreed that hardship cases should be looked at sympathetically
– although it couldn't accept that it had surrendered. The Admiralty re-
ciprocated this view by sending a signal to be read to all ships'
companies of the Fleet that gave them a *bollocking*, and warned them to
be better boys in the future. The New York papers got hold of the mutiny
story and named it as such, rather than calling it unrest. And a subse-
quent run on gold couldn't be avoided; it was being withdrawn from the
Bank of England at an alarming rate, such that on Sunday the 20th of
September Britain was forced off the gold standard.

Austen Chamberlain had tried to play things down by making a statement declaring an amnesty for those who'd taken part, so that the Board
could take no disciplinary action relating to the events at Invergordon.
There would be no court marshals! The Naval Discipline Act, with its
'Death or other such punishment as is hereinafter mentioned', could not
be applied. There was an important exception to this however – if it
could be shown that subversive activities had been continued after the
fleet had returned to their homeports, the Board of the Admiralty *could*
get their own back.

Now naval Intelligence set out to prove that the mutiny was not spontaneous but was planned in advance by the Communist Party directed
from Russia. Rear Admiral Tomkinson felt that this was the case; he was
confident that there had been: *Organisation in the actual outbreak*, and
he believed *that the preparation must have been made over a consider-
able period.* (235) This was a view wholly shared by many of the
Dartmouth-trained and indoctrinated officers who believed that the
lower deck were incapable of organising the strike without assistance
and that subversive elements were attempting to secure the downfall of
discipline in the Royal Navy. The reds, they believed, were already under the bed and the SIS was busy compiling a dossier of – *Ratings under
communistic influence.* On *Nelson*, (by the 12th of November), thirteen
had been identified. (202) Austen Chamberlain even considered closing
the gates at the dockyard ports to try to stem the spread of insurgency
back to the ships. The panic spread from the Admiralty to the Cabinet;

everyone had been wound up to believe that the plot would erupt in the fleet on the morning of Tuesday the 22nd of September. But – there was no plot, so of course it didn't, but meanwhile the Cabinet had authorised the Admiralty to restrict the cuts to a maximum of 10 per cent.

It was rumoured that the King himself, (an ex-naval captain with a reputation for severity), had influenced the appointment of the Commander-in-Chief of the Atlantic Fleet, Admiral Kelly, so that he could sort out the fleet. This he did, but since Chamberlain had made it clear that there could be no recriminations for Invergordon, the 121 men who were removed from their ships just before the fleet sailed again must all therefore have been involved in a post-mutiny revolutionary plot! Here, in barracks, they underwent a 'training course' – a thin disguise for punishment, and a month or so later 24 of them (including Wincott and Copeman) were discharged onto the streets with no prospect of employment – under the regulation that permitted the navy to get rid of undesirables without trial. In October, at the very time Dad would have seen Admiral Kelly aboard *Nelson* at South Queensferry making jokes about the Admiralty to the men and boosting the morale of the fleet, almost 400 men from around the world were being sent into barracks for being a nuisance to the navy. They would later be dismissed in a general clear out. Some were homosexuals – which indicates that more than a few things have changed since Invergordon – because these days the navy advertises for recruits in the gay press. (236)

The group of people who probably gained most from the mutiny were the teachers – they'd automatically had their pay cut reduced from 15 per cent to 10 per cent *at a stroke* – but without giving the government any *stick*.

✦ ✦ ✦

I followed the Cromarty Firth to Dingwall and then turned onto the A835 to head west across Easter Ross towards Ullapool where I was hoping to camp for the night and be ready to board the ferry next morning for Stornoway. With eighteen miles to go I pulled into a snug wooded lay-by, made use of the log-cabin-styled toilet, wrote up a few thoughts about Invergordon and then, as my original itinerary had changed, decided I'd better telephone Malcolm in Stornoway. As I switched on the mobile phone I noticed the little envelope message sign in the top left hand corner of the screen and opened it up – it read:
HAPPY FATHERS DAY GRANDAD
GRANDMA HAS GONE 2 LIVE WITH US.
JASMINE

21. Part Of The Union

'It's good out there,' said the young girl, shovelling chips into the little greaseproof bag until they spilled out onto the newspaper. It'd started to rain again – and I wasn't sure whether she was teasing or serious.

'If that's good,' I said, looking behind me out the chip shop window, 'I'd hate to be here when it's bad!'

'Well at least it's not blowing a gale or swimming with midges,' she said, deftly rolling the newspaper.

Outside, I found a friendly wall on which to lean, pulled up the hood of my anorak, and had just started to nibble the first rain dampened chip when the mobile rang – it was Ruth.

'Where are you?'

'I'm in Ullapool.'... (There was no response, perhaps she was unfolding a map, I thought I heard a sort of rustling sound)...'I'm catching the 9.30 ferry in the morning to Stornoway on the Isle of Lewis,' I said.

'You're determined to go then?'

'Well, I'm here in Ullapool and I'd like to go – it's what I'd planned to do.'

'You'd better go then hadn't you – can't interfere with your little plans can we!'

'I won't go if you don't want me too!' I said.

'No, no, I'm not having you say I stopped you doing your precious trip. You go and don't worry you about the consequences.'

'What do you mean – consequences?'

'Nothing...nothing...'

'What was the text message from Jasmine all about then?

'What? Oh that ... Nothing, I'm at Sian's, that's all,' she chirped. 'I have to go now, we're going out for a meal... Bye!' And the phone went dead.

There was a long queue to purchase the ferry ticket to Stornoway for the next day, not helped by the fact that each potential passenger had to complete a registration form. I asked the lady in front of me about the form.

'That's in case we go down,' she said disconcertingly.

✦ ✦ ✦

The name of Seaforth cropped up several times as I tramped around Ullapool – Seaforth Road, Seaforth Lane and now here I was sitting in

The Seaforth Inn...places named after the Earls of Seaforth, (the title itself having been taken from Loch Seaforth on the island of Lewis). The title of Earl of Seaforth was first bestowed upon Colin Mackenzie of Kintail in 1623, the Mackenzie family having taken ownership of Lewis in 1610.

The names of streets and pubs are all that now remain of the Seaforth line, due, it's said to the actions of the third Earl who on a visit to Paris dallied with a French lady, as sometimes happens. Unfortunately for the Earl, his enterprising wife engaged the services of a seer called Coinneach Odhar who, placing a white divination stone to his eye, told her and others present, of her husband's Parisian capers. Lady Seaforth was not best pleased with this public revelation and decided, a bit harshly perhaps, to have the seer executed; if he'd consulted his divination stone a bit sooner, perhaps he might have seen this one coming and told a few white porky pies instead. On this occasion honesty had definitely not been the best policy, but before he met his end he predicted the end of the Seaforth line in a peculiarly accurate level of detail, which became known as *the curse of Coinneach*. It all came true. (237)

In the bar of The Seaforth Inn a loud Irishman had put a curse on the ginger-haired barman who'd just told him off for swearing. Perplexingly, and as loudly as possible, the Irishman began to sing John Denver's *Country Roads*, or at least those parts of it he could remember. Then he picked up and rang the brass barbell in town crier fashion declaring:

'Oh yea, oh yea – It's the ginger times,' and pointing at the barman.

✦ ✦ ✦

It was still light when I returned to the campsite. From the pink-brick chimneys of white cottages that bordered the camping field, coils of smoke streamed lethargically into the damp night air – fires were still blazing in the hearths of the abodes of many of the 1,500 townsfolk of Ullapool; it was the middle of summer and tomorrow would be the longest day.

At 12.30 a.m. there was a loud bang and a whoosh, very close by, followed by two more bangs and whooshes – and then the en masse unzipping of tents – including mine. It must have been signal flares, but there was nothing to be seen. Perhaps those gales that the chip-shop-girl referred to were about to blow-up. Instead though, it began to rain, slightly and sporadically at first, but then with a now familiar constant patter on the tent, heightening at times to a machine-gun rattle. At that moment, lying there rain-swept in a soggy tent perched precariously on Ullapool Point, I began to wish that Captain Watson hadn't decided to sail *Nelson* to Stornoway seventy-three years before, and half wished that those pages of the ship's log pertaining to the visit had been stuck together.

◆ ◆ ◆

The ferry, the MV *Isle of Lewis*, the largest ship in the CalMac fleet, was built on the Clyde in 1995 and registered, (so her hull claimed), in Glasgow. She was capable of carrying 123 cars and 970 passengers – so she was no tub and I worried less about the registration form.

As she sailed out around Ullapool Point the little islands at the mouth of Loch Broom were bathed in glinting sunshine, whilst behind, in the distance, the dark storm clouds remained, stubbornly clinging to the mountains of the mainland. The islands, as we passed them, were a piebald mix of red-grey rock and yellow-green turf blotched with brownish-green bracken and, in the steep white rock crags above, sea birds nested precariously on slim ledges. The ship moved out into the open sea and suddenly the riffles turned into a swell. At this point I knew I'd made the right decision by avoiding the cooked breakfast at the Frigate Café, which had included the dubious, (to a southern palate), northern delights of haggis and black pudding.

Approaching Stornoway aboard MV Isle of Lewis, June 2004.

For the two-and-three-quarter hour voyage across the Minch, I strategically positioned myself in the forward observation lounge and watched the blue and white flag on the bow jiggle around like a Scottish reel in the wind and the shoreline of Lewis gradually emerge from the horizon. As we crept into the shelter of Stornoway harbour the sea gradually flattened into a millpond mirror and, sailing in past Goat Island, I felt a strange intoxication overtake me as the enigmatic, white blurred convex strip on the shore materialised slowly into individual buildings. Suddenly then – there I was, re-living that panoramic view seen from HMS *Nelson* in 1931. The magic then suddenly began to unfold and I was Dad, sailing into this cloistered United Kingdom outpost, looking forward to watching some football.

HMS *Nelson* had arrived in Stornoway on Sunday the 7th of June 1931 and the crew had played two football matches – on the Monday night and again on Wednesday, just before she'd sailed. The local team she played was made up from four clubs in the Stornoway league at the time: Stornoway Athletic, Stornoway United, the Nicolson Institute and Grays, (a team composed of mainland players from a firm of contractors who were then extending the King Edward Wharf in Stornoway harbour). (238) I just knew that with Dad's passion for the game, he would have been there.

Passion for football is an impossible concept to explain to somebody who doesn't already have it, to those who see the game as twenty-two grown men pointlessly chasing a piece of leather around a field. It used to be a working class game with a working class stigma attached to it; all the public school boys of course played rugger and cricket. But once you've acquired the passion, you have it for life. Not that Dad was much of a footballer, by the fifties at least, he was too big and heavy to run much, so he'd just bumble along in the park, side-footing the ball back to me with his great bellbottomed turn-upped trousers billowing and flapping about in the wind. But still, he loved *the beautiful game* with an innate passion that he passed onto me (and I passed onto to my son).

I was convinced that Dad would have gone to the games *Nelson* played in Stornoway, so I wrote to Stornoway Athletic F.C. and today I was to meet the club's current secretary, Malcolm, underneath the Clock Tower in town.

◆ ◆ ◆

The island of Lewis is part of the Western Isles, or Eilean Siar, as they're known in Gaelic; they were sold to the Scots by Norway in 1266 and have a population of just over 27,000. The largest island, Lewis, has a falling population of 23,000, 35 per cent of which live in Stornoway. By the year 2016, it's estimated that the population of the young and middle-aged on the islands will have shrunk by around 40 per cent, whilst those over sixty will have grown by around 15 per cent, so the social services are presently in a process of planning and re-adjustment. (239) My guidebook again said little to recommend the place: *The best thing about Stornoway is the convenience of its services*, it said. (240)

The Western Isles used to be known as the Outer Hebrides, a far more expressive description of the place for me anyway, conjuring up an association with the wildness and desolation of Outer Mongolia. The islands are supposed to be one of the safest places in the UK in which to live according to the Area Police Commander, (who had as one of his most important targets for 2002/2003 – *The reduction of dog fouling*). You wouldn't have believed this fact though if, like me, you'd purchased a copy of *The Hebridean*.

Perhaps because of lack of any other newsworthy items, this newspaper seemed to roister in the misdemeanours of islanders; in two half-page spreads entitled: *On the Beat* and *Justice Files*, it succeeded in depicting the place as a hotbed of petty crime. I counted four drink-driving offences, three drug offences, three cases of carrying offensive weapons, one burglary, three assaults – including a woman who head butted another in a bar, and the case of a 16 year old male who let off a fire extinguisher without there actually being a fire – a lifetime ambition of mine…and one I'd no doubt have achieved long ago if I'd spent my youth in the Outer Hebrides.

I'd spread out and flipped through the pages of *The Hebridean* on my bed in a comfortable Smith Avenue guesthouse on the eastern outskirts of the town. Everything was going to plan. There were four whole hours in which I could potter about the place before my clock tower appointment with Malcolm. Then a collusion of weird happenings occurred and I found myself transformed into a dotard, incapable of coping with anything, with time frittering away before my eyes. The first happening occurred as I sauntered down the path from the guesthouse and reached Smith Avenue. Suddenly I stopped dead in my tracks, struck by blind panic. Where was my wallet? Rushing back to my room I ransacked the place, tossing things from the rucksack into a dishevelled heap on the floor in a blind frenzy. Nothing…God, I must have left it on the counter in the tourist information centre! It would take me ten minutes to get back down there – I'll telephone them – every minute might be crucial. What's the number? – Don't know – I'll ask the landlady.

'Hello,' I called at the entrance porch… Nothing…'Hello, Hello – are you there?'…Still nothing… perhaps she was asleep. 'Hello…'

I couldn't wait any longer and for the second time in five minutes I walked down the path from the guesthouse, again stopping dead in my tracks as I reached Smith Avenue. Then, tapping around my pockets, I discovered under the flap of a side-pocket of my anorak – the missing wallet. Multifarious relief swept over me, not only because I'd located the wallet, but also because I hadn't located the landlady, telephoned the tourist information centre, or worst still made it all the way back there to rant at the counter. Silly old fart!

I wasn't expecting the library to be much of a place, and the drab concrete façade certainly confirmed my worst fears, it was a dump. Worst still, it possessed one of those dreadful press-button voice box devices that you have to speak into in order to gain entry. Unbelievable I thought, but then this *is* the Outer Hebrides after all.

'What are your opening hours?' I asked the crackling voice from within the box. There was a pause...

'We're open *now!*' the woman replied. There was another uncomfortable pause...

'Well how do I get in then?' I asked with some frustration.

'Go to the *front* of the library,' she replied, somehow managing to restrain from laughter at this thick Sassenach who'd tried to gain access via the rear mobile library loading-up point.

The front of the library was actually painted an impressive lilac and maroon, with a pillared outer and inset inner glass entrance; inside it was modern, well organised, spacious, and equipped with a plenitude of computer terminals.

I plunged into the 1931 archives of *The Stornoway Gazette and West Coast Advertiser* where I found that the officers and men of *Nelson* had been offered facilities for recreation, including – angling, golf, tennis and bowls for the officers – and football for the men...As well as *free use of the Town Hall,* it added, *where a dance was to be held on the Monday – after the football.* (241)

An earlier advertisement in the gazette, two days before the arrival of the ship caught my eye: (242)

```
TALKIE, TALKIE, TALKIE
THURSDAY, FRIDAY & SATURDAY
A great sensational picture, in 9 parts
THE SHIP FROM SHANGHAI
A cargo of thrills such as you have never seen before
in the first talking picture to be filmed on the HIGH SEAS.
```

The odds were, I thought, that Dad would have seen this, and I wondered how many others from *Nelson* would seen it too; this was just three months before certain events were to unfold at Invergordon, and I was pretty sure that William J. Pigg would have seen it. It was set on a yacht sailing from Shanghai to the Unites States when the sailors, led by a megalomaniac steward, revolted and took control of the ship.

The picture had been shown in the, then recently constructed, Lewis Picture House, known as the Playhouse, amid much controversy from many of the townspeople. The churches were grimly set against the opening of the picture house and many saw it as a den of iniquity. Coinneach Odhar, (remember him? The Brahan Seer who couldn't predict his own downfall), prophesied that a picture house would be built in Stornoway and that it would be burned down, with only one little fair-haired child being saved. The second part of his prophecy never transpired, it's still there, although it closed as the Playhouse Cinema in 1977. (243) Now it was the British Legion Club, and it was where I was heading – or it would have been if I'd known where it was; instead I returned to the tourist information centre.

'I wonder if you can help me,' I said to the young girl, who produced a bonhomous smile for me through braced teeth, 'it's a bit of a strange enquiry – I'm looking for the British Legion Club,' and with that I whipped out of my pocket a map of Stornoway and spread it across the counter.

'It's *there*', she said gleefully, pointing ...and indeed there it was...clearly marked in bold capital letters – **BRITISH LEGION**. For the third time that day I felt a complete *plonker*.

The club was located on South Beach, not far from the ferry terminal; a white block bottomed, pebbledash topped building with a wrought iron balustrade, drainpipes, windowsills and other adornments all painted in the contrasting pale blue and white of Scotland's flag. The blue was sadly peeling from the windowsills, but still the Union Jack and the St Andrew's cross flew proudly together. So I trod the ground, walked up to the brown wooden door and stood there for a moment – the furthest I could go, without making a written plea to the Legion.

◆ ◆ ◆

There have been a number of sons of the Hebrides who've gained notability in distant lands and for diverse reasons. One in particular had caught my imagination enough to divert me from *footsteps* for a while. It was the reason I'd walked back up Francis Street to stand outside the old Victorian double-storied building, once part of the Nicolson Institute, which was now the Museum nan Eilean. He was Sir Alexander Mackenzie – a motherless boy of twelve when he'd left Francis Street for New York in 1774 on the emigrant ship *Peace and Plenty*.

Alex wound up in Canada in 1779 at the age of sixteen, sent by his father to escape the American War of Independence. (244) In 1789 he became the first European to canoe, (with a twelve man crew of French-Canadian voyageurs and Indian hunters), the full length of the 2,630-mile long river. Mackenzie had by then become a fur trader, head of the firm of Gregory, Macleod & Company. With money and a passion for exploration as his motives, he was trying to discover the Northwest Passage to China and had started out from Fort Chipewyan, now in north-east Alberta, hoping to paddle out into the Pacific Ocean. Instead he discovered he'd developed extraordinarily large biceps, a liking for bear meat and blubber, and had unwittingly taken a wrong turning to finish up in the Arctic Ocean. He named the river – The River of Disappointment, and later he booked himself on a course in London for a year to study navigation – (this is no lie). The Arctic explorer Sir John Franklin later re-named the river the Mackenzie.

In 1792-93, Mackenzie, with the help of the native people, became the first European to cross the American continent north of Mexico from east to west via rivers and on foot, to eventually reach the Pacific at Bella Coola, and although he would never know it, this feat would lead to the French eventually surrendering their holdings in Louisiana and Texas (Napoleon needed the money) and to the Spanish doing likewise in California. (245)

Mackenzie was knighted in 1802 and moved back to Scotland, (near Inverness) permanently in1808, where he married and where he died. But its on the map of Canada that the man is most prolifically remembered: Mackenzie River, Mackenzie Valley, Mackenzie Bay, the Mackenzie Mountains, Mackenzie Point, Mackenzie District, the Mackenzie Highway, Mackenzie Pass, Alexander Falls, Mackenzie Place, (the hotel that's the highest building in the Northwest Territories) and the Sir Alexander Mackenzie Provincial Park, which has within it the Mackenzie Rock. (246) It was on this rock that Alex marked the end of his epic journey to the Pacific by mixing melted bear grease with red pigment and painting – ALEXANDER MACKENZIE, FROM CANADA BY LAND, 22ND JULY 1793. (247)

◆ ◆ ◆

The ground floor of the museum housed the early history of the island, complete with a predictable collection of Norse and Viking artefacts dug out of the peat, but, as I climbed the wooden stairs to the first floor I became excited that here I'd find some previously unknown fact about Stornoway's most famous son. I meandered around the gallery, passing a display of the history of the weaving industry on the island, complete with an old loom shed, followed by a display that chronicled the life of the herring industry from around 1844 until its decline after the First World War.

During my entire circumnavigation of the first floor gallery an attractive blonde lady in her early thirties had been engaged, behind the staff counter, secreted in quiet conversation on the telephone, perhaps in Gaelic, (which is taught in schools by parental choice, and which now as few as 100,000 Scots speak). I was loathed to interrupt vital museology business but hovered by the counter so that eventually she'd notice me. When she did, the telephone conversation seemed to get even more subdued and simultaneously sped up. Then she hung up abruptly.

'Can I help you?' she asked in a lilting Scottish accent.

'Yes, perhaps you can,' I said. 'I don't know if I've missed something, but I don't seem to be able to find anything in the museum about Sir Alexander Mackenzie.'

'Who? She said, frowning slightly.

'Oh dear,' I said politely, 'he was a famous explorer, born here in Stornoway.'

'Oh, I'm sorry', she said, as if I were a train spotter in a bus station, 'we're only a small museum and we're limited for space.'

'That's a shame – I'll just take these then,' I said, handing her two Stornoway Historical Society Journals.

Mackenzie didn't think enough of Stornoway to return there at the end of his life – I wonder if they'd have given him a small corner of the museum if he had?

✦ ✦ ✦

Malcolm was already waiting under the clock tower when I arrived – late. He was the secretary of Stornoway Athletic FC and they were playing that night. He drove us to the Caledonian Hotel, a sober looking establishment on South Beach, where we both ordered a cheeseburger and chips. Whilst we sipped our pints and waited for the meals, he explained how football worked these days in the north of Scotland.

'It starts in April and finishes in September,' he said, 'the pitches are unplayable in the winter – waterlogged and frozen.'

'I didn't know they played in the summer,' I said, 'has it always been a summer sport up here?'

'Well, coincidently we switched from winter to summer the year that your Dad was here – in 1931. In those days the teams in the league were all from in and around Stornoway – now they're from all the islands' he said, taking a slug of McEwens.

'How many teams are in the league?' I asked.

'Ten at the moment – the leagues in the north of Scotland play for the Highland Amateur Cup, the widest spread amateur competition in Europe.'

'Where's the dividing line between the islands and highlands?' I interrupted.

'The islands are from Orkney down to Barra and across to Skye – and the highlands are the rest, including Inverness which is both the southern and eastern boundary,' he said.

I'd noticed the exclusion of Shetland and, although I didn't pass comment, I imagined that all the *Guisers* up there donned Viking helmets and played in the Norwegian fjord league.

'It must be difficult – the travelling,' I said.

'Yes, but the kick-off times take account of any potential ferry problems, and in the cup competitions there are no replays – it's down to penalties,' he said.

The cheeseburgers and chips were better than McDonalds and were delivered almost as quickly, but I didn't say that to Malcolm because McDonald was his surname, (although spelt differently).

A lightning car tour of Stornoway followed the fast food. Malcolm's penultimate stop was on a promontory at Battery Point where the sky at 7 p.m. was a balmy blue with a scattering of puffy white clouds. An old cannon, mounted on a concrete plinth above a sloping green, pointed seaward. It was a remnant of the largest RNR battery and training depot in Great Britain that had stood there from 1876 until 1919. Thousands of men from the Hebrides received their training there for service in the Royal Navy.

Stornoway Athletics' kick-off was fast approaching, so we drove on to Goathill Park. Here it was that HMS *Nelson* had twice taken on and defeated the Stornoway League Select of 1931 – seventy years before. But actually the Goathill Park of 1931 was a different one to the present, just a few metres further along Goathill Road and closer to the town centre than the new one, which had not opened until 1934.

The old Park was now overbuilt partly by an all-weather sports pitch and partly by a house. I took an uninspiring photograph of it and then stood for a few moments savouring a rare *footsteps* moment, imagining Dad and the rest of the *chucking-up* party cheering on the team. *Nelson* had outclassed the locals on both occasions, winning 2 –1 on the Monday night and 5 –1 on the Wednesday. If *Nelson* had played Stornoway Athletic instead of the League Select team there might have been an even bigger deluge of goals, but that probably wouldn't have worried the Athletic team because it included no less than seven Macs.

Malcolm arranged to meet me later in the Lewis Hotel; then hurried inside Goathill Park as the teams were warming up. I marched on down Goathill Road towards the quay; 'my' match was also due to start, in about half an hour – England was about to take on Croatia in one of the last qualifying group B matches of Euro 2004.

The bar of the Lewis Hotel was narrow; a sturdy brass tubular foot-rail ran its length and two middle-aged Lewis men were sitting on bar stools facing it with their knees bent so that their feet planted themselves resolutely on the rail. I slid onto the spare bar stool to the left of them, with the television set high up behind the bar. A disquiet creep over them as I ordered a pint of McEwens, a kind of aggressive curmudgeonliness. The one closest to me had the sort of face that looked as if he was just about to shit a box of tintacks. Mentally I'd named him MacNasty. They both completely ignored me.

After two games, England was lying in second place in the group B league table. France was leading and, with Switzerland to play, they were expected to qualify in top spot. Croatia had drawn both their games, so their match against England was the qualifying decider; if Croatia won they'd qualify – if the game was a draw, qualification for England would depend upon the French result and maybe goal difference. In essence, England had to win to be sure of qualifying.

On the screen, the teams were lined up fidgeting, jumping up and down, and waiting for the national anthems to be played – and already John Motson had begun pontificating on whom England would be likely to play in the quarterfinals once they'd disposed of the paltry Croats. It seemed that Spain might win their group and be England's next adversary. *No-hopers* Greece, who'd, (unlikely as it may have seemed), somehow accumulated four points and had qualified for the quarterfinals were, according to Motson, likely to be *massacred* by the French.

The game got underway and after a fairly even first five minutes Croatia was awarded a free kick. James in the England goal had forgotten to wear his Velcro-like gloves so couldn't hold onto the ball and suddenly England was one-nil down. An omniscient smirk crept over MacNasty's face. This was England *going down the drain* again, already – Ha!

After ten minutes play, Gerrard went down on the edge of the Croatian area and Motson swore it was a penalty; unfortunately Mr Collina, the goggle-eyed, bald, Italian referee didn't agree with him. England continued to press forward and spent most of the next half-an-hour in the Croatian half of the field without getting a return for their efforts – Rooney, Beckham, Lampard, Gerrard and Terry all had attempts on goal which for various reasons were thwarted. The twisted smirk remained on MacNasty's face. It looked as if the game would be one of those desperately frustrating ones, familiar to all England fans, in which they'd be lucky to scrape a draw.

Then, as the game approached half-time Owen fired a shot, the goalkeeper parried, Rooney headed the ball on and Paul Scholes headed it in. MacNasty scowled and contorted his face to shit some tintacks. It got worse for him on the stroke of half time as *boy-wonder* Rooney drove the ball from twenty-two yards into the Croatian net – and England went in one goal to the good.

'Basteds – basteds!' cursed MacNasty, slamming his glass onto the bar, not bothered at all by the fact that I was English, (which he'd gleaned as soon as I'd ordered my first pint).

At half-time Motson began to prattle on uncontrollably with an un-apologetic nationalistic fervour, whilst Alan Hansen, the tamed Scot, nodded and agreed obsequiously. Motson unbelievably, now well out of control with his fantasies, began to compare Rooney with Pele; this was the last straw as far as MacNasty and his mate were concerned – they thought this outrageous.

'Agh – what the fuck's he bletherin aboot – he's off his fuckin heid!' Snarled MacNasty.

'Rooney's shite!' concurred MacNasty's mate, who I'd mentally named MacGruff – 'He could be on drugs next year. I'm an advanced driver, but it's like comparing me wi Michael Schumacher.'

As the second half began, I noticed that the striker Ivica Mornar was on as a substitute for Croatia. He was a Pompey player who I didn't rate, but I feared that just to show me, he'd do the damage against England. Sure enough, within a minute Mornar had put in a cross and forced a Croatian corner; then a little while later, he charged forward, like a dog about to be castrated from behind by two house-bricks, and won a free kick. At this, I decided to have some sport with MacNasty and Mac-Gruff:

'He's useless,' I said, bending slightly towards MacNasty ' he plays for my team, but knowing England's luck he'll probably score against us.' There was a long pause whilst MacNasty thought whether to ignore me or not, before curiosity finally overtook him.

'What's yer team then?' he asked finally, but still without looking at me.

'Portsmouth.'

'What're ye doing right up here?' asked MacGruff, 'don't tell me it's sailing?'

So now it seemed I was forced to relay my mission. MacNasty had decided that he wanted nothing further to do with the conversation and continued to stare towards the screen like a zombie.

'What sort o book is it?' asked MacGruff – I tried to explain cumber-somely.

'Oh! Ye mean like Bill Bryson? Said MacGruff, almost managing a smile.

'Something like that,' I said.

'Ye'll be on a lottery grant then, aye?'

'No.' – Unfortunately the thought had never occurred to me until that moment.

'Hu!' grunted MacNasty in contemptuous disbelief, still not looking at me.

Events on the screen curtailed further debate; Owen played a ball through to Rooney, who stormed forward again with fire in his belly and slotted the ball confidently past the keeper to put England two goals clear.

'Basteds, basteds – fuckin basteds!' MacNasty cussed whilst tintacks spattered out across the floor, and his beer, which he almost knocked over, jounced across the bar, its contents sloshing like the sea off Stornoway in a storm ten. His head had slumped to the bar. 'Basteds' he mumbled again quietly and almost to himself.

'Are you alright Rab?' asked the barmaid.

'Aye – apart from they basteds' answered MacNasty, raising his head and nodding at the screen.

An elderly Dutch or German couple had meanwhile come into the bar and asked the barmaid if there was anywhere in Stornoway to eat. Before she could draw breath and everyone laughed, MacGruff answered:

'Its afta nine!' he said, 'there'll only be the Indian or Chinese open now.'

'And the Thai in Church Street,' added the barmaid reflectively.

'Oh aye – and the Thai.'

The Germans or Dutch, (I never heard them say *no* amongst themselves, so I was never able to discover their nationality), did not look happy tourists as they left. Obviously Scottish ethnic food did not altogether appeal to their Germanic (or otherwise) palates.

But things took an interesting turn on the screen – Croatia had won a free kick, and Igor Tudor, lurking at the back post, headed the ball into the England net. Croatia was back in the game and English fans everywhere – even the one on Lewis – began to sweat and crave for Mr Collina to blow the final whistle. Luckily the sweating only lasted another four minutes before Frank Lampard smashed in the fourth for England, and MacNasty drained his pint and gripped MacGruff's arm.

'Och! I'm not aboot to listen to Motson talkin through his arse, gaun on aboot they basteds,' said MacNasty, sliding off the bar stool, 'I'm away to ma hoose' and, still without looking in my direction, he disappeared quickly out the door – probably on the trail of the Germans, who by now would be heading reluctantly to join the queue at the Chinese takeaway.

As MacNasty walked out the door, Malcolm came in.

'What can I get you?' I asked.

'Oh, I'll have a pint of McEwens please,' he said, 'they're winning are they?'

'Yes, they are now, I said, but it was looking dodgy for a long time. How did your team get on?'

'Drew, one each,' he said.

We watched the end of the match almost in silence. I relayed to him, at some point, the highlights of the MacNasty moments and the fact that none of the English team were apparently born of parents who were in wedlock.

'Ah! Said Malcolm philosophically, 'we don't hate the English – just your arrogant commentators.' (248)

Next morning, at the bottom of the path from the guesthouse I hitched up my backpack. The sky was blue, blotched only by rolling cumulonimbus clouds that suggested I might have to wrench the anorak from the bottom of the pack at some point during the day. But at that moment the sun was shining, and I felt good. On the corner of Smith Avenue and Springfield Road school children were tumbling out of buses, gathering into groups and meandering into school.

On the way down to the town centre several estate agents windows caught my eye; if you really fancied a quiet life combined with a frequent change of scenery you could buy about ten, five bedroom houses up here for the price of one in London. I passed The Whalers Rest on Francis Street, also known, (Malcolm had told me), as the Carlton; it was closed of course, but I remembered Donald of Clydeport and thought I might catch him in there before the ferry would sail that afternoon. I took a tourist photograph of the bronze statue of the herring girl at North Beach, and a *footsteps* photograph of the steps up from the quay, where I believed Dad must have come ashore off a drifter from *Nelson*, and then I set out on the long walk out to Arnish Point, out from which (Malcolm had confirmed) the warships used to anchor.

Crossing the bridge over the Bayhead River, I began to follow the orange, gravel track past the golf course and Lews Castle out to Cuddy Point.

To spoil the morning I switched on the mobile and called Ruth.

'Why didn't you phone last night?'

'Because I was out with Malcolm Macdonald and I didn't get back until twenty past eleven,' I explained.

'You're always the same when you're with somebody – that's how you are!' she screamed – and hung up.

I'd just seen a sign to the Creed River Iron Well when I felt the first splatters of rain descending gently and vertically. A large black cloud loomed above, out of a pure blue-sky – it was the strangest thing. Then without further warning, and before I could sprint for the cover of a tree, the rain hammered down unmercifully like space impact bullets. It was just a shower, the sort that makes everything smell fresh afterwards and soaks you in seconds.

The path swung inland to follow the white foam, gushing, narrow Creed River that crashed noisily over silvery-black rocks. It swept along fiercely below, its steep rising banks thronging with overhanging trees. Beautiful pinkish-mauve flowers garlanded the trees; I wasn't sure what they were, so at Matheson Pool I stopped an old man who was passing and asked him.

'Rhododendrons,' he said, with obvious surprise at my horticultural ignorance. Adding '...They come from India.' Well, I thought even I would know a rhododendron when I saw one – but obviously not – at least not the Lewis Indian Creed River variety. Anyway they were spectacular.

I crossed a new looking redbrick coloured wooden bridge, climbed over a stile, up a small rise and found myself on a narrow road that headed gently uphill towards some distant hills, behind which I hoped was hidden the lighthouse at Arnish Point. The road was of surfaced stone interspersed with a patchwork of tarmac repairs sealed with bitumen, wet and slippery following the shower. The road became steeper as I progressed and I soon began to puff and sweat a bit.

During the twenty-five minutes I was on this road I saw just one car and a lorry carrying aggregate. The lorry came up behind me, almost brushing my right shoulder and swirling spray up from the road over me. The driver was bored and was having a reckless laugh on me. Ten minutes later however he returned back down the road. Here he came, barrelling along... From a distance I transfixed my eyes on his, daring him to have another go at me...He bottled it.

To the side of the road and following it, was a boggy, water filled ditch up from which climbed a steep cross-section of black peat – the fabric of the whole island. Deposits of peat began 5,000 years ago on Lewis. The Gaelic name for the island is actually Leodhas which means marshy. Malcolm told me though that the people of Lewis use little peat these days; apparently it's too much trouble to get the tractor out and go dig it up.

I caught sight of the lighthouse over to my port side, but the road I was on began to leave the coast and I started to worry that I'd have to hike across the wild boggy land and scrubby machair. Then I realised that the lighthouse and Arnish Point were on a peninsula that curled back up into Stornoway harbour and, that if I stayed on the road, I'd eventually finish up back on the coast.

The bleak looking oil storage tanks and buildings of Arnish Generator Station appeared suddenly around a bend like part of a weird moonscape and, a little further on, the road curved around another sharp left hand bend and dead-ended in sight of the sea. To the left was a large pair of gates guarded by a gatehouse and a sign that read ARNISH POINT INDUSTRIAL ESTATE. To the right, over marshy ground and up a small but steep hill was a monument erected to commemorate the landing of Bonnie Prince Charlie. Charles Edward Stuart had wandered around here in May 1746 after Culloden, before his escape to France, but the inscription was so weatherworn that the record of his roving on the isles was indecipherable.

To the seaward of the industrial estate was an unfenced strip of land occupied by an eight-metre high pile of rocks and rubble. I scrambled up and picked my way across it, moving slowly and precariously northward, back (as the crow flies) towards Stornoway. At the end of the rubble bank I edged gingerly up to a cliff-top by squeezing around a fence post on a narrow ledge with a sheer drop down to a rocky cove below, to emerge onto a grassy bank sprinkled with buttercups and sheep.

Far below me, to landward, huge aircraft-hanger workshops loomed up – part of the industrial estate. It was in fact a recently opened engineering concern manufacturing wind turbine towers on a redeveloped site of an erstwhile oil industry fabrication yard. Outside, a man was working away at a huge construction, generated sparks with a hand-grinding tool – noiselessly (for me up there), drowned out by the wind and the crashing waves on the rocks below. Shetland ponies roamed the site, rambling between the factory buildings, finding grazing grass amongst the reedy land that surrounded them.

I was nearly there; it had taken me over two hours of walking and scrambling, but ahead, over the springy cliff-top grass, past the concrete remnants of wartime fortifications and around another cove, was the 32 foot high, white towered, black domed top beacon of the Stevenson lighthouse at Arnish Point. It was designed and built by Alan Stevenson, a member of the famous engineering family that also spawned Robert Louis, whom his family perhaps considered odd for producing novels instead of lighthouses.

Arnish Point had been one of the anchorage co-ordinates of HMS *Nelson* on Sunday the 7th of June 1931. Now, today, the slightly loco son of a Royal Marine, who'd been on that battleship when she'd anchored approximately half a mile south east of this point, had finally made it back. Not exactly the feat of Mackenzie in crossing the continent of North America, but still, if I'd by chance stumbled upon some melted bear grease and red pigment I'd have painted on a rock – MIKE PINNOCK, FROM PORTSMOUTH BY SEA BY LAND, 22ND JUNE 2004.

I set up my little compass on the grass bank above the cliff on the headland, just before the land tucked in again and ran away towards the lighthouse. I let the needle settle, its tip pointed north towards Stornoway. One or two gulls swooped around the cliffs below, perhaps kittiwakes or guillemots, I couldn't really tell and wasn't about to get too near the edge to find out. The sea was a burnished dark blue, almost black, carpeted by shimmers of silver ripples, glinting like a shoal of herrings that once might have been seen here. As if to mirror my thoughts a single fishing trawler chugged out from behind the foreland, working its way slowly southeast.

I sat for a very long time staring out across that water towards the anchorage of *Nelson*. She'd sailed on from here to Lamlash having arrived from my next goal – Scapa Flow. I sat there spinning out the time because I didn't want to leave. I'd fallen in love with the place and knew it would be at least a year before I'd be this far north again – at least a year before I could reverse the journey of *Nelson* and travel back to Scapa. A lot could happen before then, and I began to think about what Ruth had meant by 'the consequences'.

Then I packed away my compass and slowly began retracing my steps to begin the long trek back from this far-flung part of the union.

22. Going With The Flow

'Could Mr Green and Mr Pinnock please make themselves known to the cabin staff by pressing the overhead call button.'

It's Ruth – I thought immediately, she's contacted the airport with some fictitious concoction of a personal emergency and they're going to frogmarch me off the plane to take a phone call in the departure lounge whilst the not-so-Easyjet, (that had by then been delayed by two-and-a-half hours), finally takes off. Either that or they've discovered a planted, wired and dangerous looking package Ruth had cannily concealed in my case between boxer shorts and handkerchiefs.

Ruth's threats of 'consequences' had melted away after my return from Stornoway the previous year, but they'd begun to solidify again about a month before my departure for Scapa Flow and Norway.

'It's up to you,' she'd said, 'If you go, I'm going to leave you. It's up to you – you've got a choice.' But I'd gone anyway, and now Ruth was getting her revenge.

'Do you have your boarding pass please sir?' asked the stewardess who'd appeared suddenly by my shoulder. Then she whisked it away like a cheating schoolboy's copy sheet and faded away with it to the cockpit.

But why was Mr Green implicated? Had he also been caught by the hidden CCTV camera with trembling hand hovering suspiciously over the 'YES/NO' buttons on the machine that finally spits out your baggage tag and boarding pass after asking those fatuous questions 'Did you pack your luggage yourself?' and 'Could anyone have interfered with your luggage?'

'Thank you Sir,' said the stewardess, handing me back my boarding pass and disappearing without an explanation... Then I remembered that they'd logged us through the gate by boarding pass numbers, but had stopped the procedure immediately after I'd got through because of some sort of irregularity with the pass handed in by the man in front of me, (Mr Green, I now supposed).

The whole incident served me right anyway, I was just about to break my first ground rule – not to fly, even if it was only a short hop up to Edinburgh from the East-Midlands to save some time.

✦ ✦ ✦

Dad had *sailed* all the way to Scapa Flow in 1930, from Portsmouth; it had taken *Nelson* two days. My journey was to take a day and a half by plane, car, train, foot, bus and ship.

The train from Inverness left next morning at 0714 prompt, and the journey I was making that bright Monday morning followed the route of most servicemen who were posted to the Orkney Islands during both wars. In the First War the trains trundling them up north were called the *Jellicoes*, after the Admiral of the Grand Fleet in Scapa Flow at the time. They were stuffed full with unwilling unfortunates and cluttered with kit bags; they were cold and were without corridors (no good for me, with my bladder). (249) Those unpleasant journeys contrasted markedly with mine; the buffet car attendant soon passed with his trolley and offered me a coffee. I felt special, and apart from a young girl who slept for most of the time, I was the only passenger in the carriage.

It was a beautiful morning; we slowed approaching Beauly, especially it seemed so that I could take a wonderful photograph looking out over the Beauly Firth to the dotted white houses in the distance and the lapis blue of the millpond flat water merging with the blue of a cloudless sky.

The train zigzagging up through Fearn, Ardgay, Lairg, Rogart – all names I'd not heard of before, all places I'd probably never see more of than the flash of their station name on the platform, all populated by people I'd never meet; hills, rivers, streams, a scattering of farmhouses, sheep, but no roads or people. And then suddenly the descendants of the sheep Bryson had spied a decade before flooded away down the bank at the side of the track, frightened by the sudden appearance of the *First Scotrail* train. Miles of barren land with the occasional group of trees, a wind farm in the distance and a ragged farm that had somehow acquired a red London double-decker bus.

The sun butterfly-flitted through the trees onto the pages of my *Scapa Flow* book, whilst we drifted up the east coast to Brora, then tracked back inland again and north, passing through Helmsdale, Kinbrace, and Forsinard to Georgemas Junction, where the lines from Wick and Thurso meet. I panicked as we went backwards but then checked the rail map in the carriage – we *were* going to Thurso.

Thurso is located about fifteen miles from Dunnet Head the most northerly point on the mainland of Britain. It was the end of my rail journey; now I had to catch a bus to Scrabster for the hop across the Pentland Firth to Stromness on the Orkney Island mainland.

The Pentland Firth is the channel that separates the Scottish mainland from the Orkney Islands, where the North Sea and Atlantic meet, it usually runs a nine-knot tide, and it's reputed to be one of the most dangerous stretches of water in the world (250) From 1918 until 1981 there had been a recorded 347 incidents of shipping in distress in the Firth. (251) I was not looking forward to the crossing at all and expected it to be rough. Seasick tales of the Firth have grown into folklore. A remark made by the captain of the *St Ola* summed up the experience pretty well: *It was only the hope o' deein' that kept him alive!* (252) In the event my fears were unfounded – the voyage was smooth, helped by the Northlink's 110-metre long, well-stabilised car ferry – *Hamnavoe*.

✦ ✦ ✦

Nelson crossed the Firth from the east and entered the 120 square mile stretch of sheltered water known as Scapa Flow via Hoxa Sound; she, together with *Centaur* and *York* had sailed from Portsmouth and had met up with ships that had steamed from the Forth and the Cromarty Firth. They'd then sailed into the Flow with the destroyers leading, followed by the cruisers and battleships. (253) *Nelson* was one of 34 ships of the Atlantic Fleet that entered the Flow in 1930. Its primary purpose was to indulge itself in the annual regatta – the biggest sporting event to be held in Scottish waters. Ships competed primarily for the coveted chanticleer – known as *The Cock*, but a heavy ships' regatta was also held where the prizes were the Rodman and Battenburg cups. These events were designed to keep the fleet both motivated and amused during the sterile inter-war years. (254) The destroyers and cruisers dropped anchor on the west side of Scapa Bay, whilst *Nelson* and the other battleships anchored off Gaitnip Craigs (252) The problem was – I had no idea where Gaitnip Craigs was.

✦ ✦ ✦

Arthur, a thin, grey-bearded, grey-haired Orcadian cattle farmer, met us from the ferry in a four-wheel-drive – us being a pair of American honeymooners from Georgia, and myself, the English gooseberry. I'd pictured all of Orkney as being flat, but not Hoy – its name comes from the Old Norse for High Island. The three-mile drive was undulating, and terminated up a stony inclined track at an isolated farm.

Our hostess, a bubbly Dutch lady named Louise, met us at the doorway smilingly, greeting the honeymooners with impassioned hugs, as if she'd known them all her life, and much later, me, the ageing English *bachelor*, gooseberry – with a staid handshake. She'd cooked us a fine pasta meal for that evening, (claiming that she hadn't catered for three, but still providing more than sufficient portions for us all). It was during the meal that I gleaned some impressions about the honeymooners, Kerry and Scott. Scott apparently, legally spied into company's hard-drives and presented expert evidence in high-powered courtroom cases. He related how his uncle had once been a heroic World War Two Luftwaffe pilot, which led us into a conversation about the Scapa Flow Visitor Centre and Museum that I planned to visit next day, and which Scott *wanted* to visit next day – but couldn't, because he'd just got married and, if he did, he wouldn't get anything that night except earache.

'If you want to go around the museum – go ahead,' said Kerry – but a secret female code warned against it with a silent regard.

Kerry had been trained as a *Rolfer* (a therapy developed by Ida P. Rolf, a Columbia University trained biochemist in the 1930s). She explained that Rolfing was all about realigning the body by intense pressure, and stroking, to stretch shortened and tightened fascia back into shape. (255) She claimed that just by touching a person's shoulders, she could feel whether or not they needed this therapy. I kind of hoped she'd try it out on me. After the 27 hours of travelling it had taken me to get here, I fancied a good Rolf.

✦ ✦ ✦

By morning the honeymooners had hatched a vague plan to discover an archaeological site – Dwarfie Stane. But like me they'd made two fundamental miscalculations. Firstly they'd misjudged distances without the aid of motor transport, (Hoy is deceivingly ten miles long and five miles wide), secondly – they'd assumed yesterday's good weather to be infinite.

'I take no notice of the weather forecast,' Louise said, 'but my barometer is falling badly – you have a mac?' she called after me as I started down the stony track.

'Yes,' I called back, thinking her over pessimistic – it wasn't raining – just a bit dark and overcast that's all.

After half a mile the road turned sharply north towards Lyness and, as I passed a long thin flat-topped house named The Garrison, I felt a few spots of rain ushered along by a little gust of wind – nothing to worry about! But then, within a few minutes, the wind increased, as did the spot frequency so that I thought it wise to don my anorak. After another few minutes the head wind was driving relentlessly at a forty-five degree angle into my arched body, bringing with it torrents of the wet stuff, so that within a further few minutes my trousers, below the anorak line, were completely soaked and sticking to my legs. To add to the misery I was cold and some of my fingers had developed a touch of white finger. If they started to turn black with frostbite, I was definitely heading back.

Louise had said that because there is no public transport on the island, car drivers always stop to give lifts – particularly in bad weather, but to disprove this claim, about four cars passed evanescently down the road, and it wasn't until I was in the home straight, heading downhill into

Lyness, almost in sight of the museum, that a car stopped and I dripped in.

'I thought you must either be a farmer or a tourist,' he said, 'but you weren't wearing rubber boots so I assumed you were a tourist.'

The museum was free. The building reminded me of an aircraft hanger, but it was once actually a pumping station. Built in 1917, it took over the role of naval headquarters in 1919 when the Admiralty relocated from Longhope. To its rear sat a restored and converted oil storage tank, one of 16 that once existed on the site giving a total storage capacity of 228,000 tons, with 6 more tanks, squirreled away inside Wee Fea hill holding a further 100,000 tons. When Dad had been in these parts there would only have been 4 tanks, the remaining 12 being built from 1936 onward. The oil was delivered to the jetty at Lyness by tankers, pumped up into the underground tanks – and from there down into the tanks at the pump house. (256)

The museum reflected the importance of the base at Lyness during both world wars, but between the wars I discovered that Dad would likely have seen the activities of Cox & Danks whilst they endeavoured to raise the German High Seas Fleet that had been scuttled on the 21st of June 1919. By the time *Nelson* and the rest of the Atlantic Fleet had arrived in Scapa Flow in May 1930, Cox had already raised 26 destroyers as well as the battlecruisers *Seydlitz* and *Moltke*, the light-cruiser *Bremse* and the battleship *Kaiser*. He was at that time working on one of the largest ships in the Kaiser's navy – the 26,000 ton *Hindenburg*.

I spent the greater part of the day in the museum, whilst the rain hammered unmercifully on its metal roof, but I only found what I was looking for unexpectedly, just before I was about to give up and leave. It was a caption above a photograph that was part of a display in a corner of the restored pump room dedicated to the *Royal Oak* disaster. The battleship *Royal Oak* was torpedoed and sunk by a German submarine – *U47* in the early hours of the 14th of October 1939 with the loss of 833 men. The display featured the letters of the ship's nameplate that had been illegally removed by an amateur diver in the early 1970s and had been taken to Canada, to be guiltily returned in 1995 and presented to the Orkney Island Council. The caption read: *Looking from the cliffs at Gaitnip to the wreck site over which a Naval vessel stations for the annual service of remembrance in October.* (256) So the final anchorage of the *Royal Oak* in 1939 was the same as that of *Nelson's* in 1930. I now knew where Gaitnip Craigs was – it was on the eastern shore of Scapa Bay and what was more, a turquoise buoy, identifying *Royal Oak's* resting place, marked the spot.

The rain eased when I finally left the museum and it had stopped completely by the time I found my way along stony lanes bordered by barbed wire fences, fields of sheep and a few derelict cottages, to the Lyness Royal Naval cemetery. There weren't many *Royal Oak* graves there though – most of the bodies lay aboard the ship, many of their body bones still floating in their hammocks.

✦ ✦ ✦

It was late afternoon when I made it back to the farm, and Kerry had her feet up on a stool in the conservatory of the farmhouse reading a book. Scott was nowhere to be seen; perhaps he had a hard-drive on the go in the bedroom or maybe he'd been Rolfed a bit too much! They'd been caught by the same storm as me and had soon abandoned all archaeological explorations for the day, retreating hastily to dry off and warm up in the snug farmhouse.

'You said you might be walking to the hotel for a meal tonight?' I queried.

'Oh, I don't think so,' Kerry said, 'it's a six-mile walk.'

'OK', well I think I'll go anyway – would you tell Louise that that's what I've done,' I said.

'Well, yes – but are you *really* going to walk the six miles there *and* back?' she quizzed incredulously. 'You're very brave.' Or stupid, I thought!

The restaurant, one of the few on Hoy, was part of the Stromabank Hotel on South Walls – which had actually been a separate tidal island until a causeway had been built in 1900 connecting it to Hoy. It was directly opposite the farm, over the Longhope inlet and behind a hill that rose above Longhope, about a mile-and-a-half at most as the crow flies. But to get to it I had to walk southwest to North Bay, negotiate my way around the 180° loop of the bay, then head back northeast, traversing the causeway and climbing the hill to reach the centre of South Walls, where Arthur told me I'd find the hotel. Not a single car offered me a lift. It took me an hour-and-a-half of brisk marching. Dad would have been proud of me.

As I passed a landfill site and began to climb the hill from the crest of which I was sure I'd be able to see the hotel, a seagull dive-bombed me, swooping treacherously across my face and almost rasping off my nose. I waved my arms about like a demented scarecrow on acid and shouted, all the while puffing on up the hill as fast as my little legs would take me.

On the way down the other side of the hill I scoured the land that fell off sloping down to the sea for any building that looked remotely like a hotel – there were just a couple of farms. I telephoned Stromabank on the mobile, puffing while I walked.

'You must be along just a little bit from us – Oh yes I can see you,' said the landlord.

'Can you?' I said stupidly.

'No – I'm pulling your leg. But you can't be far away – we'll be on your left.'

And so, after about three minutes, I was staggering to the bar dripping sweat.

'You found us then!' beamed the landlord, with an unspoken pride at his little joke.

'Yes – a pint of lager please, and a look at the menu,' I said, without realising that a couple of elderly tourists were before me.

'You look as if you need a drink more than us anyway,' said the elderly man smilingly.

'Have you walked a long way?' asked the landlord.

'About six miles,' I said, gulping a quarter of the pint down, 'got attacked by a seagull coming up the hill.'

'That wouldn't have been a seagull, it would have been a bonxie,' said an unshaven dark-shadow-faced man next to me wearing an open denim jacket over a RNLI tee shirt.

'A what? I've never heard of a bonxie!' I said.

'A bonxie, a great skua, I've seen one swoop down and take out a sheep's eye,' said the lifeboat-man.

'Farmers used to catch em and eat em didn't they Robbie?' said the landlord.

'Aye, but you're not allowed to touch em these days,' groused Robbie taking a slug of his Guinness. He was seated on a bar stool next to a grey-haired man with a south-of-England accent who it seemed was trying to run a bed-and-breakfast establishment somewhere on the island and had suffered a downturn in trade.

'I phoned up the tourist board,' he said, 'and asked them what was happening – and do you know what they said? They said – well there's nothing to do on Hoy is there, apart from the museum in the south, and the *Old Man* in the north – and that's the tourist board for you, so what chance do we stand!'

'There are plenty of things to do,' said a third man at the far end of the curved bar, 'but it's the insurance that kills it. There's that cave over at Garth Head for instance…'

'Where the locals used to hide out from the pressgang?' chipped in grey-hair.

'Yes – but as soon as you advertise it as a tourist attraction you'd have to get insurance – and that'd kill it.'

The conversation continued in this bonhomie vain for some time until the landlady led me into the restaurant, which looked like a cross between a conservatory and a ship's bridge.

The hotel was elevated, with a good view out from the restaurant across Hoxa Sound, which runs between the islands of Flotta and South Ronaldsay, and is one of three main shipping entrances into Scapa Flow from the Pentland Firth. The others are Hoy Sound, (through which I'd sailed into Stromness aboard *Hamnavo*), and Switha Sound. But it was through Hoxa Sound that *Nelson* and the other ships of the Atlantic Fleet had sailed into The Flow in 1930.

After the meal I returned to the bar, which had been deserted by the other locals, and sat on a stool next to Robbie, who was part way into another pint of Guinness. Something in the waters of the Pentland Firth was distracting him from his pint.

'It's a yacht,' he said, peering out the window and then slipping off the bar stool and leaving the hotel to get a better view.

'She's very slow out there,' he said when he returned.

'Are you a member of the lifeboat crew?' I asked dumbly.

'Yes,' butted in the landlord, who was ear-wigging, 'he's ...', but at that moment Robbie slid off his seat again with some sort of urgency and disappeared outside, this time with me following hard on his heels.

'Ah, she's OK,' he said. 'For a while there I thought she was in trouble. I'll buy you a drink?' he offered as we returned to the bar.

'Thanks, I'll have a Trawler rum please,' I said.

'Sure,' and he ordered it – together with another pint of Guinness for himself.

'What happens if you get a call out?' I asked.

'I've got a buzzer,' he said. (I was thinking more of his intoxicated inability to crew the lifeboat).

'Mmm – what work do you do? I asked nosily.

'I work on the ferry – I'm an engineer – work two weeks on and two off – that suits me fine; – when I'm working I work a hundred hours a week.' – (No European working hours directive in this outback then!).

'Ye, and when he's not working he's drinking a hundred hours a week,' chipped in the landlord.

'I'm on my second week off at the moment,' Robbie said, ignoring the interjection. Then suddenly he asked me –

'Can you drive?'

'Yes.'

'OK, well you can drive us back in my car after we've finished this one – I've had a few of these tonight.'

'Tonight!' scoffed the landlord with a smile.

'OK then,' I said, grateful that at least I'd not have to make the six-mile hike on a full stomach.

'Take your time,' said Robbie, as he saw me ease a slug of the hot dark stuff down my throat, 'no hurry.'

Outside we climbed into an unlocked old Renault and I cast about frenetically for the seat belt like an angler with a tangled line.

'Ah – don't worry about that,' said Robbie, 'nobody bothers over here.'

I went with the flow and spun the car out of the car park with a balletic uncertainty, driving east gingerly as he directed me down the narrow road.

'Take a left here and stop,' Robbie said after a short while, and compliantly I parked adjacent to a two-metre high grey stone wall.

Without saying anything he led me into a graveyard, and picked a path through the graves to stop at a tiered memorial topped by a bronze statue of a lifeboat-man. On the bottom tier was engraved:

GREATER LOVE HATH NO MAN THAN THIS
THAT HE LAY DOWN HIS LIFE FOR HIS FELLOW MEN.

'This is to the Longhope lifeboat,' Robbie said, 'she capsized in 1969 – eight men drowned – left seven widows and ten orphans – the Queen Mother came over.'

I silently read the crew names of the lifeboat *T.G.B.* that had been launched to aid a Greek crewed Liberian tanker in a force-nine southeasterly gale. (257)

Then we both stood there quietly for some time before Robbie drove us on along the alternative tourist trail to the Martello Tower at Hackness. The tower was one of two, erected either side of the mouth of Longhope inlet during the Napoleonic wars to protect shipping from American privateers; it took its name from similar fortifications at Cape Martello in Corsica where it had proved itself strong enough to drive away two British warships. By 1814, when Napoleon had been defeated and American hostilities had ceased, work on the tower had still not been completed. (258) They're a bit laid-back up here! The tower was closed at that time of night so we circled around the gravel car park and drove on. Turning right out onto the road for Longhope, I habitually flicked the indicator.

'No need to bother with that either,' said Robbie, there'll be nobody there – nobody for miles.'

'How many people live on Hoy?' I asked.

'Four-hundred and fifty,' said Robbie unhesitatingly, 'Half native and half English – we don't mind the English – and the good thing is there's only one policeman on Hoy and he's fifteen miles away. We're all professional drunk drivers over here – you're no driver at all unless you can drive with six pints inside you. On the mainland though it's a bit different – you stand more chance of being breathalysed there than anywhere.'

'The mainland?' I asked.

'Aye – Kirkwall.'

Just then, as if to contradict him, ahead in the road appeared a posse of fluorescent yellow jackets that looked to me like police on a drink-drive crack down. They turned out to be waterworks workers (thankfully) and we drove on, past a scattering of dwellings called Wyng, with the Longhope inlet on our starboard side, to the Royal Hotel. Once called The Ship, it was later known as The Longhope until it was again re-named after King George V had spent two nights there in July 1915. At that time it had been the house of Admiral Colville. (259)

'Leave that,' said Robbie, as he saw me grappling with my rucksack, 'it'll be safe enough.' But my rucksack had in it all my money and my passport, and I wasn't about to leave it outside a pub in an unlocked car – so I dragged it in with me.

We joined half-a dozen locals choking the small bar. The Guinness and Trawler rum was served by a barmaid in her early thirties.

'Best looking girl on the island,' said Robbie flirtingly as she handed him his pint.

'Well – best looking barmaid anyway,' he whispered to me, (there are only four pubs on Hoy)! Of course Robbie knew everyone in the place, and next to us at the bar lounged an unshaven scruffy young lad with long straggly hair, projecting ears, a missing front tooth and an incomprehensible Orcadian accent. His name was Raymond. Between them, (because Robbie had to interpret most of Raymond's questions for me), they explored my reasons for being in the surreptitious world of South Walls – and of course I disclosed my *footsteps* quest and *Nelson's* visit.

'Can you send me a copy of the book?' asked Robbie, and tried to write down his name, address and telephone number on a slip of paper he'd pulled from his pocket; tried – because he started to write it in such big letters that he ran out of paper.

'Write it down for me,' he asked the barmaid and, turning the slip over, she obliged – then handed it to me.

'He's interested in local history,' Robbie said to the barmaid, and from under the bar she handed me an album of old black-and-white photographs. I thumbed through them slowly, hesitating over one that caught my eye because it pictured an old man posing by a rusty torpedo.

'That's Johnny Meil,' said Robbie, catching my interest, 'he lives over on the mainland at Dyke End – if anyone around here knows about *Nelson* it'd be Johnny.'

'He could tell you a few stories' added Raymond with a chuckle.

'Give him a ring,' said Robbie, draining his glass, 'come on let's get you back.' – and we left, weaving out slalom-like between the locals. Raymond followed and now I began to seriously worry about the rucksack because there was nowhere I could put it except on the back seat of the Renault that, I suddenly realised was to be occupied by Raymond.

We drove back along the road I'd walked much earlier that night, Robbie and Raymond taking swigs from a half bottle of whisky they passed backwards and forwards between them. When we reached the track that led up to the farm, Robbie suggested that we might give the third of the four drinking establishments on the island a shot and with subdued English politeness I drove on past the farm in silence. But by now my paranoia about the safety of the rucksack alone on the backseat with Raymond had reached a level that far exceeded that of being stopped by the supposedly non-existent police force. On several occasions I fancied I heard a zip being pulled behind me and rustling noises – but Raymond could have been doing anything back there – nothing seemed beyond the bounds of possibility; he could have a knife or even a gun. I tried to get a glimpse of him in the rear view mirror, but almost swerved the car across the road and into the sea – (I wanted to be buried at sea – but not just yet)! Everything felt surreal, like a wild American road movie.

'It's pash,' Robbie grouched as we approached the uninspiring looking flat roofed Hoy Hotel at Lyness, 'there's no atmosphere – it'll be dead.' Then as we got out of the Renault he spotted a car he recognised.

'There could be trouble in here – leave it to me!' he said.

Now my anxieties intensified – this was all a set-up; we'd picked up Raymond at one pub *not* by accident, then we'd be picking up a second accomplice here – and then I'd get mugged, relieved of my rucksack and left in a soggy ditch somewhere…and of course the only policeman on the island was fifteen miles away…

This time I ordered the drinks – Robbie took a whisky, Raymond a Guinness and I another rum. When the drinks came I had desperate need of the toilet and, slinging the rucksack on my back, headed off towards it, realising that it was difficult to disguise this act, and that either I was justified in my fears or they might think me very untrusting and be offended. I peed hands free, ready to swing around at any moment.

The other car apparently belonged to another lifeboat member who, when I returned to the bar was in a serious discussion with the other two

– I fancied I heard the word *rucksack*, before they dropped into a suspicious silence as I approached. The third man though was about to leave and, as he walked to the door Robbie pulled a silent sign from his forehead that I recognised to mean *dickhead*. Was this a ruse to put me at ease? Would the third man actually be waiting outside in ambush? Flickering shadows of *The Wicker Man* sprang up in my mind like burning phantoms.

'You know...' said Robbie, 'that up there...' he nodded out the window '...is a tunnel cut into the hillside where they used to store the fuel oil during the war – in a minute we'll drive up there – but it's a windy old track so I'll drive – OK?'

'OK,' I said – not knowing whether to worry more about his intoxicated driving or being mugged – because short of running off down the road, I had no real option.

So then we were off, careering up the track towards Wee Fea picnic area on the wild alternative tourist trail again – or maybe to the ideal place to dispose of a tourist's dead body. Loose stones shot out fiercely from the tyres as Robbie swung the Renault up the track, then he veered right, scattering more gravel, onto an even rougher and more rutted track. He was driving well for someone who'd probably consumed six pints and a few whiskies. We stopped abruptly at the entrance to the tunnel and Robbie and Raymond got out and made towards it enthusiastically. I hung about in the front passenger seat, fearing that this was probably where the deadly deed would be done, but also making sure that I took my rucksack with me lest they should both dash back to the car and escape with it down the hill.

The tunnel entrance was a pedestrian arch cut into the rock, fitted with stout iron gates, padlocked and hung with a PROHIBITED – NO ENTRY sign in red lettering.

'I can get in there,' said Robbie, but it was obvious that he had neither a key nor torch with him, so we all three just stood there peering through the bars into the dank blackness beyond – well, actually I made sure that I stood a little behind them. Had they expected the gates to be open? Was it here that the bodies of other itinerant tourists had been disposed of? A shiver ran down my spine.

'The tunnel goes straight in for about half a mile,' said Robbie, 'then it turns right – I think there are still six oil storage vessels in there somewhere.'

Now I knew he was lying; I'd read in my *Scapa Flow* book that civilians had dug out the tanks in 1944... (260)

✦ ✦ ✦

Back down the track, a splendid view unfolded of Gutter Sound and the now uninhabited island of Fara. It was then that relief, followed shortly by guilt and shame began to creep over me in waves.

Robbie said to give him a ring if I wanted to go to the cave at Garth Head. He drove me right up to the front door of the farmhouse, where I reached behind to clasp hands first with Raymond in the back and then with Robbie, feeling more than a little sick now about my sad city suspicions. I should have known better, Robbie was after all a lifeboat-man; the engraving on the memorial in the graveyard said it all. As for the maverick that was Robbie, could he have been anything other, to accept those unknown risks taken each time the boat is launched out into the wild and awesome Pentland Firth.

❖ ❖ ❖

A flotilla of ducks meandered their way through the riffles, punting slowly along the seaweed foreshore that glinted in Houton's early morning sunshine. I wearily wheeled my case (containing, amongst other things sleeping bag, bedroll and tent) from the ferry and sat savouring the fresh sea air – legs, swathed in shorts, pendulous above a low sea wall, shirt open and the warm sun on my chest.

When I switched on the mobile, the call-tone broke the tranquillity unexpectedly; it was a voicemail message, this time from Ruth – the other Ruth, the soft one that I loved, not the reproachful, threatening, vindictive one. I was relieved. Perhaps she hadn't left me?

❖ ❖ ❖

The person camped next to me that night in Kirkwall was a serious contender for the world snoring championship – in fact he or she would have won palate down. It was the worst night's sleep I could remember since Glen Rosa over a year before, so that it was early when I rang Ruth – the soft one, who told me that she'd returned home from Wales and that she missed me. Perhaps she rumbled my clumsy attempt to change the subject, but if she did, she didn't let on.

'My dentures have turned fluorescent yellow,' I said, 'it's something to do with the sauce they put in the chicken buna I had at the Indian last night.'

'Well at least you'll be able to find them in the dark,' she laughed.

'It's not funny,' I said chuckling – 'I can't get it off.'

❖ ❖ ❖

At a road junction a mile south of Kirkwall, the main road curled briefly east before turning south again to lead out to Burray and South Ronaldsay – both once islands, but now connected by the Churchill Barriers. I continued south at the junction on a flat and almost straight B road that led for another mile down to Scapa Bay. Sheep grazed both sides of the road; on the eastern slopes that led eventually back up to the main road, and on the bay's marshy river basin to the west where, in the foreground and stretching into the distance, masses of reedy stalked yellow flags leapt in bunches out of the short grass.

There was no doubt I was now truly walking in Dad's footsteps – this was the very road that he and the others would have taken from the liberty boats at Scapa Bay pier to walk into the relative metropolis of Kirkwall. Re-surfaced of course, but this would have been the very road.

Since Dad's visit, the pier had, before the Second World War, been both lengthened and widened on its seaward side, and now it was being widened again by Balfour Beatty who'd barber-taped off sections of it and implanted a crane and several Portakabins. I walked to the end on its pristine white concrete – uninspired. It was all too new.

The walk from Scapa Pier to Gaitnip was around four miles; the sun was strong and I was sweating profusely by the time I stopped to get directions from a young man who was systematically mowing a large lawn, guarded by a large dog that barked furiously at me.

'See the top of the hill, where that car top is shining in the sun?'

'Yes,' I said, puckering my lips like a ventriloquist to hide my dentures.

'Take a right there by a stone wall,' he said convincingly, 'there's a large house; you'll be able to see it when you get to the top of the hill – that's Gaitnip.' But his instruction proved difficult to follow because, when I reached that point, no stone wall revealed itself.

A little further on though a compacted yellow shingle drive led off from the main road, bounded at its entrance by two imposing sculptured plinths; it flowed down seaward for what looked like about half a mile, then curled left to terminate at a mansion whose tall apexes were shrouded in the green gauze and the cloistered scaffolding of a major renovation. Two horses, ridden by young ladies attired in jodhpurs and riding hats, trotted and pranced down the private drive.

I walked on, now worrying that I'd never get to see *Nelson's* anchorage of 1930 from the vantage point of Gaitnip Craigs, but at the brow of the next rise a man was unloading building materials from a van.

'It all belongs to Paddy Casey,' he said, as I interrupted his labours, 'he'll probably be all right about it. Why don't you go up to the house and ask?'

'Well it's a long walk back if he says – *no*,' I said smiling – remembering then too late that I probably looked like a *before* advert for *Pepsodent*, (for those of you of a certain age who might remember). 'It'd be better if I could phone him – do you know his number?'

'I may have it...' he said, rummaging in the back of his van. 'No,' he said after thumbing through a dirty, dog-eared book...but... I'll tell you what...just along there,' – he pointed further up the road, 'on the right, is a workshop where you'll find some of Paddy's men. Ask them, they'll sort you out.'

The workshop was part of a farm, and my apprehensions began to spiral at the thought of the inevitable black-and-white collie dog attack that would follow at any moment. The building was of semi-circular corrugated iron construction, so that the walls and roof were one. I entered at the open end, calling stupidly: 'Is there anybody there?' Like a medium at a séance – discovering, after weaving between equipment and fabrications strewn across the floor, two of Paddy's men in the middle of a tea break at the far bricked-up end of the workshop.

'Do you work for Paddy Casey?' I asked.

'Yes,' said the elder one.

It was easier to say that I wanted to look at the *Royal Oak* buoy than to mention an obscure reason connected with the anchorage of *Nelson* nine years before. Paddy's men didn't seem too surprised at my request; there is still a lot of interest from relatives in the war grave site. Ex-seamen in their eighties who'd survived the sinking come back to visit the site and get very emotional, thinking of all the years of life they'd savoured whilst their shipmates remain young but dead down there, skeletons for all those years. Some old-timers have even asked for their ashes to be laid with their shipmates – so divers have gone down with urns and have slipped them into crevices. (261)

'They generally just walk off down the side of the track there,' said Paddy's elder man.

'Yes, but I don't want to trespass,' I said. 'Do you have Paddy's phone number?'

'Use this phone,' he said, pointing to the black dumbbell hanging from the wall, but I'd already started to dial it on my mobile when a slim diminutive man picked his way nimbly towards us.

'Ah, here's Paddy now...' said the elder.

Paddy shattered my stereotype image of a farmer; he was a jovial and friendly Irishman who'd obviously fallen well on his feet on the Mainland.

'It's all right as long as you don't damage anything,' He said.

'I'm only going to take a photo,' I said.

'I'm only pulling your leg,' he laughed – perhaps leg pulling was a common Orcadian sport played upon English tourists! – (It's rumoured that the saying began in Scotland anyway – as to draw the leg – but nobody seems to know for sure).

I climbed over two metal-tube five-bar gates and followed the rough track until it veered off right to Paddy's house. Then I clambered into a field populated by sheep, and headed straight ahead, down towards the sea, bounding impulsively, risking twisted ankles, through a deeply rutted field of heather, with a sweaty brow and a sticky shirt.

A white striped, black-hulled ship with an amber bridge, derrick and twin funnels skulked silently a hundred metres south of the turquoise buoy that marked the war grave of the *Royal Oak*. What was she doing there? I didn't know; – perhaps she was fishing? (I found out later that she was the MV *Cameron*, owned by a company in Fife but working for the Admiralty. She accommodated divers tasked with removing oil from *Royal Oak's* tanks that had sixty-six years before been fully fuelled ready for her to sail. Last year the hull-side tanks had been emptied and taken to the terminal on Flotta, and now the divers would be burrowing further inboard).

The cheese and pickle sandwich I'd purchased in Kirkwall slipped down unceremoniously, washed down with a carton of fruity drink. I sat within the heather for a long time looking out from Gaitnip Hill to the buoy; somehow it all felt like an anti-climax: It'd taken me four days to get here – four days I thought, so that I could look out on an almost vacant expanse of sea, a buoy, and what at the time I thought to be a fishing boat.

Then I thought of Dad, who's past life I was still discovering as I drifted into my old age. I wished we'd talked more – but all that was left now was a terrible silence…

◆ ◆ ◆

Sheep shit is a particularly unpleasant substance to put your hand in, but its what happened as I stopped to remove the bits of heather and prickly needles that had invaded my shoes and forced their way through my socks. I tried to console myself with the thought that at least I hadn't sat in it, but that didn't compensate much for the fact that it smelt bloody awful and that all the way back towards Kirkwall I had to be careful not to wipe sweat off my forehead or scratch myself with my right hand.

Dyke End is a couple of miles northwest across Scapa Bay from Gaitnip, but to get to it I had to walk north to Kirkwall, then south again. Louise had looked Johnny Meil's telephone number up in the directory, and I'd given him a ring. I could see my destination clearly but there wasn't a civilised way to cross Scapa Bay's river plane without a lengthy inland diversion. So by the time I rounded a bend in the lane that wound its way down to Johnny's place almost at the water's edge, I'd trudged a total of fourteen miles that day and was two hours later arriving than I'd told him.

Johnny was an eighty-one year young, balding, grey-haired, grey-bearded man who stood at the entrance to his workshop wearing pale blue overalls supported by stud secured braces and for additional security (or perhaps to hold tools) a well-worn, sloppy leather belt. He looked like he'd stepped straight out of a road movie shot in the American mid-west. Instinctively, I held out my right hand and gripped his firmly, smiling fluorescently – then remembered too late my sheep-shit hand.

His Orcadian accent was so deep and strong that I had to sharpen my ears to understand him. I followed him into the workshop, past two dummy torpedoes that had been washed up in the Flow, to his boat, from behind which he lifted out the deck-board and carried it out to the entrance to his workshop. The part that would have been trodden on by the top brass at the end of the ship's gangplank was a nicely varnished three-sparred wooden frame, in-filled with lattice, but when he turned it over, on the board's central spar, if you looked very closely, you could pick out the faint letters that spelled – NELSON. I photographed the board and ran my hands over it – to feel a bit of the old ship.

'I just touched it up a bit with a pencil,' Johnny said, 'but you can see it was from *Nelson.*'

On the way to his place, I'd had this romantic image of Johnny pulling the board from the sea himself as a young man, but in fact it transpired that an old salt – an artist – who'd lived over on Hoy, owned *Nelson's* deck-board and when he died, it had been sold as part of the contents of his house. It had reportedly been washed up at Lyness, but nobody knew for sure exactly when.

Nelson herself saw an illustrious Second World War career that included Marshal Badoglia signing Italy's surrender in the admiral's quarters in 1943 – and two years later, Rear Admiral Uozumi signing the surrender of Japan's Penang area forces. She was finally scrapped at Inverkeithing in 1949, but bits of her still survive like donated transplant organs: The ship's bugle rests in the RN museum at Portsmouth, her crests and flags are in All Saints church in Burnham Thorpe – Norfolk (Lord Nelson's birthplace), whilst the ship's silver bell, which was returned to her donors at Tyneside when she was scrapped, now lies in HMS *Nelson* barracks – Portsmouth. Few people knew about this deck-board, and I wondered how many more bits of that famous old ship survived around the world in private hands?

Johnny lived with his wife amongst nautical artefacts, books and photographs in a homely boson's locker of a house set above the western shore of Scapa Bay. It was the house he'd been born in and had lived in all his life. I was just glad to sit down on a settee for a moment and re-lax; the tea and biscuits were a bonus.

'Help yourself,' said Isobel, Johnny's wife – 'we say over here – put in a hand.' I did – more than once; the biscuits were accompanied by tasty cheese, and there was even a *Kit Kat*.

Johnny was very knowledgeable about *Nelson*; he knew more about her than I did and remembered the warships in the Flow from his youth.

'They'd get their food brought aboard in big wooden boxes,' he said, 'then they'd take the food oot and throw the boxes overboard. All the Orcadians had boxes then – see boy,' he said in a beautifully deep, slow, broad accent.

◆ ◆ ◆

Johnny and Isobel drove me back to the campsite in their four-by-four.

'Bye,' said Johnny, 'hope you find what you're looking for.'

I smiled then, too late remembered again my yellow glow, and waved as they drove away. They both waved back. Then I thought I saw Johnny smelling his hand.

Johnny Meil outside his workshop with a deck-board from HMS Nelson.

23.   An Odda Way To Go

HMS *Nelson* left Scapa Flow on the 8th of June1930, heading for the
Hardanger fjord and Odda, a small industrial town locked in by mountains at the bottom of Sørfjorden, one-hundred miles from the open sea.
It seemed a curious choice of summer cruise, and the Royal Navy's motive for it was as intriguing as Dad's perspective of the Norwegians. He
told me that they were a strange lot.

On the way, the battleship held an inter-part tug-of-war competition on
the upper deck, consisting of four rounds, which the Royal Marines won
by beating the topmen, (whoever they were), in the final. The winners
each received from the chaplain the spiritually healthy gift of a tin of
cigarettes, (any unlikely non-smokers obviously entering the bartering
stakes). The topmen runners up wouldn't have been very lit up with their
gift awarded by the commander of a sheet of emery paper, perhaps so
they could sharpen up a bit for the Commander-in-Chief's pending inspection. I bet there were no prizes for the suggestions they made about
what he could do with his prize, but I suspect they might have been a bit
abrasive! (262)

Nelson entered Hardanger at 9 a.m. and steamed for eight hours to her
anchorage at Odda – passing Norheimsund at around 1.30 p.m. and the
village of Utne, at the northern end of the Folgenfonna Peninsular, at
around three in the afternoon before she'd turned south towards Odda.
Utne was at about the same latitude as Bergen, my port of entry into
Norway; it was the furthest point north that Dad had ever travelled to in
his life – and it would be for me too.

◆ ◆ ◆

The fast-boat from Norheimsund took forty-five minutes to reach Utne,
a journey that had taken *Nelson* twice as long, although to be fair she'd
have been sailing at nothing like the 23.8 knots speed she'd achieved
during her trials – if she had, a few Norwegians at the side of the fjord
might well have been drowned.

Along the fjord the same thin white-lines of waterfalls traced their distant paths, thundering down between rock and forest just as they'd done
seventy-five years before. Although it had been early June when *Nelson*
had made this journey, the correspondent of the *Globe & Laurel* had
reported that it was cold, and that: *The mountaintops were thick with*

snow. (262) Now too it was cold, but only because of the fast-boat's speed across the water and my exposed position on her aft deck.

I was the only passenger to disembark at Utne. It was 9.45 a.m. and the clean, tidy streets were deserted. One general-purpose store seemed to be the only shop around and, apart from a restaurant, the Utne Hotel, (the oldest in Norway – dating from 1722), and a very clean toilet, the place seemed to possess no other public buildings. I'd come via Edinburgh, Aberdeen, Inverness, Thurso, Kirkwall, Lerwick, Bergen and Norheimsund. Now here I was in Utne – it had been an odd a way to go.

I sat on a spotless wooden slatted teak coloured seat next to the bus stop guarded by a cylindrical green litter bin, (that was probably empty because everyone in Utne took their litter home), and waited for the bus to arrive. Then, as the deadline passed, I waited and waited…thinking of all manor of statistically improbable reasons for its non-appearance. There was still nobody around. Then unexpectedly it arrived … ten minutes late – stopping down the road, outside the Utne Hotel, from where a quartet of German hikers suddenly appeared.

The bus wound its way tightly along the west bank of Sørfjord in Hardanger as it thinned-in towards its cul de sac at Odda. The roads we drove had been built by the workers of the town – made redundant in the 1920s by the temporary closure of the carbide factory. (263) We juggled our way scarily around bends and through shallow rock tunnels that between-times offered fluttering glimpses through the trees of the fjord where *Nelson* had freewheeled slickly towards her anchorage.

My first view of the industrial town was glimpsed from the bus through a gap between white wooded houses – it was of the church. Above it rose the now familiar pattern of houses dotted up a wooded mountainside with the white-ribbon of a waterfall weaving its way down into the fjord. The bus pulled up on a vacant quay where I imagined the great warship must have moored.

I'd finally arrived. Across the tranquil blue-green water was the centre of the little town of Odda, sometimes cited as the most ugly town in all of Norway. (264)

✦ ✦ ✦

In the late nineteenth century five small cottar's farms sat on the east, and six on the west side of the River Opo that flowed from the Sandvinsvatnet lake, through rapids down to the fjord. It was an idyllic place – an isolated haven; there were no roads to the north of Odda, which itself was a mere crack in the mountains inhabited by thirty people on two farms.

The first English tourist came to Hardanger in 1826. He was a gentleman by the name of Edward Price, a globetrotter and artist, whose sketches and writings started to popularise the area, so that by the mid nineteenth century hundreds of foreign tourists were discovering the wonderful gushing waterfalls above the little community of Tyssedal, and by the end of the century Odda had become a major tourist draw. (265) The wealthy came by boat and cruise ship that were in effect floating hotels; tour operators brought large groups with professional guides.

The tourists – boat loads of 150 on occasions – dashed from the ship when it docked at 9 p.m. and raced each other desperately along the quayside to ensure a good room in one of Odda's twelve hotels. One of these was the *Hardanger* then the largest hotel in Norway, boasting 96 windows, 110 rooms and a dining room large enough for 250 guests. Half of all the foreign tourists visiting Norway in 1900 came to Odda. (266)

Odda, at the head of Hardanger fjord, July 2005.

The Norwegians had used their waterfalls to turn millwheels from as far back as the middle ages. But in the 1870s, at just the time that Odda found itself to be the equivalent of Norway's Blackpool, Lester Pelton an American carpenter and millwright made a discovery that was to change the town forever, by developing a highly efficient water turbine that was to be eventually named after him.

By around the 1890s it started to dawn on some people that one thing Norway had plenty of, was water – and waterfalls that could be used to generate power. Odda had more than its fair share of waterfalls; three of

Norway's largest and most famous lay within the boundaries of the region. So even as the wealthy tourists flooded into the area, an engineer from Tønsberg, Nils Henrik Brun was spending his summers in the mountains near Odda fiddling around with his instrument and sometimes making water flow calculations. He and another engineer, Per Larssen Aga both acquired waterfalls *for a song* from the farmers of Tyssedal, which later they sold for large profits, (although Aga handed over the rights to one of the waterfalls to the Norwegian Tourist Association in the hope that it would be protected). It didn't do much good though, because by 1906 *everything* had finished up in the hands of a Mr Hiorth, the director of a newly founded power company. (265)

This company, AS Tyssefaldene, aimed to tame the river Tysso by constructing a dam to deliver electricity to a new carbide factory in Odda. The carbide factory was to be built by the British Sun Gas Company – on the understanding that AS Tyssefaldene would develop and deliver 20,000 horsepower of electric energy to it by the 1st of May 1908. (267) Construction of the hydro power plant began in 1906 and by 1908 the waterfall had been channelled into pipes that fell 400 metres almost straight down the mountainside into the blades of the Pelton turbines in the plant below. On its completion in 1918 it was the largest power plant in the world with an average annual production of 700 million kilowatt hours. (268)

✦ ✦ ✦

The little tourist information centre on Odda quayside directed me to the campsite situated on the banks of Sandvin Lake, with a view out over the valley of waterfalls to the Folgefonna Glacier. On the way to it I looked through a tree clearing, across a green quadrant and past an unlovely block of ochre flats to get my first view of the unnatural, gaunt skeleton of an industrial plant squeezed below a lushly forested mountain backdrop. This was my first close-up view of the carbide factory. It must have been about as welcome a sight to the hoteliers of Odda in 1908, as a sewerage plant would be suddenly appearing in Mayfair. Today, the only tourist accommodation apart from the campsite is a guesthouse, an apartment block and the Hardanger Hotel – but not the original; *it* was torn down in 1978. (268)

I'd contacted the bibliotek (library) by Internet months before, so they were expecting me. The deputy librarian Sim, like many Norwegians, spoke perfect English interlarded with the endearing Nordic trait of inserting little intakes of breath between sentences. She swiftly pulled from under the counter a folder, upon which was written my name. It contained two documents: The first was a treatise written in Norwegian, entitled *Arbeiderklassen – og de engelske matroser* by Nils Moldøen. I had great hopes that this would yield an explanation of the reason for the visit of HMS *Nelson* to Odda. But of course I couldn't read Norwegian, and so instead spent the remainder of the afternoon in the bibliotek, crouched awkwardly over the second, English, document – absorbed by and absorbing the potted history of the carbide factory.

◆ ◆ ◆

By 1929, the year before *Nelson's* visit, the carbide factory had nine furnaces in operation, with sales reaching a maximum of 69,000 tons; one of its most important customers was Allen-Liversidge, a UK company soon to be taken over by the British Oxygen Company. But by the time *Nelson* anchored at Odda in 1930, the first signs of the world depression were beginning to be felt and the number of operational furnaces was already in decline, having been reduced down to seven, (a year later it would be down three). (269)

But the carbide plant would not have been the only factory Dad would have seen as *Nelson* sailed up the Sørfjord; there was an aluminium factory (DNN Aluminium) at Tyssedal, and four kilometres from Odda, on the little peninsula of Eitrheimsnet, jutting out at an angle of forty-five degrees into the fjord stood a shiny new zinc plant. If *Nelson* had made the same trip a few years before, nothing more innocuous than fruit growing and farming labours would have been seen on the peninsula. But the year that *Nelson* sailed past the factory it employed 470 people and the production of electrolytic zinc had already reached 34,000 tons. Today the plant is known as Boliden Odda A/S. (270)

◆ ◆ ◆

The Vertshuset Hardanger was the only bar I could find open, (apart from the one in the Hardanger Hotel which I never ventured into for fear of its probable extortionate prices). I'd scoured Odda unsuccessfully for a bar that looked as if it might have survived from the thirties, where I would find a garrulous ninety-year-old English speaking Odda old boy who would vividly remember the visit of a British warship one summer seventy-five years ago. It was a fanciful dream – I couldn't even find a likely *bar*, and ended up in the contemporary styled Vertshuset (meaning lodging house) by default.

From the pavement outside I could see that a football match was on the TV, which in truth was the other reason I went in. Stephen Gerrard had just scored for Liverpool. Inside, in a room at the back, a group of seven young Norwegian lads were clustered around a large screen that was also showing the same match. Two had no drinks at all, one was swigging (very occasionally) from a bottle of Coke and the others were attempting to break the slowest drinking record, to gain entry into the famous Guinness book.

I ordered rum, which appeared to be an extraordinarily unusual request, because the barmaid had to ask several people where it was kept. Eventually a bottle *was* located in a cupboard behind the bar, unveiled, (after being unlocked), via a sliding glass door. It was Bacardi of course, and before I could stop her, the tall glass had been three quarters filled with glacial water cubes and embellished with three miniscule but long, coloured straws. The price was astronomical – at least twice the UK price.

'There would be a revolution if we had to pay that price in England,' I said, undiplomatically.

'You are in Norway now.' replied the barmaid unflinchingly – putting me in my place.

I managed with some difficulty to spin the Arctic drink out until half time, retiring then to my tent to savour the cheap but loving company of a bottle of dark Lerwick rum. If ever I feel the need to go on the wagon, I'll remember to take a long holiday in Norway.

✦ ✦ ✦

I spent most of the next morning in Odda bibliotek, learning what I could of the rest of Odda's industrial past from a photographic display of its early history, and from the documents I'd been given, (trying to pick fragments of meaning from the Norwegian one). Anyway, it was raining and I'd formulated scant plans for the day.

The bibliotek had sent me some local newspaper clippings before I left England that had actually answered one of my questions; they covered the visit of *Nelson* in June 1930 and, after I'd had them translated, a picture began to emerge that gave some clues about why Dad might have formed his generalised derogatory view of the Norwegians.

The first report, appearing on Saturday the 7th of June, was terse enough – it was simply headed *Det første Orlogsskib*, (The First Warship) and it read: *Monday, the first warship will arrive at Odda. It is a large Englishman 'Nelson' of 750 feet. It will remain here about a week.* (271) On the following Wednesday another snippet appeared: *Mellemofficerene på HMS Nelson – The petty officers of HMS Nelson will arrange a dance in the Folkets Hus, Friday at 8 p.m. All ladies who like to dance to the music of the English jazz band are invited free of charge. They ask us to urge that this offends nobody, as it is the only way they can manage to organise an event.* (272) On Saturday the 14th there were two clips – one, uncontroversial enough, advertising a football match that *Nelson* would play between themselves at the Almerket the following day, but the second put a completely different slant on the visit. It was headed *O.K.U. protesterer*, and read: *O.K.U. has, on the meeting of June 11th considered the notification of the English officer's party on Friday and will direct a protest against it as we are aware that sooner or later these officers will be the butchers of English Citizenry in the war against the Soviet Union and who are today taking part in shooting down our Indian comrades and revolutionary workers. We demand that this is not repeated.* (273) It was a good job that Norwegian wasn't a language taught in the public schools of England, or a degree of offence might have been taken, by Jove!

HMS *Nelson* weighed anchor to sail from Odda at 11.33 a.m. on Wednesday the 18th of June and coincidentally, (just in case there *might* have been somebody aboard who *did* understand Norwegian), it was on that very day that the *Hardanger Arbeiderblad* let fly with its, until then, suspended political polemic against British Imperialism: *The British Navy always occupies a leading position when it comes to bringing the oppressed people who fight for their freedom to silence with their cannons. The bombardment of Chinese cities by English warships is still fresh in one's memory. Today the entire Indian population are struggling against British Imperialism. The freedom fight of the Indian population assumes more and more harsh forms, but every day more and more is brought under the direct leadership of the Indian proletariat. The gunfire of the British Imperialists is belching forth to kill the struggling Indian workers and peasants – at the moment no less than five battle cruisers are in India.* (274)

The 1920s were a time of communist growth in Europe and elsewhere, (since the Russian revolutions of 1917), helped by the scourge of rising unemployment. In 1927 the army of General Chiang Kai-shek entered the city of Shanghai, following prolonged strikes organised by the Nationalists and their Bolshevik allies. In Austria that same year, workers took to the streets fuelled by the communist press, (following the outcome of a political murder trial), setting fire to the Ministry of Justice. In Britain too its presence was felt; the Welsh miners on their walk from the Rhondda Valley to London were noted to be holding up banners that sported the hammer and sickle – and even in Germany, two years later, communists fought running battles with the police in Berlin. (275)

The newspaper article went on to perhaps answer why Dad felt the Norwegians to be a strange lot, but it still left unanswered the reason for *Nelson's* visit to Odda, (which was my real curiosity). It identified the Norwegian workers of the town with the working class boys of the lower deck of the Royal Navy who it said had joined up to escape unemployment, suggesting that they should be directing their aggression not against their colonial brothers but against the ruling classes in Britain:

Their real enemy, it continued, *is in their own country; it is English capitalism, its servants, the so called 'workers government*, (referring to MacDonald's labour Government), *and the higher ranking officers within the British Navy who are preparing to force them into battle against members of their own class in the British colonies and against the Soviet Union*. It almost encouraged mutiny, a year before Invergordon. *The path to freedom for the working class crosses over the bodies of the present ruling class*, it said. *This path also the English workers and sailors must follow*. Finally, the article recorded the act that was to be the upshot of these proclamations and which was undertaken as a finalé to the visit: *The friends of the Soviet Union and the communist youth movement in Odda had printed a manifesto in English, it said, copies of which were distributed yesterday during the dance on board the warship*. (274) The boys from Odda who mingled amongst the sailors and marines, slyly slipping them pieces of paper, must have got some very funny looks. Usually such a clandestine act would be an invitation to an address where some local female hospitality might be sampled for a price. I can see why Dad thought them a strange lot... Many of *Nelson's* men handed the leaflets into the ship's office, so that the officers and even Captain Watson got to see them – they apparently provided a delightful source of amusement in the wardroom.

Odda and Tyssedal it seemed were red through and through. Sim told me that the Communist Party remained strong in Odda right up until after the Second World War, fighting bravely against the Nazis during the war – and even now, she said, it's second only to the Labour Party in Odda.

✦ ✦ ✦

They told me in the Tourist Information Centre where the worker's cottages were located, and I found the guide Lars doing a spot of gardening. He was a tall, grey-curly haired man with a bubbly face, wearing glasses over which he peeped at me with one good eye and one crooked one. He reminded me for some obscure reason of Pinocchio's carpenter father Geppetto. Although I was pretty sure I was his only customer of the day, I still received the full tourist treatment, commencing with the film show. After he checked that the film was running all right and in English, (he'd started off with the Norwegian version by mistake), Lars sneaked back to his gardening, leaving me alone in the little darkened cinema. Here all the history I'd researched in the bibliotek was vividly brought to life by dozens of old photographs interlaced with the commentary.

✦ ✦ ✦

Between the turn of the century and Dad's visit, the population of Odda had increased five-fold; people came from all over the place, and especially from Sweden, to run the kilns of the smelter works both night and day, including Sundays. The plant was the largest of its kind in the world at the time and the wages were good; production workers could earn ten times as much as they could get from labouring on a farm. But the work was dangerous and unhealthy; it was dirty, dusty and noisy. The carbide brought the skin up in sores and got into the eyes, a tiny spec of it could leave a hole in the retina. It also ate into the bodywork of the few vehicles there were around and it was impossible to get off. (276)

There was a marked difference between the standard of living of those at the top and those at the bottom of the pile. The managing director lived in a large house on a hill with servants. His managers too had fine hilltop houses with good views and fresh air drifting up from the fjord, whilst the workers houses were down by the factory amongst the grit and grime. A barbed wire fence separated the two extremes with a locked gate that could only be opened from the manager's side. If a worker died, his wife and children were evicted from their tied houses at short notice and had to exist on relief. Maybe it wasn't so surprising then that the communists became so strong. (277)

✦ ✦ ✦

Lars was still gardening when I found him again, and now he led me on the official tour of the cottages; each was typical of the years 1910, 1920, 1930 and 1950, decked out with period-dressed dummies, furniture and articles. He told me that the museum was opened in 1985, before which the buildings had been used to house refugees for a while. He spoke good English and, when the official tour was over, I explained about the visit of *Nelson* and pestered him with questions.

'What about the carbide factory now?' I asked.

'An American company owns it,' he told me, 'but it's been closed down for three years – lost the market to the Chinese who make it much cheaper. For three years they have been discussing what to do with the buildings – at a similar factory near Oslo it took them twelve years to make a decision.' He said he'd gone into the factory the day after it'd closed and (like Pompeii after the eruption of Vesuvius) everything had been left fossilized just where it was.

The petty officers had held their dance in the Folkets Hus or the peoples house. Maybe, (I hoped), the marines had been invited to, so I asked Lars if it still existed.

'No,' he said, 'I will show you something – come...' and he led the way to another cottage and up some stairs to a room that was not included in the official tourists' tour – (the red room I named it). It was as if Odda was now ashamed of just how red she'd once been, yet was still secretly fervent about her past. In the room the white wood panelling was draped with red flags, dripping blood red from red flagstaffs hanging from the sloping white wooden roof; and where the roof met the walls a red frieze ran around the room. White lettering set into the red declaring FOLKETS HUS – and below were sepia photographs of the inside and outside of that building.

Folkets Hus was a great Victorian-looking building topped with chimney, domes, and long rectangular church-like windows. Inside, it was multi-functional, used for everything from political gatherings to Christmas parties. Workers too sick to work were even allowed to hold bazaars there to support themselves. At one end was a small stage and around the building's sides was a gallery that seated 400 people. Where the stalls should have been, instead – in the photograph – banquet tables had been set out in rows.

The local labour unions had built Folkets Hus themselves; it was completed in November 1914 and was their Grand Union Hall, or assembly building. Dr Petersson, the director of the carbide plant and one of the founders of modern Odda, lent the worker's movement 15,000 Krone of his own money (269), but otherwise they raised the rest themselves by organising raffles and arranging bazaars. Voluntary communal workers helped dig out the site and the workers themselves brought all the materials there. (278)

Lars left me alone in the room for some time, (whilst he probably did a bit more gardening), and the ambience of the red room seeped into my mind; I was almost back there with the workers – the socialists and communists, feeling their struggle, tasting the carbide in their lungs and feeling the sweat on their brows. I could almost hear the verses of Jim Connell's song swamping into my brain…

The people's flag is deepest red,
It shrouded oft our martyred dead,
And ere their limbs grew stiff and cold,
Their hearts blood dyed its every fold.

The old photographs of the Folkets Hus seemed too to almost disgorge the characters that had spoken there into my head. There was comrade August Magnussen, a Swede, who came to Norway in 1897 – he was a sturdy fellow, a staunch communist, and powerful orator, leader of the Odda Co-operative organisation and chairman of the Folkets Hus building committee. His obituary summed him up: *Every revolutionary union member can remember Magnussen* it said, *he was sound and straightforward…only death could keep him from the struggle for the working class.* Karl Holmberg was also a Swede; he was one of the key figures in the founding of the Odda Worker's Union almost as soon as he arrived, in 1906. He fought for the building of both the hospital and the Folkets Hus and for a cooperative grocery (the Co-op to you). After a dispute in 1913 the management refused to let him back in the factory – until the union threatened to strike. He died in 1962 aged 92. (278)

'It was demolished in 1971,' Lars said, reading my mind. I hadn't heard him return – and he'd found me with a glazed look standing in front of the photographs of the Folkets Hus.

'If you come to the window I think you can just see where it was,' he said. It was at the far end of a street called Folgefonngata; a low flat-roofed building, out of character with the surrounding architecture. 'It's a supermarket now,' he said.

'And what about the Almerket?' I asked, 'the sailors from *Nelson* played a game of football there.'

'Yes – it is opposite the church,' he said, 'It is not a field anymore – it is a car park.'

✦ ✦ ✦

I bought my next morning's breakfast at the supermarket at the end of Folgefonngata; it was named the 'COOP', but the 'Os' were interlinked. I supposed it was the Norwegian equivalent of the Co-op – appropriate in the circumstances. I *floated* through the aisles in the same air space that was once above the floor of the Folkets Hus, where Dad might just have danced with a young Norwegian lady of communist persuasion and where he'd perhaps pocketed those strange Polo Mint ore coins that I'd found in the old brown case. I found myself smiling as I placed the items on the conveyor belt. The young checkout girl smiled back at me po-litely, no doubt oblivious to the history of the place in which she toiled. Then a macabre thought uncontrollably crossed my mind: Mum had organised Dad's funeral through the Co-op – I wondered if she ever got her divi?

I wandered past the horizontal-white-boarded wooden church to the concrete car park of the Almerket that had once been the venue of a rau-cous Royal Naval football match. Then strolled up through the Røldalsvegen, (Odda's small pedestrian shopping street), to explore the fenced-off facets of the factory from its various approaches. I sneaked a look through padlocked gates to verify Lars's description of its demise. It was accurate – wooden pallets were stacked haphazardly just where the fork-lift truck had left them, red-and-white traffic cones marked the site of some incomplete works that had stopped that day, three years ago, when the factory had closed. And as I stood there, I could feel the his-tory of the place permeate from within the gates.

It made me think about August Magnussen and Karl Holmberg again, of the syndicate unions run by the Swedes operating from the *Svenske-brakka* – the Swedish barracks in Skjeggedal, nicknamed *Rødbrakka* – the red barracks. The workmen were roused not only by August and Karl but by all sorts of other radical movements that grew like fungi around the carbide plant – the socialists, the communists and the anarchists. These were men who knew their real worth to the bosses but who still had to fight all the way to win their rights, they were men who would not take their hats off for anyone. The first large strike was held at the plant in the summer of 1913, but the growing labour movement was soon to be driven from Russia.

◆ ◆ ◆

The Comintern was inspired by Lenin, the leader of the Bolshevik faction of Russian socialists, who'd observed bitterly the collapse of the Socialist International in 1914. This had been an organisation whose ideology, (that the working class would together resist the war), had crumbled within hours of its declaration. Lenin then announced that a new Third International had to be constructed to take its place, and so in 1919 the name *communists* was adopted and the Comintern was founded in Moscow with the slogan: *Proletarians of all countries unite*. Delegations from 37 counties were invited to the first congress in 1921, including representatives from the United States, Japan, Germany, the British socialist parties, (including the Socialist Labour Party) and the Norwegian Labour Party. The central policy of the Comintern was that communist parties should be established across the world to aid the international proletarian revolution. The Comintern congress was held just a year before the republics of Russia, Ukrain, Georgia, Azerbaijan, Armenia and Byeloruse met at the Bolshoi Theatre to form the Union of Soviet Socialist Republics (USSR). (279)

In Odda, in 1923, there was a vote as to whether membership of the Comintern should be continued. Its supporters won, and took the name of the Odda Labour Party, together with control of the newspapers and the Folkets Hus. Others with opposing views formed the Norwegian Communist Party (NKP) and when *Nelson* visited Odda in 1930 the strengths of these two parties were about equal.

Leading up to this time, Russia saw Britain as her main enemy and was paranoid about being attacked by Imperialist Britain – hard to believe taking into consideration relative country sizes – but there was a fear that another great war was coming. In 1925 there had been raids in London on the Communist Party offices, where Russian ideas for generating strike action had been seized, and in October of the same year

British communists had been arrested under the 1797 Incitement to Mutiny Act.

In May 1926 the Conservatives were in power in Britain and experienced the general strike that highlighted the struggle between the working class and the middle class. And when in May 1927 the UK severed diplomatic relations with Russia – accusing the Soviet mission in London of espionage, the gap between the classes became even more apparent, evidenced as Labour MPs sung *The Red Flag* when Soviet diplomats were chaperoned out of the country via Victoria station. A month later the Russians retaliated by executing twenty alleged British spies. It took until September 1929 before diplomatic relations between the two countries was restored. (280)

This was the background then that sparked the reaction of the NKP to the visit of *Nelson* to Odda in June 1930; they'd opted for confrontation rather than cooperation. This explained the outbursts from the *Hardanger Arbeiderblad* about the visit and why those Odda boys had handed out the flysheets. But it still didn't explain why *Nelson* had made the visit there in the first place…

✦ ✦ ✦

Friday morning – rain began to pound the tent in the early hours and didn't ease up until mid morning. Average precipitation in Norway is 1,500mm a year, twice the European average, although I'm not sure if they included Wales in the statistics? (281) Ninety per cent of rain stays as water, which is odd; all that free water, yet beer, (the majority of which is water), is an extortionate price. Rain, a comrade of mountains, was obviously a frequent visitor here and on my way down into the town I even spotted a dog wearing a red raincoat. The weather decided that my last full day in Odda be spent on a visit to the Norwegian Museum of Hydropower and Industry in Tyssedal.

What the longhaired blonde, English-speaking male guide didn't know about the place wasn't worth knowing. I was surprised to learn for instance that up until 1967, the electricity distributed from the power station to Odda was not at 50-Hertz frequency but at 25 Hz. When Dad had visited, this would have meant that everywhere would have been lit by flickering pale yellow lights – Oh, except in the Managing Director's house and those of his managers – they had their own separate 50 Hz frequency generator it seemed.

✦ ✦ ✦

Sunk deep into the recesses of a black leather settee I spent my last evening in Odda amidst the relentless background din of rap music, facing a table with a glazed surface top lavished with burnishes that reminded me of the scraped surfaces of test pieces I'd produced as an engineering apprentice. I was back in the Vertshuset bar on a slow Bacardi straw drip again. The place was empty apart from a fat twenty-something girl and a blonde lad of a similar age sitting around what to me looked like a computer screen. That evening I'd again searched in vain the streets of Odda for anything that might take me back to the thirties. Not many of the 8,116 people residing in the district were about. So I gave up and flopped out into the settee.

I was melancholic as I left the Vertshuset bar; tomorrow I'd be leaving Odda. I'd learnt a lot of its history, tasted its damp weather, trudged its streets and met some of its people, but when I'd leave tomorrow, its heart would remain a mystery. Dad's words still rang in my ears, as queer as that *Polo Mint* shaped ore coin.

Slowly, I climbed back up the hill to the campsite for the final time, past the horizontally slatted wooden houses where, inside, the Odda folks would be watching TV. A sports car romped unbridled over speed humps and chased an unsuspecting seagull that skewed skyward to escape. The car swerved and skidded to a halt – Friday night entertainment over. Silence returned. Dark grey puffs of clouds hung ghost-like and motionless around the trees on the lower slopes of the mountains. An imperceptible drizzle leaked silently. I felt my tee shirt – it was already wet through.

✦ ✦ ✦

The journey from Odda to Haugesund took over three hours, but now there were another three to wait before the ferry sailed. For a moment I wondered if the taxi driver had dropped me at the right place – the Fjord Line office seemed so small and there was nobody behind the counter. A slightly built fair-haired Norwegian man, (whose name I later learnt was Jan), was the only person in the office.

'I have been here twenty minutes,' he said, '...and nobody...' He looked around, as if someone might appear by magic.

'I wondered if I had the right place,' I said.

'Where are you going – to Newcastle? Asked Jan.

'Yes – you as well?'

'Yes... It is unusual, there is normally someone here by this time.'

'You've done this before then?' I asked.

'Yes, several times, I'm going with my girlfriend across for the trip – we'll buy some things in Newcastle and then come back. They are good crossings, plenty to eat and drink,' said Jan. He was going on a Norwegian booze cruise, the equivalent of the British popping over to France. He worked, he told me, as a merchant sailor – it seemed a bit like a busman's holiday to me.

'Where have you been in Norway?' he asked. So I relayed the trip to him and my reasons for making it.

'Odda eh! That's a strange place,' he said, 'alright to visit, but not I think a good place to live.' We both took a seat as it looked like being a long wait. Then a thought crossed my mind...

'I have a document in Norwegian,' I said, 'about the visit my Dad made to Odda – I wonder if you could take a look at it for me?'

'Sure – no problem,' he said, 'lets have it.' So I pulled from my ruck-sack the copied document *Arbeiderklassen – og de engelske matroser*. He began to browse it and spent a long time nodding, grunting and flicking the pages of the sixteen-page document back and forth.

'What does it say?' I asked eventually, 'I mean – generally.'

'Well Odda was very red... very red...and it says that ...the boys of Odda well, they did a good job on the English sailors.' I looked at him intently.

'Yes, that's it really,' Jan confirmed, flicking the pages again, 'they reckon they did a pretty good job on them – in turning them red.' I wasn't going to let him off the hook that easily.

'Does it say why the ship visited Odda?' I asked.

Jan looked at me, saw the seriousness in my eyes and nodded.

'Yes,' he said turning the pages more slowly now, 'Here...' he said pointing to a heading, 'it asks the question – why would the fleet visit Odda?'

'And does it answer the question?' I asked persistently. Jan looked at me smiling, and then looked around the room. There was no sign of anyone appearing – either other passengers or Fjord Line officials – maybe he was looking to escape interrogation, but then he seemed to resign himself to the task and returned to the document, reading it silently again, this time more intently.

'It says...' he said slowly, 'that...it thinks the sports competitions, the dances, the concerts and the cocktail parties were all a cover up... and that really the visit was to protect the British Empire's strategic interests.'

'What strategic interests?' I asked, almost to myself.

'Well,' he said... 'Norway was dependent on coal from England to fuel her shipping industry and because of this... she wanted a good relationship.' He looked up at me briefly, then back at the page. 'Britain herself wanted...it says... to control the marine activity in the North Sea,' he said. 'The visit to Odda was to mark Britain's strategic interests.' I looked puzzled – I couldn't see how a visit like this could do that.

'It says that a few observations would have been made during the visit, but that most of the military intelligence work would have already been done by travellers disguised as tourists.' There was a long pause whilst Jan read on through the rest of the document, then slowly he said:

'OK, I will try and read this bit to you – the best that I can.'

'OK,' I said, and Jan started his translation.

'From what is known about the industrialisation of Norway… it is likely…that Odda was viewed as a perfect example… of how investments from abroad could merge with local interests and create work for the people. But… whether this investment relationship… implied that the English fleet was invited or not, we do not know,' he said. (282)

'So,' I said, (remembering that Sun Gas had originally been built by a British company, and that one of the most important customers for calcium cyanamide at the time was the British Oxygen Company), 'perhaps the British Government were worried about the communists in Odda?'

'Hmm. maybe so,' said Jan smiling – 'or maybe it was just… that the captain's father had told him that Odda was a nice place to visit…'

✦ ✦ ✦

A thick black coil of smoke had billowed up into the sky above Newcastle as the ferry transfer bus neared the train station. I was just beginning to wonder if this was normal for Newcastle, when a fire engine wailed past.

In Odda, conversations with Ruth had been amiable enough, but the North Sea had somehow become a medium of transmogrify.

'There's just been an announcement,' I said, 'we've been delayed – they've closed Newcastle station because of a fire – we were the last train out.'

'Delayed! You're having a laugh aren't you?' Ruth screamed.

'No, listen Ruth,' I said, trying to whisper so that the other passengers didn't stare, 'we're waiting to change engines from an electric to a diesel or something, but it means I'll probably miss the connection in Peterborough.'

'I don't believe you – you get back here NOW.'

Two taxis and seven-and-a-half hours later I finally made it home – at one in the morning. It took about a month for Ruth to come around.

24.   A Ball At The Grand

The sweat beaded on my forehead and began to trickle down the sides of my face into the chicken chilli masala. It was the hottest curry I'd ever attempted to eat and it should have been described as a chilli chicken, chilli chilli masala. It numbed my tongue and throat and was heading for my brain so that at any moment I thought I was going to be rushed off to hospital in a *korma*.

The hottest curry ever is supposed to be a phal; a dish not found in India, but devised purely as a source of Saturday night entertainment by Anglicised voyeur Indians, Pakistani's and Bangladeshi's up and down the land who like to watch machismo, pissed young Brits attempting to demonstrate their phallic prowess by tackling it. The phal, it seems, contains more chilli powder than either a vindaloo or a tindaloo, none of which I've ever ventured to try. But I reckon that someone must have distracted the chef at the Scarborough Tandoori whilst he was adding the chilli to the masala – either that or he fancied some light entertainment because not too many young male Scarborians order phals. Anyway, It was good to be back in England.

When I caught my breath – I enquired the whereabouts, and was given directions, to one of Scarborough's most famous landmarks – the Grand Hotel, not that I was staying there of course!

At the bottom of St Thomas Street I zigzagged down through terraced gardens, past diagonally panelled wooden fences and pseudo gas lamps that attempted to rekindle Scarborough's Victorian age. On the sea front at South Bay I turned south along Foreshore Road, the multi-coloured flashing lights of an amusement arcade soon destroying any Victoriana persona. The Grand Hotel now towered above me like a castle out of a Dracula film, its flagpole domes balefully piercing the charcoaled night sky.

This was the hotel where, in June 1930 The Commander-in-Chief Atlantic Fleet (Admiral Sir Michael H. Hodges, K.C.B, C.M.B. M.V.O.), and officers of H.M. Ships *Nelson*, *Barham*, and *Malaya* attended a ball. The *Scarborough Mercury* advertised it: (283)

Scarborough – Naval Visit, 1930

A BALL Will be given by the Mayor and Corporation
at the GRAND HOTEL on TUESDAY, 24TH June 1930
Dancing 9 p.m. to 2 a.m. Victor Haythorne's Dance Band.

◆ ◆ ◆

On the preceding Friday HMS *Nelson* had arrived from Odda. She'd left on the Wednesday morning, making the cruise to Scarborough at the required inter-war economic speed of 12 knots an hour. *The Scarborough Mercury* reported that:

His Majesty's Ship Nelson, Flagship of the Atlantic Fleet, which, with its sister ship Rodney, is the most powerful warship in the world, and HMS Barham, flagship of the second battle squadron, arrived at Scarborough this Friday morning, dropping anchor at five minutes to ten. Immediately on arrival a salute was fired, which excited the interest of the crowds gathered about the east pier and other vantage points, to whom it seemed an unfamiliar proceeding. (283)

The report went on to reassure its readers that the gun salute was purely a naval courtesy, but for those of the gathered crowd who were around a little more than fifteen years before, the sound of gunfire from *Nelson* must have sent a shudder down their spines. Looking out to sea through binoculars in June 1930 they might have seen the shimmering white shock-wave flashes followed by dense black smoke pools billowing out and rolling almost majestically across the sea. Then they might have recalled a cold misty December morning in 1914 when two German battle cruisers and a light cruiser appeared off North Bay and in a brief period of half an hour fired 489 high-explosive shells from their 11 and 12 inch guns into the town, castle and harbour. That's one shell every 3.7 seconds. Eighteen people were killed, 84 injured and 209 properties were damaged. The Grand Hotel copped for 36 shells alone – a nice looking target I suppose.

Nelson's salute would have been a salute to the Flag, probably because of the arrival of The Commander–in–Chief Atlantic Fleet; it would have been a 19 gun firing. There was a strict etiquette as to how many guns could be fired and when salutes could be given; all 32 categories of salute were laid down in a six-page table in Article 66 of King's Regulations and Admiralty Instructions. A foreign Consul for example got only 7 guns, whilst Governor-Generals received a good 19. But the ships could really *go to town* with a 21gun blast when entering a foreign port and saluting that country's national flag – but only on being first satisfied that the salute would be returned. (284) How would they know that, I wonder?

A lady who'd been a teenage girl in the crowd by east pier on that Friday in June 1930 wrote to me: *It was a great event when the huge battleships visited – the natives thought they were wonderful – so large! Why are they so small now? I can remember three of them standing off in the South Bay – Nelson, Rodney and I can't remember the third –*

would it be Barham? It was so long ago, but I was there! She signed
herself – A true and proud Scarborian. (285)

✦ ✦ ✦

The Grand loomed somewhere above me as I walked on along Foreshore
Road (where tramway lines had once run) and passed the funicular
which had been virtually new in 1930. It was closed at this time of night,
so I had to climb though the chicanes up the steep Saint-Nicholas Cliff
to arrive breathless at steps that led to the doors of The Grand Hotel. It
was 9.30 in the evening, but they appeared to be locked; I swore I'd just
seen some people leaving, but I pushed and pulled the doors in vain. The
Victorian fortress appeared to be riff-raff proof – designed especially to
debar the son of a bootneck.

The Grand Hotel, Scarborough. [Photo: Britannia Hotels, Altrincham].

Dad's venue would have been more like the Lord Nelson, a hotel strategically situated at the root of West Pier. The smoke-yellowed,
patterned ceiling paper and dirt ingrained pattered carpet in the bar had
probably both been there in 1930. The walls were embellished with photographs of fishing smacks and black-and-white Victorian street scenes
where groups of people posed for the photographer with Cheshire cat
smiles.

It was karaoke night (Dad would probably have approved). A book of songs appeared, card requests were made and there were no shortage of volunteers – although not one of them could vaguely be described as a singer. Apparently karaoke started in Kobe city in Japan and in Japanese it's an abbreviation of a word that means *empty orchestra*. Certainly a few empty vessels made a lot of noise that night in front of the screen in the Lord Nelson. Four very fat ladies, that I surmised may have comprised two sets of mothers in their late fifties – and their daughters, took turns to entertain themselves by wailing and flat-noting their way through a string of seventies hits, whilst a young male poser in a blue denim top and jeans gyrated to impress in front of one of the daughter 'singers'. When a tone-deaf man who wasn't even Welsh unbuttoned the front of his shirt to reveal his jet black chest mane complete with gold medallion and began to whine his way through *Green Green Grass of Home* I decided to head back to my hotel, one of Scarborough's seventy or more such sleeping establishments.

I'd spent part of the afternoon in the library and not wishing to pay for entry into the castle, I'd walked on an elevated footpath around its walls. From there I'd looked down on the little harbour, much as the Royalists had looked down on the Parliamentarian troops in 1645 during their five-month siege of the castle. Then of course I'd looked out to sea – *Nelson* had been anchored three miles out from shore.

✦ ✦ ✦

The next morning wiled itself away. It began with a stroll along the seashore via Royal Albert Drive and Marine Drive. Lunch was a bag of chips eaten by the miniature fairground at the harbour (surely not *the* Scarborough Fair)! But eventually I found myself back at St. Nicholas Cliff, where I prowled around outside the Grand Hotel again. Something drew me back to the place.

The hotel, after financially enforced delays, had finally been opened in 1867 and had been named, (no prize for originality), the Cliff Hotel; it had taken four years to build and was the concept of a group of Yorkshire businessmen who'd formed a syndicate with the object of building a magnificent hotel (and incidentally making lots of brass), their vision inspired by the changing times.

The advent of the Industrial Revolution meant that *mucky* northern manufacturers became loaded with brass that put them on a financial par with the landed gentry. Combined with the coming of the railway in 1845, it meant that the town was set to become accessible to many more visitors.

The architect engaged to design the building was Cuthbert Brodrick, of Leeds; apparently his original concept was that the building would comprise four towers, twelve floors, 52 chimneys and 365 rooms, representing the seasons, months, weeks and days of the year, (the leap years had him stumped though). But anyway, it didn't quite work out like that, although upon completion it was never- the-less described by a Victorian (semi-illiterate) as: *The largest and hansomest hotel in Europe*. It was also said to incorporate an Italianate feel to it with elements of the French Second Empire thrown in – and it was the Continent's largest brick building with six million bricks and 40,000 cubic feet of stone used in its construction. (286)

I caught sight of a sign that no doubt explained why the hotel's doors had been locked the previous evening; it was mounted at the side of the hotel by the little souvenir shop and it read: THE HOTEL IS NOT OPEN TO NON-RESIDENTS. Perhaps the guests had been issued with bar-coded passes that opened the doors. But today I wasn't to be deterred; I watched and waited, and when an elderly couple climbed the steps under the Romanesque arch of the main entrance, I scooted along and tagged on behind them as if we were all together.

Inside, I cheekily strolled by the reception desk and sallied forth to the bar. Above, the huge domed ceiling had changed little from how it would have appeared in 1867, whilst behind the wide main staircase the ornamental cast iron balustrades stretched away sumptuously. I ventured seaward, took a right turn past the dining room and followed departing guests into a corridor. There I stumbled upon a little coffee shop.

The man behind the counter looked as if he'd once served as a butler in the *La Belle Epoque* days before the First War; at any rate he looked and talked like a gentleman. He was tall, elegant almost, and greyed at the temples – only the Edwardian sideburns were missing. I wondered how he was coping in these Butlinesque days.

'Have you had lunch Sir?' He asked as I stood trying to decide what to order.

'Err…yes thank you,' I said, trying not to think of the bag of chips.

'Do you fancy a scone Sir?' Now *that* was a strange thing to say I thought, although he'd seen that I was eyeing them up.

'No…no thank you.'

'Quite a big lunch I expect Sir?'

'Yes.'

'What can I get you then Sir?'

'Oh…just a coffee please.' He dispensed the coffee with an efficiently rarely witnessed in England these days and handed it to me with two small biscuits slid daintily onto the saucer.

'Thank you,' I said, proffering a note.

'No, that's alright Sir,' he said.

I waved the note towards him again.

'No that's quite alright Sir.' Now, suddenly, the penny dropped… and I had to bite my lip hard not to say: 'I'm not actually a resident.'

He'd thought I was offering him a generous tip, so now there was little option but to play out the situation. Either that, or I was going to be thrown out for sure, coffee-less and biscuit-less onto the street.

The corridor opened out into an impressively huge room at the extreme southern end of the building, which he saw me peeking into.

'You can take your coffee into the Ballroom,' he said – so I did.

It was an amazing room, once called the Coffee Room, and it was completely deserted. I sunk into a plush high-sided armchair, rested my coffee on a little table, nibbled a biscuit and stared up at the domed roof with its ornamental plasterwork. Ruth would love it here. Cherubs blew on long horns in decadent opulence somewhere up there, but my mind was already wandering… Had this been the room in which the ball had been given by the Mayor and Scarborough Corporation in honour of the visit of the fleet in June 1930? I was sure it was.

That week in June 1930 had been memorable for the town in many ways – not only because of the Fleet visit. It was also *Home Week*, incorporating the Peasholm fair, the coronation of Scarborough's Queen of the Roses, together with swimming displays and aquatic sports at the bathing pool. To top the lot, the National Association of Master Bakers had held a conference in the town. Nothing was half-baked though – the Mayor rose well to each and every occasion.

Sitting alone in the coffee room I could almost feel eerie vibrations floating through the air towards me: The foxtrots and waltzes of Victor Haythorne's Dance Band permeated the room, suffused my mind. The officers of *Nelson*, *Barham* and *Malaya* were here too with me. The Commander-in-Chief Atlantic Fleet, Admiral Sir Michael Hodges had just made a short speech and had pronounced a toast; it was a Tuesday, so it would have been to – *Our Men*. Now the officers partook of supper and some wandered over to the large windows on the seaward side of the room and peered out to where, three miles out to sea, the sailors and marines were already in their hammocks.

I sipped my coffee – an intruder here I knew. Dad could never have dreamt of these surroundings, and I'd cheated to get in here now. I pulled out from my pocket a photocopy of the newspaper report of *Nelson's* departure from Scarborough, stared seaward and read the report:

HMS Nelson sailed for Guernsey at 8 o'clock on Wednesday evening. Crowds assembled at various points to see the Flagship of the Atlantic Fleet depart; it is no doubt true to say that there were regrets on both sides at the end of a remarkably successful visit.

It continued: *The Nelson steamed slowly past her consorts, inshore of them, and then turned and headed directly out to sea, where she was lost to view within an hour. (287)*

It was the last time I'd visualise the spectre of *Nelson* out at sea during this small-circle circumnavigation of the UK and beyond – Guernsey and all points south would be for another time if I had enough of it left in my life. But for now I had to pick up the tracks of one of Dad's other ships for a last time – *Tiger*.

I almost had to wipe a tear away from my eye. Almost – but the trouble is, nostalgia's not what it used to be.

25. Coincidences

When I was a boy my parents bought me a book. It was one of those books without a sleeve, bound instead with covers of thick board; it would probably fetch quite a bit these days at an antique fair – that is if I hadn't used it as a dartboard when I was a boy. It was a very British book, English even. On its inside covers St. George was portrayed in silver armour with a flowing red cape, wearing a basinet from which flourished red, white and blue ostrich plumes. He was mounted on a dashing white steed that reared up with its mouth gaping as his lance pierced the heart of a purple winged dragon with a long-curled red tongue and smoke puffing from its nostrils.

I still have the book – it's called *The Boy's Book of Heroes*. On its cover a boy lays in a meadow reading that very book, gazing into infinity whilst all around him the images of heroes float in the air like phantoms. I would never sell the book because it crystallises the things that made the world I'd grown up in and the people who'd made it that way. But I always wondered about these great people, the heroes in the book – what made them tick, drove them, influenced them. Was their greatness something they'd been born with, or did the environment or *their* heroes influence them? My hero was Dad of course, but a close second came a schoolmaster named Mr Martin. I was thirteen and devoid of academic interest, languishing in the *relegation zone* of the class table, but he stirred something within me – made me believe in myself.

The librarian at Southend Central Library sent me a microfiche photocopied extract taken from *The Southend Standard* that brought back all these thoughts, but then also (unfortunately) made me cynically question the motives of the captain of HMS *Tiger*, Captain Campbell, V.C., D.S.O., RN.

A party of 80 schoolboys, the pupils of Alleyn Court School, Westcliff on Sea, had visited the ship, (*fetched off in Tiger's drifter*), together with their headmaster – a Mr Wilcox, who'd been an *auld acquaintance* of the Captain's when he'd taught him at Dulwich many years before. The article concluded:

Before the party left the ship, Mr. Wilcox expressed hearty thanks to Captain Campbell and his officers; the boys giving loud cheers for them. Responding, the Captain remarked that if Mr Wilcox had not at one time been his own master, he, himself, would probably not have been where he was that day. (288)

Had this relationship between master and pupil been the real reason why *Tiger* had anchored off Shoeburyness for a fortnight in the spring of 1927? How much licence did the Captain have in determining where the gunnery training ship would carry out her program of heavy gun practice? Why hadn't Portsmouth been the venue, after all HMS *Excellent* was where the Navy's gunnery school was based? Or was I just being unfair? Had it just been a coincidence? After all a battery had been built in 1918 at Yantlet Creek on the Isle of Grain in order that the navy's heavy guns could fire up to the top of the Maplin Sands off Foulness Island; it was where ammunition development trials had been carried out prior to the manufacture of the production pattern of the guns for *Nelson* and *Rodney*. (289)

✦ ✦ ✦

Whatever the reasons for Shoeburyness being chosen, it determined that I found myself sitting one lunchtime in The Shore House, a modern family pub with a high apex teak roof, positioned opposite the coastguard station, just off the promenade. I felt totally out of place here, alone – surrounded by noisy Essex families heartily devouring Saturday lunches, whilst their sticky toddlers ran up and down to the fun factory. It was early autumn and I'd driven down for the day to try and capture a brief taste of the place.

I confess, I'd never heard of Shoeburyness until I'd seen it on a page of *Tiger's* ship's log. I'd heard of The Nore – an anchorage situated south of it, just off the Isle of Grain and much frequented by the English fleet during the wars of the 17th and 18th centuries. This had been where Richard Parker, an ex-officer had led a mutiny in 1797 and where he was hanged two weeks later from the yardarm of his ship HMS *Sandwich* – in fact he'd had the good sense to jump, to avoid the otherwise slow strangulation. (290)

Tiger had, in 1927, been anchored just north of The Nore – in Lea Reach, at latitude 134°, just out from the end of Southend Pier, and although I'd been to Southend before, I'd never been on the pier or made the four-mile trek further east to Shoeburyness. (291)

The beach at Shoebury was a mixture of shingle and sand, banked by the high tide and dotted with upturned rowing boats. Small craft were moored out from the shore whilst a few unmoored ones scudded about with no apparent aim other than to enjoy the sunny day. To the east of the coastguard station was a palisade fence, the other side of which was still MOD property. Warning signs abounded, one read: WARNING – THIS AREA MAY CONTAIN UNEXPLODED OBJECTS WHICH

MUST NOT BE TOUCHED OR MOVED. It was what I expected, because Shoeburyness was known as *Gunners' Town*.

After the end of the Napoleonic wars in 1815, the artillery-testing site at Plumstead Marshes near to Woolwich Arsenal was becoming a hazard to passing shipping in the Thames – not to mention farmers complaining about their hay fields catching fire. So in 1849 the Board of Ordinance purchased land at the Ness to set up a new testing range at Shoebury. (292)

At the time, things were developing fast in ship design and in ordinance. In 1837, the French had introduced a shell gun; a powder-filled projectile that could make big round holes in little wooden ships. A naval race was now in progress between the French and the British, so that by 1860 both countries had built ironclads, (the first action between armoured vessels though in fact took place in 1862 during the American Civil War). The first rifled breechloader had arrived in Shoebury in 1854, and the arrival of the ironclad inevitably led to the desire for a more powerful gun, the development of which was largely undertaken on the marshes at Shoebury.

One of the more famous trials involved the bolting together of three, 5 inch steel plates to represent the hull of HMS *Warrior*, which they then preceded to pound with 300 lb. shells. The first weapon that could penetrate this armour at 1,000 yards was brought to Shoebury in about 1864; it was called *Big Will* after its designer. He was indeed a big boy, with a 15-ft. barrel, he knew how to penetrate, the problem was he was so big and heavy that nobody had yet built a warship that he could mount himself on to do the deed. (293)

In 1876 the *Terrible Infant* arrived, this was the latest in a series of muzzle-loading guns that were known as the *Woolwich Infants* because they were looked after like a baby and because of the cradles that were used to transport them. When this 81-ton monster was fired, it let out a deafening roar, accompanied by a volume of flame and a cloud of smoke, whilst the ground beneath it shook. It recoiled over thirty feet, twenty of which were up a steep incline. The inhabitants of Shoebury were not exactly enamoured by this noisy baby – it shattered the windows of their houses, wrenched doors from their hinges, showered them with plaster from ceilings and cracked shop plate glass windows from top to bottom. (294)

By 1927 then Shoebury residents had had over fifty years to get used to the banging that went on thereabouts, so that when HMS *Tiger* arrived for two weeks of heavy firing they already knew the score. The Admiralty though covered themselves by informing *The Southend Standard* and issuing warning notices. *The Standard* reported: *Warning notices have been issued to residents on each side of the Thames Estuary to open their windows when signals are hoisted to indicate that firing is to take place, as the Admiralty will not take responsibility for any damage that might be caused by the shattering of panes of glass.* (295)

I drove from The Shore House into Shoebury itself to take a peek at what was left of the *Gunners' Town* and the Garrison. The High Street area had been designated a conservation area in 1981, as also had much of the old Garrison, including Horseshoe Barracks, the Gatehouse and the Clock tower. The ramparts of the Garrison probably go back to the Iron Age, and it seems that just about everyone invading England used the site for military purposes, from the Romans to the Saxons and the Danes.

The last regiment left the station in 1976 and the MOD sold off the majority of the 180-acre site in 2000 to Gladedale Homes. As I drove past, the signs were out advertising: *Stunning new and refurbished homes, parkland and nature reserve on a site steeped in history. 5 bed Victorian homes and 2 large refurbished apartments.*

Leaving the car parked back at The Shore House, I walked into Southend. The prom was bordered by a seawall from which the occasional set of concrete steps led down to the beach, whilst on the landward side, I passed a row of highly prized possessions, hundreds of them – beach huts. Although mostly white with black roofs, many had been painted externally in alternating colours and personalised with quaint and cosy names like Dels Den, The shoe box, Bilz hut, The Shambles and Just 4 us.

Despite the time of the year, the promenade was still busy with strollers, dog walkers, joggers and aged leather clad motorcyclists who sat around in groups on the seawall catching the late-season sun. The transition from Shoebury into Southend was evidenced by the emergence of beach stalls and amusements, (all of which were open and doing good business), that led the way to Southend's focal point, its pier.

The anchorage of *Tiger* had been at Leigh Reach, somewhere at the end of the 1.34 mile long pier, which I proposed to walk. I didn't have to pay for this privilege, but still had to obtain a ticket to get through the turnstile. Most people caught the train.

The predecessor to the present train was an electric tramway known as the *toast rack*, which came into service in 1890 and which in its 59-year lifetime carried 65 million passengers. The tramway was opened a year after the new iron pier was constructed as a replacement for the original 1830 wooden one. The new pier was extended, eight years later, to a length of 7,080 feet, making it then a world record length for a pier. When *Tiger* had anchored in Lea Reach in 1927, the eastern (Prince

George Steamer) extension, that would make it even longer, was still two years away from completion. (296)

It was a long, windy and boring walk to the end of the pier and I continually expected to see the quarter-mile-markers a lot sooner than they actually appeared. The passing back and forth of the little white and maroon train was all there was to break the monotony. It passed, tooting its horn provocatively, four times during the walk out, loaded with old fogies like me, and kids waving candy-stripe windmills. By the side of the world famous McGinty's pub and restaurant I stopped to purchase a hotdog at a snack bar; half-cooked for an obscenely short period of time in a microwave, it was disgusting, no less than a disaster.

Disasters it seems were a frequent visitor to the pier; it'd suffered four major ones since the end of the war but unlike the hotdog, mostly of the overcooked sort. In 1959 the wooden pavilion at the shore end of the pier caught fire, cutting off three hundred people who had to climb down the pier structure and board boats to escape. In 1976 another fire, this time at the wet end, completely gutted the 1908 pier head, whilst in the summer of 1995 yet another finished off the shore end bowling alley where bowling balls could be seen sizzling into the sea. (296)

At the end of the pre-1929 pier I continued on the slim connecting walkway, passing through a *Polo Mint* of a building and emerging onto the 45° angled steamer extension. Here, a bubbly young foreign foursome asked me to take their photograph against the sandwich-backdrop of dark blue sea, chalk blue sky – and with the thin smear of Southend in the middle for a filling.

At the very end of the pier I climbed some steps to what looked like the newly timbered transom of a ship, but which was in fact a sun deck, enclosed by rails painted carmine red. Half-a-dozen wrought iron seats faced out to the three seaward sides, all freshly painted a shiny black. At the end of the deck, cantilevered from a concrete post, hung a ship's bell inscribed: M & S LONDON 1929, placed there to commemorate the opening of the extension by HRH Prince George, the Duke of Kent, (although I couldn't imagine why Mr Spencer and Mr Marks might have attended the ceremony?)

During the war, the Admiralty, who'd taken over the pier, renamed it HMS *Leigh*, after Lea Reach; it had then served as a convoy assembly point. So now, actually below me, clear of the shallow-water mudflats, would be the Reach itself – the anchorage of HMS *Tiger* in 1927. (298)

I stood for a moment, realising that I'd tracked my last anchorage of the great battle cruiser. I'd followed this *old lady* from the Isle of Wight along the south coast of England to Scilly, over to Bangor in Northern

Ireland, up to the Isle of Arran in Scotland and back down to Shoebury – It was a poignant moment.

From the end of the pier I looked across the Thames Estuary to Sheerness in Kent; to the right, I picked out the Isle of Grain, and between the two was, I knew, the mouth of the River Medway, narrowing as it snaked its way through mud flats the twelve miles or so, more or less west, to Chatham – my last port of call before the run home back to Pompey.

✦ ✦ ✦

JINXED – SOUTHEND PIER RAVAGED BY FOURTH FIRE, read the headlines. The fire, on Sunday the 9th of October 2005, shortly after my visit, destroyed the entire pier head, its railway station and an amusement arcade. McGinty's pub, a restaurant, an ice cream shop and toilet facilities collapsed into the Thames Estuary, taking part of the pier's wooden floor, (and I hoped the half-baked hot-dog snack bar), with them into the sea. The heat buckled the tracks of the railway and eyewitnesses said that the flames leapt 40 feet into the air. Seventy-five fire fighters tried to quell the flames. The blaze, the newspaper said, was *the biggest setback in the pier's 175-year history.* The owners of the pier, Southend Borough Council were, it was reported, in the grip of a financial crisis, so officials said that (even optimistically) it would take two years to repair the damage.

The report said that the cause of the blaze was not yet known: *...but it is certainly being treated as suspicious. This is a routine assessment until arson can be ruled out.* (297) (298)

Now Guv, I know I'd visited the Grand Hotel in Plymouth a month before it caught fire, and I know I was in Newcastle the day they had to close the station, but honest Guv, it wasn't me. It was a coincidence Guv, honest – just like the coincidence that made Captain Campbell choose Shoeburyness as HMS *Tiger's* venue for two weeks of heavy gun practice in March 1927.

Looking west from Southend pier.

26.   Squaring The Small Circle

'Everything you organise is for what *you* want to do isn't it,' Ruth chided, 'its all for *you – you – you*. You're a TOAD.' She shouted.

We were staying in the Holiday Inn on the outskirts of Rochester. The weather had taken a turn towards winter and a chilling wind cut into us as we made our way across the car park to reception. In the morning Ruth preferred the warmth of the hotel to tramping around Chatham, so I set off early and alone along the A229.

Dad, it has to be said, only spent two days in Chatham – well two days one hour and three minutes to be precise. According to the ship's log, this was to enable the Vice Admiral to make some official calls and to inspect the Reserve Fleet ships. (299) It was June 1935; rumblings of strife were heard from all around the world, and everyone felt there were darker days ahead. War was to be just a matter of time…the only ray of sunlight was the celebrations for King George Vs Silver Jubilee. (300) Dad had joined HMS *Effingham* in Rosyth; she had been on her way down to Spithead for the Jubilee Review Day and had just popped into Chatham. He never even made it into the dockyard proper.

At the beginning of Queen Victoria's reign, when Britain ruled the waves with an expanding navy, the only direction in which the dockyard could grow was east, in an area known as St Mary's Creek, below a marshland known as St Mary's Island. The creek was converted into three interconnecting basins each 700ft. wide. The Corps of Royal Engineers headed its construction, although convict labour did the spadework. The undertaking was completed in 1885. (301) It was where *Effingham* had moored and where I headed after I'd parked the car.

A disenchanting pedestrian shopping precinct and spew pools on the pavement along Dock Road didn't endear me to the place during the half-an-hour walk to the basins. Only the old dockyard gates, a bleakly situated pub called The Royal Marine and the figure of Field Marshall Earl Kitchener, proudly mounted on his horse on the slopes of a hillock, made an impression.

Dock Road leads into Maritime Way that divides, as it runs onto St Mary's Island, the western No.1 basin from the eastern No.2 basin. The western basin was the first to be opened in 1872 and is now Chatham's Maritime Marina, but I trod the deserted red and grey block-paved edge of No.2 basin towards *Effingham's* 1935 berth in No.3 basin. Lining its northern edge were blocks of smart and expensive waterside apartments, whilst Chatham Maritime Quayside bordered its southern edge, an assortment of large red brick and glass constructed office buildings. The waterfront leading past them was dotted with dual-cantilevered pseudo gas lampposts and brightly painted black and white mooring posts that would no longer fulfil their designed use.

No.3 basin is the longest of the three basins and is connected to the river Medway by two locks. I could see cranes in the distance but, as I approached, noticed what appeared to be a black painted, spike-topped, steel palisade fence and a locked gate. I climbed on a mooring post to get a better view and imagined HMS *Effingham* moored there. It was the closest I could get to the basin; beyond the locked gate were parked cars and the land was privately owned.

I walked back disgruntled – south, and then tracked east along the pavement of the A289, climbing a pedestrian road-bridge to cross it. Unexpectedly, a view emerged of the elusive No.3 basin. Medway Ports owned the land now; forklift trucks stood amidst stacks of sheeted, steel-banded, number-stencilled timber.

At the next roundabout, I took a brief look at the entrance to the basin and the quayside that I was unable to tread. A Portakabin, complete with security guard, stood in the central island between two red-and-white barber-pole security barriers that barred my way. I turned south – the scenery was bleak. Dad would have thought himself lucky that he only had to spend a couple of days here. For one thing, I came across only one pub standing silently at a strange looking road junction; it was called Bridge House – but its windows were boarded up and its pub days were definitely over. Now, it was just a sad and lonely building. It seemed to me to symbolise the loss of the Royal Navy in Chatham.

✦ ✦ ✦

We left early next morning; it was going to be a long day. I pulled off the M25 at Leatherhead onto the A24. Then at Beare Green, I headed down the A29 into West Sussex towards the South Downs.

Cousin Michael, who I'd contacted via cousin Eric, had sent me a well-researched genealogy of the Pinnock family going back to 1791. My great, great, great, great Grandfather, Thomas, had lived in a little village that we eventually found still nestling snugly below the downs, just as quiet and rural now as it had been in his day almost 250 years before. Ruth stayed in the car reading, whilst I stalked around the churchyard squinting at lichen-covered headstones above the bones of many strangers – none of whom was my ancestor.

We continued to drive west, along dangerously snaking, one-car width lanes, tooting the car horn madly through blind bends to the next village, this time the home of my great great Grandfather Francis who was born in 1816 – where I repeated the unsuccessful churchyard process.

Now driving southwest, we crossed to the southern side of the downs, across the Midhurst to Chichester road, to where my great Grandfather Frank had lived, (all the time following the sign of the hedge sparrow) and stopped at one of those low-oak-beamed country pubs. We ordered food and, whilst awaiting it, I studied the family tree and read the notes cousin Michael had sent me.

There were a few surprises: My great Grandmother Emily, who'd given birth to my Grandmother in a workhouse had, it appeared, become a bigamist upon marrying my Grandfather. Another of my ancestors had drowned in a quicksand, whilst a few others had died in the madhouse. But the real gem was a farmhand called Luke, who'd married my Grandfather's sister. He, so local gossip said, was an adulterer and whilst working in the harvest field one day was struck by something. It was lightening, and it killed him – an event that was regarded by the local community as a divine punishment from God. I must remember not to walk through any harvest fields when there are black clouds in the sky. (302) What a family Dad had! What a family *I* had!

✦ ✦ ✦

Since 450 BC, when an Ionian called Anaxagoras (born in what is today Turkey) first tried to construct a square with an area equal to that of a circle, man had been obsessed with squaring the circle. Until that is, a German called Lindemann in 1880 finally proved that however much you try, pi will never come out even, and so the circle can never be exactly squared. (303) This is how things had proved for me too – the final leg back to Pompey would complete a small geographical circle, but it too could never be squared – not perfectly.

There were things I'd been unable to discover in my travels, things I would probably never know for sure: Why *Tiger's* visit to Scilly had apparently not been reported? Where exactly Dad had landed to carry out a covert training exercise on those islands? Whether he happened to have been on the starboard watch aboard *Nelson* on Monday the 14th of September 1931, had taken shore leave and had attended those meetings in the canteen and at Black Park football ground before the mutiny at Invergordon? And I would never know for sure why *Nelson* had visited Odda in June 1930. But the biggest mystery had been the ship to which he'd been attached for six weeks in the summer of 1944, the 'ship' whose name described what I was just about to complete, a long and eventful journey – HMS *Odyssey*.

I'd still not been able to unearth exactly where Dad had landed in Normandy. The archivist at the Royal Marine's Museum told me I needed to know the naval party number to which Dad had been attached. So I contacted the Public Records Office again, who re-directed me to DPS (N) 2, in Portsmouth, who months later returned my money and told me that the PRO actually held the appropriate record! Another circle, but one certainly not squared. For now, I'd have to be content with the visit I'd made to Bembridge on the Isle of Wight where I'd looked out at the Nab Tower to the spot where *maybe* his craft had rendezvoused with others before the landings.

My second rule also sometimes proved difficult to apply; several times I'd been unable to follow exactly in Dad's footsteps. I bitterly regretted, for instance, not walking on the Admiralty pier at Invergordon when I had the chance, (even allowing for the fact, that it wasn't the same 1931 one). There was also Haldon Pier in Torquay, upon which I'd been prevented from treading because of the Living Coasts project, and then there was the dead-end I'd reached at No.2 basin in Chatham. With those exceptions though, I couldn't think of many other pieces of space where Dad had been that I'd been unable to go. I say pieces of space because time changes everything, especially man made things; buildings are knocked down and piers and jetties are built where once there was sea.

But then I thought of the successes. I'd learnt of Dad's part in the Chanak crisis and, thanks to Steve, had trodden the ground around berths 38 and 39 in Southampton docks from where Dad had sailed to Turkey. Somehow I'd managed a tour of the Commando Training Centre at Lympstone, and I'd discovered that the MNBDO1 road to Egypt had been the correct one to take, which had led to Donald showing me around the King George V Dock at Clydeport. I'd discovered Dad's secrets about the Invergordon Mutiny and had followed his ships *Effingham*, *Tiger* and *Nelson* around the country and beyond. I'd visited Dad's tug-of-war venues at Dorchester, Bournemouth and Poole – and I'd even run my hand over a small bit of old Nellie's woodwork.

I'd done all of this because – well – I'd loved the old boy, and missed him still. I'd felt very close to him lots of times, particularly during the quiet moments after long treks: Looking out to sea from Arnish point near Stornoway and from the cliffs at Gaitnip near Kirkwall. Then there was that magic moment alone in the ballroom of the Grand Hotel at Scarborough – and of course there were the pubs.

But the net I'd dropped at the start of this quest had yielded more types of fish than I'd set out to catch: I'd found a lot of unexpected history in a host of places stretching from Scilly up to Odda, I'd seen a real live ghost in a Scottish hotel room that had changed my view of death, if not of life – and I'd met a lot of people.

There was my cousin Eric of course, Bob the young Royal Marine Commando at Lympstone, Robert, the retired Captain from Dartmouth, who, if he were now still alive, would be 92 years young. Then there was the melodious MI5 Agent Orange Sunhat in Plymouth, and Brian from Falmouth who'd greeted me at his door with a kitchen knife. My mind then spun up to Northern Ireland and to another Brian who I'd met in the Ormedu Arms in Bangor, who just wanted someone to love him and not to pity him for being disabled. In Scotland there was Stuart from the Arran Heritage Museum, old Davie from Invergordon, Malcolm from Stornoway and Robbie and Johnny from Orkney, whilst in Norway I thought of Lars from the workers' cottages. I recalled all their faces, and with each, the experiences that went with them came flooding back.

✦ ✦ ✦

These thoughts passed through my mind as Ruth and I drove slowly east along Southsea promenade. Passing South Parade Pier I turned left along St Helens Parade and drove past the Canoe Lake. It was here when I was five that, wearing a white sun hat, I'd stretched too far with my net try to scoop up a shrimp, and had disappeared into a phantasmagoric bubbly subaqueous world for what seemed like ages, before being pulled out by a leg. It was the only part of me that Dad could see above the water. I was still wearing my sunhat when he landed me. It was the first time I'd seen the amphibious world.

✦ ✦ ✦

The argument started because I'd swore several times trying to park the car somewhere off Eastern Parade.

'Where is it? – Miles away I suppose? – Can't you park any closer?'

'No – I can't,' I said grouchily – it's all double yellow lines, there's *nowhere* to park around there. We'll have to walk.'

'I don't know why we have to go there anyway,' Ruth moaned, ' I bet it's a dive! Do they do food? – I'm hungry!'

'Last time I was there I had a cheese and pickle sandwich,' I said – and you *know* why I want to go...because I went there four years ago. I want to see if something is still there.'

'Well *you* go then – I'll stay in the car.'

'No, I want *you* to come too Ruth.'

'Why, because it suits you now – you usually don't want me – you say that I just slow you down, stop you from doing things...but now, *now* – it suits you.'

We entered the RMA Tavern in a strained silence. It was empty apart from the landlord and one customer. I ordered drinks and then asked the bearded, bald-headed landlord if they served food.

'No, I'm afraid not,' he said apologetically.

'Not even sandwiches?'

'No, sorry.'

Ruth sat miserably at a little round table whilst I ordered two packets of crisps. I looked around the barroom; the pool table still stood in the centre, but the jukebox by the door had gone. The stone fireplace was still there, but it had been bricked-up and an altogether smarter looking gas fire sat on a burnished stone hearth in front of it. Above the fireplace the framed scroll that had displayed the potted history of the RMA had gone, as had the TV – replaced now by a clock, whilst wood panelling had been added either side of the fireplace.

'It's changed a bit since I was here last,' I said to the landlord.

'How long ago was that? He asked.

'About four years I think.'

'Yes – we did it up about two years ago,' he said, 'I've been here about three years.'

The most noticeable change was to the bar itself. Now wood panelled throughout and rounded. What had previously been two bars, public and lounge, was now one. The support column, whose safe structural re-moval had somehow been engineered, had disappeared along with the Royal Marine enlistment poster that had once been fixed to it – the thing I'd come to see.

I'd wanted to take another look at the poster again because, in the in-tervening years, I'd discovered what *Galloons* were – those things that had enabled: *The Private Marine to make sufficient prize money to ren-der himself and family comfortable for life.* I'd found the answer on an Internet site: *By the best Computation, that could be made of the sudden, they cannot be fewer than one hundred and fifty Ships of all Sorts; and severall of them called Galloons and Galleasses, are of a Size never seene before in our Seas, and appear on the Surface of the Water like floating Castles.* (304) The Galloons then were ships of the Spanish Ar-mada.

Ruth and I sat munching our crisps sullenly and in hostile silence at the table.

'So what other little plans have you got lined up for us today?' Ruth finally asked sarcastically – 'apart from you, for some weird reason, wanting to go swimming?'

'Just a walk down onto the beach,' I said – and I *really* want you to come down with me.'

'For what? You did that last time we were here!'

'That was years ago. I just need you to come down, that's all.'

'It's too cold and there's nothing to see.'

'It just seems appropriate that's all – the end of the book – you know?'

'What the hell are you going to amuse yourself with then Mike – once that's finished? You'll be lost.'

'That's why I want you to walk down on the beach with me...it's kind of a symbolic moment – you know – the start of a new life.'

'Hmm, I can guess what sort of a life you're thinking of. I bet it involves us travelling around like tramps.'

'No, not really...I was thinking more...more of a motor home.'

'A motor home! I'm not going to live in a bloody motor home!'

'Not live...well not all the time... but we could have very long holidays – travel around Southern Europe – you like the sunshine don't you?'

'How long are you thinking of, three weeks?'

'No...I was thinking... of about... three months.'

'Three months! You must be joking! You think I'm going to leave my house for three months!'

'Why not?'

'Who's going to mow the lawns and clean the house then?'

'We could make some arrangement – pay someone to come in. We could even rent it out.'

'No way – I'm not going to have strangers roaming around *my* house.'

'But we could...'

'No way.' She said. 'You can forget *that* idea.'

'You won't even consider it then – think about it for a while?'

'No way.'

'OK,' I said, 'I need to go to the loo.'

I was gone longer than usual...

The framed scroll describing the potted history of the RMA had been preserved, I discovered, relocated on a wall en route to the gents. In its centre was a leaf, each frond of which contained a letter of the alphabet crammed with the names in miniscule of all those who'd served in the Corps. At the bottom of the leaf was the globe, granted by King George IV in place of 109 battle honours earned by the marines, and around the globe was wrapped their motto: *Per Mare Per Terram* – By Sea By Land – believed to have been used for the first time in 1775 at Bunker Hill. The leaf was encircled by two laurels, granted to the Corps for gallantry at Belle Isle in 1761, when they obtained their Royal status. Around each laurel was entwined the names of the places in which they'd served. Some were places to which Dad had also travelled: Gibraltar (1704), Jamaica (1782), Brest (1794), The Nile (1798), Malta (1799), Navarino (1827) and Canton (1858)...

By the time I returned to the bar, Ruth had her coat on and was ready to leave.

✦ ✦ ✦

Opposite the one-time barracks, where the ghost marine bugler is supposed to have emerged from the wicket gate before sunset and crossed the main road on his way down to the water's edge, I too crunched down through the shingle that occasionally poked up brown fern-like marine weeds. A pale sun squinted through innocent looking clouds that clung low in the sky above the Isle of Wight and pooled a glinting silver strip across the sea to the shore. Groups of seagulls stood on the shingle facing the stiff north wind. Below the ridge of shingle washed up by high tides, two joggers, togged out in woolly hats and gloves, were making their way towards me along the firm strip of sand that ran parallel to the shore.

I looked across towards Bembridge. It had been three-and-a-half years since I'd sat outside that little café and looked over to the Nab and then across to where I now stood. Crossing Spithead to the Isle of Wight had been the first of twenty-one sea trips I'd made on thirteen craft.

I could never become a Royal Marine – George Eliot was wrong – but I reckoned I'd travelled by sea and by land undertaking amphibious operations *like* a marine and so in my mind I proudly wore the badge of the Royal Marines – the Globe & Laurel. But the gut-wrenching travel thing was still there, and a larger circle beckoned. To the east of Bembridge across the open sea, the next landfall was Normandy. I still didn't know where Dad had landed in June 1944, but hadn't given up hope of some-day finding out.

✦ ✦ ✦

Ruth elected to stay in the car with her Danielle Steel book, so I descended alone the steps that led down to the entrance to the pool.

Men of the Royal Marine Artillery had built Eastney Swimming Pool in 1905. It was where Dad had passed his swimming test in 1921. The roof of the main pool area had been completely re-built since then, but the building's redbrick exterior was unchanged and some tiles were missing from the roofs of the side buildings. Perhaps this was why, as I entered, I felt the cold creep into me.

Crouching in the diving position as if at the start of a race, I felt the coldness begin to gnaw into my bones. My body temperature began to fall – down – down – down – until it reached the frosty temperature of the day outside. My body too began to feel oddly unfamiliar as if it were emerging from a metamorphose; the texture of my skin felt crinkled up like an parchment, my back seemed rough and bumpy, my feet felt swollen and my throat felt saggy. My eyes too were swollen and tired. I closed them, held my arms out in front of me and took a deep breath. It did not seem like a normal breath; it swelled up inside me like a helium balloon, as if I'd sucked the whole universe into my lungs.

Hitting the water, my estranged body glided beneath it smoothly and slowly; then I began a frog kick. In that moment I knew why Dad had said that swimming was one of the most beautiful feelings in the world. I knew then how he'd performed those sub aqueous handstands. I saw his face clearly. And then that phantasmagoric bubbly subaqueous world returned again – this time with nobody there to fish me out. But it didn't matter I was with Dad now – and still I was swimming underwater – on and on, but in a way I never had before – effortlessly, on and on and on – feeling the water flow over me, under me, behind me, around me, through me. And in that moment I knew who I was, who I'd become. Now I was truly – an amphibian.

Eastney beach, looking across Spithead to the Isle of Wight.

Notes

Chapter 2

(1) www.civvie-street.co.uk. There are six elements to the badge of the Royal Marines:
1. At the top – The Lion and the Crown – Awarded the title Royal by King George III in 1802.
2. Below it – The scroll *Gibraltar* – Commemorating its capture and defence.
3. Below it – The Globe – Granted by King George IV in 1827 in place of 109 battle honours the Marines earned.
4. Encircling the Globe – The Laurels (two)– Granted for gallantry in the capture of Belle Isle in 1761.
5. Below the Globe and trapped by the bottom of the two Laurels – The Fouled Anchor – The badge of The Lord High Admiral, first worn by the Marines in 1747.
6. Below the Laurels and the Fouled Anchor – The scroll *Per Mare Per Terram*. (By Sea By Land) – The Corps Motto, believed to have been used for the first time in 1775 at Bunker Hill.
(2) The Demise of Demon Drink – Portsmouth Pubs 1900 – 1950 – The Portsmouth Papers No. 58 – Philip Eley & R. C. Riley – p3.
(3) From the Syd Goodman Collection.

Chapter 3

(4) Hail & Fairwell – Royal Marines Historical Society – Wilfred Davey – pp3 and 9.
(5) Burke's Peerage.
(6) Letter to the author dated 19th July 2001, from M G Little – The Royal Marines Museum.
(7) By Sea By Land – James D. Ladd – p122.
(8) Letter to the author dated 16th Sep. 2002, from Denise Coe, Dover Group – Kent County Council.

Chapter 4

(9) By Sea By Land – James D. Ladd – p122.
(10) Information from my late friend Pete Masterton.
(11) Portsmouth Museum and Records Office.
(12) Waterlooville and District its History and Development – A J C Reger, taken from The Rate paper – September 1961.
(13) Waterlooville – A Pictorial History – Barry Stapleton.
(14) The Norton Lightweight Twins – Andy Sochanik, (Internet site).
(15) In December 2004 I met, for the first time since childhood, three of my other cousins (all brothers), and one of them told me that the argument that resulted in my Dad not speaking to his brother had not been, as I'd thought, caused by George having Gran put in an asylum, but was because George's wife had, when Gran had died, burnt lots of the family photographs.

Chapter 5

(16) Waterlooville and District its History and Development – A. J. C Reger, taken from The Rate paper – September 1961.

(17) The Times – 7th February 1921.

(18) Hail & Fairwell – Royal Marines Historical Society – Wilfred Davey – p29.

(19) Britain's Sea Soldiers Volumes 1 & 2 – pp261-263.

(20) Portsmouth – In Defence of the Realm – John Sadden – p31.

(21) Portsmouth – In Defence of the Realm – John Sadden – p36.

(22) Public Records office Kew – ADM 157/172.

(23) The Call of the Sea – Steve Humphries – p12.

(24) Hail & Fairwell – Royal Marines Historical Society – Wilfred Davey – p40.

(25) R.M. Business No1 – 5 (Jan 1944-Aug 1945) BR1006, p40.

Chapter 6

(26) The Resurrection of the Mary Rose – Bernard Eaton – Divernet Diver Magazine – October 2002.

(27) Portsmouth – In Defence of the Realm – John Sadden – p136.

(28) Public Records office Kew – ADM 53/96593.

(29) Ryde Pier – The Heritage Trail © 1998-2005 – Heritage Trail Publications Ltd. Also – National Piers Society, (both Internet sites).

(30) BBC MM11 – h2g2 – Sandown Pier, Isle of Wight A492022, (Internet site).

(31) Isle of Wight Chronicle – 11th July 1935.

(32) My notes from HMS *Effingham's* log were disappointingly incomplete as I'd recorded only a single compass reading of 122 degrees – Yarborough Monument, (up on Culver Cliff, to the east of Sandown Bay), at a distance of 2.85 miles. Three compass readings were normally taken which then enabled a ship's exact position or fix to be established. That omission meant that I was unsure of *Effingham's* exact position.

(33) Isle of Wight Chronicle – 18th July 1935.
Isle of Wight Chronicle – 1st August 1935.

(35) The France and Germany Star was awarded for operational service in France, Belgium, the Netherlands, Germany, the North Sea, English Channel and Bay of Biscay.

(36) An old ex-marine wrote to me with a list of casualties from HMS *Odyssey*; the locations listed were various and indefinable – Normandy, Rouen, France and Belgium. I also had two e-mails. One was from a lady whose uncle was attached to *Odyssey* and who had been posthumously awarded the George Medal for his actions at Ouistreham in the Netherlands. The second was from a man who'd visited the Royal Marines Museum, had been left alone for a short period, and who'd *acquired*, (his word), certain information the possession of which, he worried might contravene the Official Secrets Act – as it broke the *Seventy Year Rule*.

(37) The Royal Marines – Julian Thompson, p323 – Ref. The Royal Marines J.L. Moulton – p79 – (Leo Cooper, 1962).

(38) Public Records Office Kew – ADM 202/449.

(39) A Rough Passage – Stan Blacker, taken from – Royal Marines and D-Day – p29 – Royal Marines Historical Society.

(40) The Nab Tower –The Forelands Homepage, (Internet site).

(41) The County Down Spectator – 14th July 1928.

(42) The Metal Fighting Ship in the Royal Navy 1860-1970 – E.H.H.Archibald – p89.
(43) Letter to the author – from F Stone, Watlington – undated.
(44) The Big Gun – Peter Hodges – pp62-63.
(45) The Royal Marines – Julian Thompson – p132.

Chapter 7

(46) First World War.com – Who's Who – King Alexander I – original material © Michael Duffy 2000-03.
(47) The Decline and Fall of Lloyd George – Lord Beaverbrook – p152 – (Collins – 1963).
(48) Naval Policy Between the Wars – Stephen Roskill – p197.
(49) Ataturk – The rebirth of a Nation – Patrick Kinross pp310-330.
(50) A Pictorial History of Southampton Docks – Bert Moody – pp 3,7,10 and 17 – (Waterfront Publications).
(51) Union-Castle Line, (Internet site).
(52) Letter to author from Alistair Arnott, Cultural Services – Southampton City Council – 12th September 2002.
(53) Southern Daily Echo – 23rd September 1922.
(54) Southern Daily Echo – 20th and 22nd September 1922.
(55) Southern Daily Echo – 25th September 1922.
(56) Ataturk – The Rebirth of a Nation – Patrick Kinross – p 334 and 335.
(57) The Southampton environmentalists won their fight in May 2004.

Chapter 8

(58) Dorset Chronicle – 7th June 1928.
(59) Dorset Chronicle – 28th June 1928.
(60) Poole & Dorset Herald – 9th August 1928.
(61) The Meyrick Family homepage, (Internet site).
(62) The Bournemouth Daily Echo – 9th August 1928
(63) The National Archives Learning Curve – The Labour Party, (Internet site).
(64) A Welsh coal miner's web page, (Internet site).
(65) The Globe & Laurel, 1928 – p201.

Chapter 9

(66) Weymouth, Dorset, England – The Dorset Page © 2000, (Internet site).
(67) Public Records office Kew – ADM 157/87564.
(68) Public Records office Kew – ADM 157/87564.
(69) Old Ordnance Survey Maps – Portland 1: Castletown 1927 – Dorset sheet 58.07 – Alan Godfrey.
(70) Letters to author from John Easton – undated.
(71) By Sea By Land – James D Ladd – pp6 & 7.
(72) Chronicle of the 20th Century – Peter Bently, Robert Jones, Denis Pits, Derek Mercer – p 368.
(73) Royal Navy – Covey Crump – Crown Copyright 2004.
(74) The South Dorset History Society – Exploring old Weymouth – a guided walk through the town's colourful past – Annette Hogan 1996, (Internet site).
(75) Letters to author from John Easton – undated.
(76) Letter to author from G Baylis – Undated.

(77) Letter to author from Dorothy Stern – 25th December 2001.
(78) Letter to author from J. Hilliard Johnson – 25th November 2002.
(79) Letter to author from Mrs Mavis Gammidge – 26th January 2001.
(80) Portland Souvenir Magazine – Edited by John Barnes, text by Rodney Legg C 1976 – pp7-11.
(81) Weymouth Underwater Archaeological Group – The Weymouth Diving Web – Torpedoes.
(82) Letter to author from I Mackenzie – Ministry of Defence – March 2002.
(83) E-mail to author from Robert Franks – March 2002.
(84) Just a Hogg's Life – Anthony Hogg – p64.
(85) Public Records office Kew – ADM 157/63122.
(86) The Royal Navy at Portland since 1845 – Geoffrey Carter – p55.
(87) Letter and e-mail to author from Alec Palmer – January 2002.

Chapter 10

(88) Lympstone 1941 – Donald A. Gibson (Rector of Berwickshire High School) – Taken from Globe & Laurel 1978 – p364.
(89) Royal Marines Training Group – Devon – Part 1: RM Reserve Depot – Anthony. J Perrett, taken from Globe & Laurel, 1978 – p162.
(90) Royal Marines in East Devon – A History of Lympstone and Dalditch Camps – Special Publication Number 9 – (Extract from The Exmouth Journal – 29 July & 12 August 1939).
(91) Public Records office Kew – ADM1/28550.
(92) Information from Mr Steve Other (Major R.M. retired).
(93) A Life on the Ocean Wave – Henry Russell.
(94) Later that day, in Exmouth's little museum, I met Steve, (who helped out there a couple of mornings a week), a retired ex Royal Marine major who'd risen through the ranks. He told me that the old wooden hut was, ironically, immediately behind the guardhouse.

Chapter 11

(95) Napoleon Bonaparte England's Prisoner – Frank Giles – p13.
(96) The Napoleonic Guide, (Internet site) – © The Napoleonic Guide 1999-2004.
(97) Memoirs of Napoleon Bonaparte – Volume 14, Chapter X by Louis Antoine Fauvelet De Bourrienne, edited by R.W. Phipps – Globusz Publishing, (Internet site).
(98) Nelson: The Essential Hero – Ernle Bradford – pp18 and19.
(99) The Big Gun – Peter Hodges, p90.
(100) Torquay: The Place and the People. 1992. – John Pike, p41.
(101) The Torquay Times – 25th July 1930.
(102) Torquay: The Place and the People. 1992. – John Pike, p44.
(103) Torquay Times, 13th July1928 – p7.
(104) The History of Torquay – J T White, 1878 – Extract from Footprints in the Sand: The Development of South West Seaside Towns – Bonaparte in Torquay.
(105) Napoleon Bonaparte, England's Prisoner Frank Giles – p20.
(106) Eliza Gutch and Mabel Peacock, Country Folk-Lore, vol. 5: Examples of printed Folklore concerning Lincolnshire (London: Folk-Lore Society, 1908) pp.383-384.

(107) Bonaparte and the English People – Taken from Napoleon Bonaparte Internet Guide – extract from The Yankee, Boston, Friday, October 13, 1815.

(108) The Fall of Napoleon – The Final Betrayal – David Hamilton-Williams, p268.

Chapter 12

(109) The History of The Castle Hotel, Dartmouth – Dartmouth History Research Group, paper 25 – Ray Freeman.

(110) The Royal Castle Hotel History – Hotel leaflet.

(111) Letter to author from Robert Franks dated 21st November 2001.

(112) Dartmouth – A Brief Historical Guide – Tom Jaine on behalf of the Dartmouth & Kingswear Society.

(113) Dartmouth Chronicle – Friday, June 3rd 1927.

(114) Letter to the author from Robert Franks dated 20th November 2003.

(115) Naval Discipline for Boys, Part II: The 1860 Ryder reforms, by 'Newjack' and Colin Farrell – PRO ADM1 – 9th September 1866 Pro H 568 – taken from Kissing the Gunner's Daughter, United Kingdom – www.corpun.com, (Internet site).

(116) The Call of the Sea – Steve Humphries – p72.

(117) History of the Rod in all Countries from the Earliest Period to the Present Time – W.M. Cooper – taken from Kissing the Gunner's Daughter, United Kingdom – Naval Discipline for Boys, Part II: The 1860 Ryder reforms, by 'Newjack' and Colin Farrell – www.corpun.com, (Internet site).

(118) Outposts – Simon Winchester – p7

(119) The Fall of the British Empire 1918-1968 – Colin Cross p216.

(120) The Navy At War 1939-1945, Stephen Roskill – p78.

(121) The Navy At War 1939-1945, Stephen Roskill – p181.

(122) British Warships, Laurence Dunn – p12. – (Longacre Press Ltd. 1962).

(123) Robert E-mailed me in April 2004 to say that Blackie had sadly passed away.

Chapter 13

(124) FOTW – Flags of the World, (Internet site).

(125) Red Pepper Archive – US influence at nuclear docks exposed – Tony Gosling – September 2002 (Internet site).

(126) Royal Navy – Covey Crump – Crown Copyright 2004.

(127) Words and music by Calum Kennedy and Bob Halfin – published in a *People's Journal* supplement, (DC Thompson, Dundee).

(128) A History of Pirates – Blood and Thunder on the High Seas – Nigel Cawthorne – pp29-46.

(129) This Information given by Ian Criddle – Assistant Local & Naval Studies Librarian Plymouth Central Library.

(130) The Devonport Dockyard Story – Ltd Cdr K.V. Burns – DSM. R.N. – p95.

(131) Letter to author from John Easton – April 2004.

(132) Journalism – Union Street Blues – Mark Simpson, www.marksimpson.com. © 2002.

(133) Memories of Union Street – Crispin Gill – Regional News Bygones (6.9.2000) – taken from HoldtheFrontPage.co.uk. – First published in the Evening Herald, (Internet site).

(134) BBC News – Thursday, 11 September 2003, (Internet site).

Chapter 14

(135) Mussolini, Denis Mack Smith – p197.

(136) Hitler – A Study in Tyranny – Alan Bullock – pp 151-161.

(137) Chronicle of the 20th Century. Peter Bently, Robert Jones, Denis Pits and Derek Mercer – p390.

(138) Battleship Nelson, Ronald Careless – p16.

(139) Lake's Falmouth Packet, Cornwall Advertiser and Visitor's List – July 11, 1930.

(140) Lake's Falmouth Packet, Cornwall Advertiser and Visitor's List – July 18, 1930.

(141) John Wesley the Methodist: A plain account of his life and work – by a Methodist Preacher – chapter XII – Wesley Centre Online, © 1999 – the Wesley Centre for Applied Theology.

(142) The Ancient Phoenicians – Pat Remler – Courtesy of Cedarland, (Internet site).

(143) West Briton – 17th July 1930.

Chapter 15

(144) Public Records Office, Kew – ADM53/87564.

(145) Walk the Cornish Coastal Path – John H.N.Mason – p50.

(146) National Weather Service Chicago – The Beaufort Scale, (Internet site).

(147) The ship's logbook did give an anchorage position based upon fixes, but the handwriting was difficult to interpret. As best I could decipher it, it read: *Pier head Light 089°, Signal Tower 116°, St Augustus Tower 189°*, but none of these landmarks meant much. *Pier head* could I supposed have been the end of the Quay, on Rat Island, or I may have misinterpreted totally; it may have read *Peninnis Head Light*.

There were three towers shown on my map on the island of St Mary's – One on The Garrison called Lloyd's Tower another near Hugh Town called Buzza Tower and a third to the north, near the golf course, called Telegraph Tower. Perhaps the names had been changed. I couldn't even begin to draw any conclusions (Ref: ADM53/87563, See Note 154 below).

(148) The Fortunate Isles, R.L. Bowley – pp44-48.

(149) Sir Walter Raleigh, Robert Lacey – p145.

(150) By Sea By Land, James D Ladd – pp29-30.

(151) Cornwall's Lighthouse Heritage, Michael Tarrant – pp35, 37 and 38.

(152) Scilly – The End of the World is Just Ahead – Luiz Eduardo Neves Peret – The Book of Sacrifices,

(153) Scilly Peculiar, Clive Mumford – p14.

(154) I later wrote to Clive Mumford at the Paper Shop and sent him a photocopy of the ship's log, on which were the anchorage co-ordinates. He confirmed that the Pier Head Light co-ordinate given as 089° would have been at the end of The Quay on St Mary's, and that the Signal Tower 116° co-ordinate would have been Lloyds Tower on Garrison or Telegraph Coastguard Tower.

The co-ordinate that had thrown me was the one I'd read as St Augustus Tower 189°, which Clive was certain would have been St Agnes Lighthouse Tower, located inland on a hill. I hadn't noticed this on my map as I'd been looking for lighthouses either at sea or around the coastline of the islands. At 189° the tower was almost directly in a southerly direction from the ship, and this allowed me to place *Tiger* between Samson, The Garrison on St Mary's, Annet and St Agnes,

None of this helped me much however with the potential landing beach – it could still have been on any island, but at least I'd learnt that there were two occasions on which I'd been close to *Tiger's* anchorage. The first had been when

I'd peeled off left, on impulse, along the dusty narrow footpath around The Garrison and had arrived at the first battery – King Charles' and had looked across to Samson. The second had been on the voyage home – when *Scillonian III* had taken the southern route back around St Mary's.

Chapter 16

(155) Lloyd George, Ian Packer – pp 4-16.
(156) Lloyd George, Ian Packer – p86.

Chapter 17

(157) An Index of Deaths from the Conflict in Ireland, Malcolm Sutton – Cain Web Service.
(158) The County Down Spectator – Saturday, July 14, 1928.
(159) Bangor Bay & Harbour – a pictorial history – Ian Wilson and Andrew Jaggers – pp35 and 39.
(160) Webmaster LOL 395, © 2002.
(161) A life in the theatre (1959), Taken from Oxford Irish quotations – Edited by Bernard O'Donohue, (Internet site).
(162) The County Down Spectator – Saturday, July 21, 1928.
(163) Friends of the Earth Northern Ireland (Internet site).
(164) From Curraghs to Catamrans – Details supplied by Ian Wilson – Bangorlocal.com.

Chapter 18

(165) History of the Villages of the Isle of Arran – Scottish Women's Institutes Arran – 2002 – p7.
(166) History of the Villages of the Isle of Arran – Scottish Women's Institutes Arran – 2002 – p9.
(167) Blackwaterfoot – Undiscovered Scotland: The ultimate online guide – © 2000-2005 Undiscovered Scotland.
(168) Interhike – Brian Henderson 21st August 2002 (Internet site).
(169) The Scotsman – Thursday 29th July 2004.
(170) Biting midge chemical ecology, Jenny Mordue and Bill Mordue – University of Aberdeen – pp159 -162.
(171) Public Record Office – ADM 1/18460.
(172) Letter to author from Stuart Gough, Archivist – Isle of Arran Museum Trust and Association – 27th October 2001.
(173) Public Record Office Kew – ADM53/87565.
(174) Scotland's Highlands & Islands, Richenda Miers – p227.
(175) History of the Villages of the Isle of Arran – Scottish Women's Institutes Arran – 2002 – p62.
(176) Hansard – Piers, Isle of Arran – pp2179 to 2188, 29 June 1948.
(177) E-mail to author from Stuart Gough – Isle of Arran Museum Trust and Association – 1st December 2004.
(178) Ardrossan and Saltcoats Herald – July 1928.
(179) When I later compared the two photographs and used the peak of Goatfell as a datum, I could see that in my photograph more of the slopes of Goatfell were exposed over the foreground hills, and Goatfell was further to the right in relation to them. This meant that I'd climbed too high and too far east around the

bay – it meant also that the original postcard photograph had been taken from somewhere on the dirt track, from between the trees, which had now grown so tall that they obscured the postcard view – it was a repeat situation to that of Marine House.

(180) Community of Arran Seabed Trust website.

Chapter 19

(181) Mussolini, Denis Mack Smith – p241.
(182) A Sailor's Odyssey – The Autobiography of Admiral of the Fleet – Viscount Cunningham of Hyndhope – p282.
(183) The Royal Marines – From Sea Soldiers to a Special Force – Julian Thompson – p256.
(184) Public Record Office – ADM 202/133.
(185) From a letter from John Wickens (former marine) to Sgt. Pete Chapman 12th May 1994, sent to the author by e-mail on 31st December 2002.
(186) New Zealand Shipping Company, (Internet site).
(187) Clyde Navigation – A History of the Development and Deepening of the River Clyde – John F Riddell – p256.
(188) No Mean City: 1914 to 1950s – Trade and Communications – The Harbour – John Riddell – Taken from TGS Internet site – (Reference: p565 – Glasgow City Council, Libraries Information and Learning).
(189) The Glasgow Story: Luftwaffe Reconnaissance – John Riddell, (Internet site) – (Reference: Glasgow Archives, TD308/2 – Glasgow City Council, Libraries Information and Learning).
(190) By Sea By Land –James D Ladd – p78.
(191) Mussolini, Denis Mack Smith – p302.
(192) By Sea By Land, James D Ladd – p81.
(193) By Sea By Land, James D Ladd – p89.
(194) Letter to author from Len Stone dated 11/2/2003.
(195) Royal Houses of Scotland – Withers family, (Internet site).
(196) The Forth Railway Bridge, Anthony Murray – p13.
(197) Letter to author from Peter Collinson, 10th December 2001.
(198) The Invergordon Mutiny, Alan Ereira – p167.

Chapter 20

(199) Scotland's Highlands and Islands, Richenda Miers – p196.
(200) Public Record Office – ADM/53/81245.
(201) The Invergordon Mutiny, Alan Ereira – p37.
(202) Naval Policy Between The Wars – Volume 2 – Stephen Roskill – p94.
(203) Public Record Office – ADM/178/112.
(204) The Invergordon Mutiny, Alan Ereira – p20.
(205) Invergordon Mutineer, Len Wincott – p 89.
(206) The Invergordon Mutiny, Alan Ereira – p59.
(207) The Globe & Laurel – 1931 – p281.
(208) The Invergordon Mutiny, Alan Ereira – p64.
(209) English History, A.J.P. Taylor – p284.
(210) Naval Policy Between The Wars – Volume 2 – Stephen Roskill – p90, taken from ADM. 116/3396.

(211) Naval Policy Between The Wars – Volume 2 – Stephen Roskill – p91, taken from CP. 205/31 of 20th Aug. 1931. ADM. 167/84 and Cab. 24/223.
(212) The Lower Deck of the Royal Navy 1900-39 – Anthony Carew – pp150-151.
(213) Invergordon Mutineer, Len Wincott – p91.
(214) Taken from 2,000 Years Of Binge Drinking, Paul Vallely, The Independent, Saturday 19th Nov. 2005.
(215) Easter Ross and the Black Isle, Christopher J Uncles – p77.
(216) This Noble Harbour – A history of the Cromarty Firth, Marinell Ash – p216.
(217) This Noble Harbour – A history of the Cromarty Firth, Marinell Ash – p228.
(218) This Noble Harbour – A history of the Cromarty Firth– Marinell Ash – p241.
(219) Public Record Office – ADM178/110.
(220) The Mutiny at Invergordon – Kenneth Edwards – p235.
(221) Britain's Sea Soldiers, C Field – p188.
(222) Britain's Sea Soldiers, C Field – pp193 – 197.
(223) Five Centuries of Famous Ships: From the Santa Maria to the Glomar Explorer – Robert G. Albion – © 1978 Published by McGraw-Hill – Taken from Maritime Archives, (Internet site).
(224) Letter to author from Davie Ross dated 4/2/05.
(225) Mutiny at Invergordon – Reason in Revolt – Fred Copeman – taken from The National Archive, Learning Curve, (Internet site).
(226) Battle-Cruisers – A History 1908-1948, Part IV – Ronald Bassett – p170. (Thanks to Geraint Bowen and John Feltham).
(227) Invergordon Mutineer, Len Wincott – pp113-114.
(228) Alness and District Times – Sep. 1991 – issue 18 – p9.
(229) The Invergordon Mutiny, Alan Ereira – pp79 -129.
(230) Naval Policy Between The Wars – Volume 2 – Stephen Roskill – pp104-105.
(231) The Royal Marines – From Sea Soldiers to a Special Force, Julian Thompson – p 235.
(232) The Invergordon Mutiny, Alan Ereira – pp115-117.
(233) Naval Policy Between The Wars – Volume 2 – Stephen Roskill – p109.
(234) To put the record straight: After my missed visit to Invergordon Library, I exchanged letters with them and received a very pleasant letter, (Ref. Gillian Rattigan – 16/02/05), confirming that the liberty boats *had* come ashore at the Admiralty Pier, and that the Naval canteen had been one of a row of huts, now demolished, which was near the Invergordon Academy Playing Fields. So the trodden ground *did* turn out to be significant after all.
    In December 2001 I received, in answer to my inquiries, a letter from the Cromarty Firth Port Authority, (Ref: Captain Iain Dunderdale – 13/12/01), recommending that I contact a Mr David Ross about the Invergordon mutiny. I never did so until I was writing up this chapter in February 2005, when it occurred to me that he and the old fellow I'd met on Joss Street might just be one in the same person. Davie wrote to me, confirmed that he remembered our meeting and gave me more details of his memories of the mutiny.
(235) Naval Policy Between The Wars – Volume 2 – Stephen Roskill – p111.
(236) The Invergordon Mutiny, Alan Ereira – p167.

Chapter 21

(237) The Brahan Seer – His Curse – The Loch Ness Home Page, (Internet site).
(238) Letter to the author from Malcolm Macdonald dated 25th March 2003.
(239) Fact File, Eilean Siar Council – www.cne siar.gov.uk.

(240) The Rough Guide to Scottish Highlands and Islands – Rob Humphreys and Donald Reid – p342.

(241) The Stornoway Gazette and West Coast Advertiser – June 12th 1931.

(242) The Stornoway Gazette and West Coast Advertiser – June 5th 1931.

(243) Going to the pictures – Chrissie B. Maclean – Stornoway Historical Society Journal – issue No.18.

(244) E-mail to the author from Malcolm Macdonald dated 2nd May 2005.

(245) 2-007: Sir Alexander Mackenzie – Dorthea Calverley – p7.

(246) Surprise Island, James Shaw Grant – p155.

(247) From Stornoway to the Pacific, Frank G. Thompson – Stornoway Historical Society.

(248) England qualified for the quarterfinal of Euro 2004 where they met the hosts Portugal in Lisbon. Rooney's tournament ended when he limped off injured mid way through the first half. The match went into extra time at 1-1 and stood at 2-2 at the end of it, England losing 6-5 after the penalty shoot out, with Beckham and Vassell missing their spot kicks.
I saw the game in a pub in South Wales, so that I'd watched England's games in all the countries of the UK except England.
     No-hopers Greece beat France in the quarterfinal, going on to beat the Czech Republic in the semi-final and Portugal in the final.

Chapter 22

(249) Scapa Flow, Malcolm Brown and Patricia Meehan – p24.

(250) Scapa Flow, Malcolm Brown and Patricia Meehan – p33.

(251) Historical Articles – Wrecks of Pentland Firth, W Bremner & D.G. Sinclair – Caithness Community Website.

(252) Scapa Flow, Malcolm Brown and Patricia Meehan – p40.

(253) The Orkney Herald – June 4, 1930.

(254) The Orkney Herald – May 28, 1931.

(255) Therapies, Whole health md.com – © 2000. WholeHealth.com, LCC.

(256) Scapa Flow Visitor Centre and Museum.

(257) The Orcadian – Thursday, March 20, 1969.

(258) Stromness Museum.

(259) This Great Harbour, W.S.Hesison – pp85-87.

(260) Scapa Flow, Malcolm Brown and Patricia Meehan – p247.

(261) Thanks to Tom Muir – Kirkwall Museum.

Chapter 23

(262) The Globe & Laurel 1930 – Correspondent: Colour Sergeant P.J. Hunt – p217.

(263) Odda – Smelteverk A/S – Fifty years – 1924-1974 – Anders Rokne – p9.

(264) Norway – Lonely Planet – Graeme Cornwallis. Andrew Bender, Deanna Swaney – p250.

(265) Kolltveit – information supplied by Tone Hesjedal – Norwegian Museum of Hydropower and Industry, Tyssedal.

(266) Charles Gill: Portrait of a magic life – Kjartan Fløgstad.

(267) Odda – Smelteverk A/S – Fifty years – 1924-1974 – Anders Rokne – p5.

(268) Norwegian Museum of Hydropower and Industry, Tyssedal – supplied by Tone Hesjedal

(269) Odda – Smelteverk A/S – Fifty years – 1924-1974 – Anders Rokne – pp4 to 18.

(270) Boliden History, (Internet site)   – © 2005 Boliden Odda A/S.
(271) Hardanger Arbeiderblad – 7th June 1930. (Translated by Lars Sal).
(272) Hardanger Arbeiderblad – 11th June 1930. (Translated by Lars Sal).
(273) Hardanger Arbeiderblad – 14th June 1930. (Translated by Lars Sal).
(274) Hardanger Arbeiderblad – 18th June 1930. (Translated by Lars Sal).
(275) Chronicle of the 20th Century – Peter Bently, Robert Jones, Denis Pits, Derek Mercer – pp 352, 356, 359 and 378.
(276) Museum Arbeidarbustader i Folgefonngata.
(277) Museum Arbeidarbustader i Folgefonngata – (Translation by Ingerid Jordal).
(278) Odda bibliotek – (Translation by Ingerid Jordal).
(279) Komintern – The Free Dictionary – Copyright © 2005 Farlex, Inc.
(280) Chronicle of the 20th Century – Peter Bently, Robert Jones, Denis Pits, Derek Mercer – pp 342,344,353,355 and 382.
(281) Taming the trolls – The story of hydro-electricity in Norway – Knut Forr Børtnes – Odin (Internet site), produced by Nytt fra Norge – Ministry of Foreign Affairs.
(282) Arbeiderklassen – og de engelske matroser – Nils Moldøen – Odda bibliotek – (Translation by Ingerid Jordal).

Chapter 24

(283) Scarborough Mercury – Friday 20th June 1930.
(284) King's Regulations and Admiralty Instructions 1934 – pp20-33 – Crown copyright – obtained from Ministry of Defence Admiralty Library.
(285) Anonymous letter to the author dated 25th December 2001.
(286) A Sense of Style – being – A Brief History of the Grand Hotel, Scarborough – Bryan Perrett.
(287) Scarborough Mercury – Friday 27th June 1930.

Chapter 25

(288) Southend Standard – 7th April 1927.
(289) Guns and Gunners at Shoeburyness – Tony Hill – pp 145-146.
(290) Mutiny at the Nore – The Napoleonic Guide, (Internet site).
(291) Public Record Office – ADM53/87564.
(292) The Shoebury Story, Maureen Orford – p39.
(293) Guns and Gunners at Shoeburyness – Tony Hill – pp38-39.
(294) The Shoebury Story, Maureen Orford – p46.
(295) Southend Standard – 31st March1927.
(296) Southend Pier – Taken from Wikipedia – The Free Encyclopaedia, (Internet site).
(297) The Independent – Tuesday 11th October 2005.
(298) Pier to cost millions to restore – BBC News UK edition – Monday, 10th October 2005 – www.News.bbc.co.uk.

Chapter 26

(299) Public Record Office – ADM/53/108470.
(300) Chronicle of the 20th Century – Peter Bently, Robert Jones, Denis Pits, Derek Mercer – pp448 – 453.
(301) Chatham Naval Dockyard and Barracks, David T. Hughes – p20.
(302) Letter to author from Michael Edwards – 7th October 2004.

(303) Squaring the Circle – www.groups.des.st-and ac.uk – © JOC/EFR February 1999, (Internet site).

(304) The English Mecurie – Published by Authoritie for the Prevention of false Reportes. Whitehall, July 23rd, 1588. (Imprinted at London by Christ, Barker, Her Highness's Printer, 1588)   © 2000-2005 WhyWaitForever.